Anthology of My Own Poems

TERRY J POWELL

ISBN 978-1-957956-13-8 (Paperback)
ISBN 978-1-957956-12-1 (Ebook)

Inquiries and Book Orders should be addressed to:

Leavitt Peak Press
17901 Pioneer Blvd Ste L #298, Artesia, California 90701
Phone #: 2092191548

To:
Best Wishes, Terry

Poems For Children

CONTENTS

A BLANK PAGE

I stare at a blank space

A piece of paper in my face Empty, all the lines look the same Borders set in a blank frame Seems I haven't got the will

For words to pour out and fill the pen lies on the page

As a sentence takes time to gage Thought's grind to a halt

It's not my fault White, square, on the sheet

I need to motivate, to make words complete Not sit here, and face defeat

Isn't life sweet?

Seems words have no respect

The bin over flows with screwed up balls that I reject Papers in piles of reams

Frustration lets out screams Just get the words rolling Get the pen controlling Let's get the flow

Get those words on the go and there lays the lazy pen

I sit and stare at the empty page again

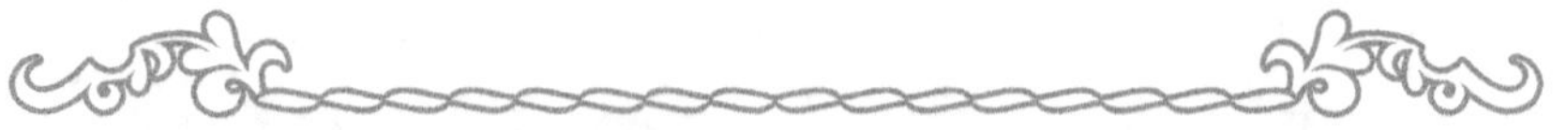

CAN YOU GUESS WHAT THIS IS?

This place of splendored Hall, its gleaming throne to greet you all. A place to ponder and depend on,

Of nature's call.

Cross words, papers, books, and puzzles, all.

A haven of dreams, ideas and thought, while face of expression and taught.

Place of rest bite,

And open 24 hours both day and night. All are welcome 365 days of the year, Privacy intended without fear.

A choice of darkness or of light, away from prying eyes out of public sight.

Time to take as much as you need, there is no time limit to really heed.

Excepts all types short or tall, Fat or thin, big or small.

Age no preference here to tell, Takes sick or healthy here as well.

No race discrimination no objection to call, Form peer, to working class, tramp and all. A place for all seasons from spring to fall, From single occasion, from party to ball.

A place that no one can do with out and would be lost, even at any cost.

Have you guessed what it is or is it driving you mad?

Then all I can say is that you've been had

THE NAUGHTY CHILD

Out when shopping you take your child You enter the store and off, they run wild

Bad enough trying to remember the shopping list but a disappearing child can be missed Wondering where and what they have done?

Being brought back by store detective is no Fun "Now child stand and walk by my side"

All red and embarrassed you want to hide Then it comes. The question you dread

"Mummy can I have?" running through your head "Because you've been Naughty!" I say NO Then the tantrums and screaming off they go

"I want it I want it" is bawled in a cry

And all in the store looking round, you want to die Tempers and tantrums screaming and fits Bringing to the end of your whit's

Trapped and no escape in the queue Nowhere to run and nothing you can do You're the OGRE parent, Mean and tight

As you battle with shopping and child full of fight The EXIT you headlong rush is the goal

Escaping the embarrassment from on lookers on the whole Then you make it outside the screaming gets worse

As parents we know the routine chapter and verse Then as you travel away from the store Child now calmed and saying no more

Getting home the child runs inside

As though nothing has happened with smile beaming wide Oh well Parents, we have all been there

Situations like this make you pull out your hair

but little darlings they are, and where would we be

As part of them growing as we can see

CHOCOLATE

The word "Chocolate" makes the most passionate woman let
out a delightful scream

Cocoa butter, milk and sugar dream Soft pink jelly, of Turkish
delight Bourneville as dark as night Almonds, fruits and raisin

Honey, and honey comb, amazing Runny fondant coffee cream
Coated by a covering of cocoa bean Liquors tantalize

Exotic shapes of all sorts set before the eye's Hazel nuts, coconut
desecrated Lemon and orange zest grated

Cherries glazed created Taste buds elated

Brazil nuts sank in caramel The urge of chocolate does compel

Mint the bitter cool Creamy strawberry fool

Thin, crisp, wafers just melt away of the senses of delicious,
tend to play

No wonder some get the chocolate urge

To treat themselves to a chocolate splurge

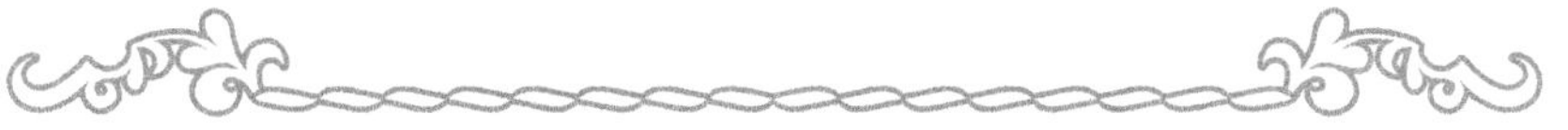

BEHIND THE FACE OF A CLOWN

Circus comes but once a year Bringing Joy and Happiness, from far to near

All manner of fun and laughs, do bring Entertainment in a Circus ring

We always remember the things we see Those Funny Clowns so clearly

But what has a clown got to hide?

His big red nose Those black, crossed eyes

That white completion Those funny smiles

Outward appearance does he deceive? An observer of life Does he preserve? Makes others laugh and what great fun Leaves others happy, till his work is done but what is his real feelings?

In life's complicated dealings Does he really run and hide?

Or keeps his tragedy hidden inside Covering it all up to create a laugh No short measures not by half

Behind the mask what does he really hide? Knowing to only himself those feelings inside So who knows? And when you see

That wonderful Clown could be me

THE COVER OF A BOOK

I am a book that sits upon the shelf

One of many, unique and a single one myself My cover looking slightly rough and worn Inside my pages tattered and slightly torn Covered with a coat of dust

With the smell of musk

My appearance leaves me on this shelf While younger, fresher, newer ones radiate wealth

I once was popular and new Neat and tidy with an exciting view

Years of reading me have made look misused Wear and tear of being abused

But if you take the time to read me well,

I still have a good story to tell

Many covers have I worn to hide to attract others to read inside but when the cover is removed, I am cast aside for looking used

So here I sit in my place Waiting for someone to show me grace

Take me off to be repaired Open my pages and make them aired

To love my story through

to read again for pleasure new So don't reject me by my cover Look inside and you'll discover

DANCING LIGHT

I lay in the darkness of my room Shadows seen to stretch and loom the lightness, taken away Outlines of black and grey

Longing for the lightness of the day to the light my room I pray

Then something catches my sight A small prism of bright light

As beams radiate through the curtains onto the wall Slender it dances a dance so small

Flickering, shimmering bright to take a where-ness of the night

And it gave me hope

For those seconds of my illness gone, so I could cope and while the light did remain

Forgotten was the pain Could this have been the sign?

For my own personal healing time? Dance oh light dance, take my attention Take me to another dimension

I breathe the air of relief Re constituted is my belief for my life is brief

But taken is the grief

Beads of sweat lifted from my brow I will survive my illness now

And the light does dance to restore life's balance Thank you small light

You helped me mend and took away my darkest night

EXAMS

Oh, Teacher what have you done?

Now that it's the day my exams have come This is my time of dread

Facts and figures of my learning thread I've studied hard these days and nights in those silent and stressful plights

My marks have to meet a demand

And all achieved by your teaching, and my own hand No one understands what I'm going through

Of all these subjects that I do Assignments set

Makes me worry and fret I really am doing my best

To win good marks and beat the rest I'm told I need to succeed

To get the best career in life indeed but every subject I can't enjoy

Some I'll pass or fail in educations ploy How I dread examinations day

This time of all my studying should pay Will this be my time of make or break?

And if I fail how and what reaction will my parents take?

As I really do want to please

As my parents have saved for the college fees and now the examination is done

Waiting for my marks to come Oh I hate this waiting game

That "have I passed or failed pain?" But teacher I know you have done your best

As your education and time in me you did invest So if I pass or I fail

At least we both done our best to prevail

EYES

Eyes the windows of your soul

Tells you what is deep inside a person as a whole Sadness inside their life they hide

Inner fears and feeling that are hidden inside Happy or sad Healthy or bad

As we meet someone familiar or new, we tend to check at a glance that optic view

Love from them can be seen and felt and deeper feelings in them can be held Reactions to the eyes can be seen

Even lies told that have been Deep emotions they do hold for untold stories they behold

Recorders of life events that have unfold in history of one's life untold

So, when you meet a friend or someone new Look into their eyes; it could be useful to you

FOUND OUT

Don't you stand there wide-eyed, with an innocent look on your face?

You know what you done and what took place It's no good acting, or starting to cry

I can hear it in your voice that you lie Sometimes I wonder if you're my child Sometimes unruly, sometimes wild

At times you wear my patience thin

The antics you've got up to and the places you have bin But, now you have been found out

It's the truth I want, without any doubt Turning on those tears don't really work with me

I've been there many times you see

I know all the tricks, and fibs that you will ever tell and all the excuses yet to come, I know very well

as adults we know all the score

We've done them all before So dry those tears and come clean

To lie to us, is just obscene So tell the truth and be true

People will respect, and look up to you

And besides it less painful, less punishing on that guilty mind

And will ease the consequences you will find Always remember tell the truth

It's all part and parcel of your growing youth

GLASS PRISON

In my prison made of glass Trapped inside a transparent mass No corners to hide your fear Cylindrical, dome shaped, and clear Shouts resound the echoes inside but silent deafness of mime outside

Strong and cold inside your silicone wall Escapeless to one and all Impregnable in all its might

Illusive to trap and holds all its light Crystal, clean, and clinical Pure, and cynical

I am looking out, as they look in

With nowhere to go, they know where I've been I see them pass by in my crystal dome

In this incarceration I call home One tiny chip is all it takes Before this structure breaks Just to make a tiny flaw

Shattering it to billions of tiny shards, to make it fall to breathe the air of freedom once again

But here in this see-through fortress, I remain and they still look in, as I Look out

No corners to hide my fears and doubt I see them walk by and pass

In my prison made of glass

GREMLIN

I got a gremlin in my cupboard because he's been here 24hrs a day

Playing his mischievous games, a spiteful way Undoes everything I do

Throws me into Confusion that's what he put me through Holds me back when I want to go forward

Makes things normally easy, difficult and hard A spoilsport, upsetting everything I try

I don't know his reasons why

I have really tried to cast him out Always about me plaguing me with doubt

Follows me everywhere Always there

He's even in my sleep, messing with my dreams Always taunting me with his sarcastic screams

He's been locked in my cupboard. or at least I thought I did He is good at escaping though, the Houdini Kid

I have learnt to live with it, as you normally do Haunting me even when I go to the loo

Well, Mr. Trouble you mostly have had your way Your days are numbered, I can definitely say

One day you will slip up, fall over, and then I will be there To Boot you on your way old son because I don't really care

Find someone else to hassle, as you're not welcome here Sorry, I seem to pass him on, it would appear

So, if he shows up on your door

Don't send him to me, I don't want him anymore So don't let him in, or you will have to pay Just kick him out and send him on his way

HAGGIS

Now that Hogmanay is drawing near It's the time in Scotland wild haggis fear Open season for the great haggis hunt is on Those fearful critters are in hiding and gone in the land that drunken Scot's women dance on tartan covered pool tables, they prance

With swinging handbags above their head

Half beaten Scot's men lay half dead and as in the land that Scotch whiskey flows

Those poor men suffer from those women's blows Fergus Mc tight wallet the greatest haggis hunter of all By Royal appointment to the King of Scotland calls The King Proclaimed "where be ma haggis for ma hogmanay feast"?

"Ye dinna hae one Fergus at least"

Fergus Mc tight wallet Said "my laird Ye canni see" Nessie their friend taught them to hide well from every Scott and me

I've set traps to tempt them with their favorite food Carrots and parsnips, sugar coated doughnuts but they still elude

The king told Fergus bring me ma haggis ready and dead or it will be your wee Sassenach Head

Time passed and on Hogmanay Day

A hundred Roast haggises on the kings table Lay Fergus Mc tight wallet rewarded for services done The Golden Caber and thistle that he had won

I sent ma women out wee her handbag

And a hundred and two Haggis she did belt wee her bag So if you're ever in Scotland and you do see

A woman with her handbag running free, spare a thought for those poor Scotsmen, Haggis and

Hogmanay

HEARTS

Take your hearts and keep them warm Keep them safe to weather the storm Protect in times of trial

Give them space, to rest a while and if it's all too much to bear A gentle touch of love will care

Hold them in both hands and make them strong So they can cope, and get along

And if the times that they get broke

Hope and time, will mend in tender words spoke as two hearts begin to share

And feelings become aware in time they will bond

Tender rare moments, of growing fond as the heart yeans for hope

The need to share, so it can cope Beating in its constant life's span

In the chest of woman, child, and man and if all can stand the test of time Those beating hearts will be fine

To rise and stand against a fall and conquer pain, love, trial, and all Then in one single heart does beat

To face what trials, and not admit defeat Then yours is the true, living part The strongest and the tender heart

HOGARTH

The old Warlock stood there in his place.
Calling the old gods and forces of nature to his face I command you to appear
I stand protected and have no fear HOGARTH does command
To help us mortals here at hand

. . . .

Rise up, rise up, I call on you as I have need Assist me with my mystical deed
I command you by all the gods that's I known Appear before me spirit of GOAN
For I have need of your services, from your grave I beckon you, my salve

. . . .

Wind, Storm, Torrent came Howling voices in moaning pain
HOGARTHS greying hair and beard tossed in winds that blew
Ghouls in a circle, Spirits flew with tempest all around
The warlock stood his ground
Once again, I shout GOAN I command thee to come You are in my power till my deed is done

. . . .

From darkest gates of hell Spawned a foul and ghastly smell
A dark silhouette writhing against his will Screaming a deathly howl in a deafening shrill I HOGATH command you not to resist
You are in my power I insist
As the creature rose on earth to full height His massive form swamped the night

. . . .

A creature with leather blue grey skin Like a crocodile covering with horns set in Tall and hunched
Face taught, twisted, and slightly bunched Deepest eyes or glowing yellow red

thick set brow and malformed head Protruding teeth yellowed with age

Thick lower lip taught with rage

…………

GOAN roared "Who has summoned my here on this night from where I dwell?"

Booming voice that shook the depths of hell

I HOGARTH warlock of the place of When lock, I have called thee

I have the power over you to do my bidding for me For You GOAN have a contract with me to fore fill The demon spoke "Hogarth I am at your will" What is this quest you will have me do?

Name this deed I do for you

…………

I have an enemy that's cast on me his hex unto me, he has angered and made me vex for this I seek revenge

I will not stop until avenged Go seek him out and take his soul

This your reward when the deed is whole for myself, I take his powers to be mine Those skills and property I can combine

…………

His name is DYTHON in the vale of dean He's cruel, ruthless, and branded mean

Go GOAN bring him to me here in this place So I can see the terror on his face

Goan roared writhing, twisting with pleasure and pain

HOGARTH waited for them to return again

…………

Time passed throughout the night when GOAN returned Dumped down a sack, inside screams and pleading was heard

Goan picked up the sack and shook it about DYTHON rolled out of the sack unto the ground and out

Mercy, mercy, he did plead

Cuts and bruises his wounds did bleed Goan Picked Dython up by his hands

Struggling foe went limp, helpless as he hangs

…………

I take your powers DYTHON for my own All your knowledge, properties, and your home

Spell now cast and all goods received DYTHON now stripped and cruelly relieved

GOAN takes the poor wretch in to the gapping ground HOGARTH listening to the screaming sound

Closed earth, now deed was done Warlock HOGATH victoriously won

IMAGINATION

Vivid moonlight casts the shadows on the bedroom wall as darkness of dusk begins to fall

Those shadows seem to twist and dance Point and mock at every glance

The imagination runs away

It's time for fear and thoughts to play the branch of the tree outside, rattle and tap

Whilst under the quilt of the beds trap Doors slam and floor-boards creak

The wind whistles through keys holes seeming to speak Lunar light catches the glint of the knife

Reflecting the light on the ceiling of the taker of life Heart pounding on the chesty drum Feverish cold sweating, struck dumb

And the cupboard door in the corner, begins to slowly open wide

Is that the place where the monsters hide? I've come for you, imagination would say I've come to take you away

Frozen with terror, too scared to scream and suddenly waking from the haunting dream

The Child wakes

To witness the day that breaks Laying there relieved and at ease

And the reality of its not for real and feeling pleased It was all pretense

Of the Childs Imaginations unwitting defense

KITTEN

Tiny little kitten how small and sweet you are Wide innocent bright eyes; you melt our eyes by far

Watching you while you romp and play Stalking and pouncing is your learning way tiny claws and needle teeth that grip and chew Makes us laugh by the things you do Everything to you is a new adventure

Lively you jump into every exciting venture Miniature paws you tap and swipe

As you run wildly about in your usual hype Then when tired you curl up into a tiny ball Fast asleep and ignoring all

When you hear the sound of food being served You rub yourself against ankles unreserved

As you tiny meows and purrs make us heed

To make us known you're hungry and need to feed Watching you grow every day

Means you will be exactly like your parents in every way Oh your tiny delicate ball of fur

Wonderful when stroked to hear your purr How your looks and antics really do appeal, we love to hold you and this is how we feel Our bonding to you as we watch you grow to an adult cat is what we know

MOTHER'S TRAITS

Dedicated to Mum, Mary Bowker. Who passed away last year 2016

Mother how you looked after us through life A faithful parent, a loving wife

Tender words to ease and help though times of pain To always be there when needed once again

You love your children as Mothers care Protective love of a parent, firm but fair

A nurse to heal wounds and take away tears A psychologist to council inherited fears

A teacher to educate in life's complicated path

A banker and lawyer to help out a financial aftermath A friend that's loyal beyond the cause

Taking time to care never ceasing to pause Provider who gives selfishly with no thought to her self

A woman of rich in knowledge's wealth A comforter in times of need Giver of happiness indeed

These the traits seen in you This your spouse does view

The heroine unique seen in our eyes Always truthful never lies

One beyond duties call

A pillar of strength that will never fall

MUSIC

How can we put the rhythm of music into word? Sounds put into describing, what you've heard Those sound bouncing in your ears

Tempo, rhythm, word and rhyme that one hears Heavy rock to purge the soul

Exciting, rhythmic, as the beat loud and whole Acid house to garage beat

That makes you dance intensely of your feet Classical takes you away to another place Slowing you down to gentler pace

Rock and Roll that's the one that makes you swing Jumping and jiving makes you do your thing Reggie that West Indian rhythm and blues Sings of slavery and going back to their roots

Soul that feeling of slight sadness of love Sung with emotions form heaven above Country and western with its lively spring

As those Cowboys and Cowgirls with a twang they sing Jazz that uniform sound

They play it as is called underground

And then their Ballads, melancholy to make you dream as you drift off to romantic scene

All the different sorts' lyrics we address Are all related to one thing no less

They all have one meaning to each role it plays to touch our emotions in different ways

Music written on a page for all time from the first to the last line

To affect us in the life and the way we live from personal experiences those artists give from the first to the last

Both in the future to the past

A poem, a verse, and written song Ever short or ever long

Now a part of history for ever more Those words of music written on a score

OLD SCHOOL DAYS

Granddad told me when he was a lad When at school in the old days, we had a piece of slate and a stick of chalk

Told to sit up straight and not to talk

No fancy pencils, pens, or books in what to write We had to learn to do things right

Our teacher were stern and strict,

Not allowed to answer back or contradict

And if played up or became a pain Was sent off to the Head to receive the Cain

We would take lunch in a little cardboard box to school or brown paper wrapping if times were hard and cruel Most times a crust of dripping and bread

Or if you had Jam, you were posh it's said at play time out in the school yard

No fancy toys, times were hard

No Game Boys, Mobile phones, or Poke man If you played football, you kicked a can

But Granddad said, "The best times of my life" Free from stress and away from strife Enjoy your childhood while you can

Things are different when you're a grownup woman or man

And how lucky you are these days

That you have all this nice stuff at your fingertips, he says you have all this newfangled technology

And he keeps asking me, what's a PC?

THE PC

The things I notice about my PC It's the stupid things it does to me

All the wrong things that you don't want it to do It does. Annoys, and plays games with you.

It does not work; you check it inside and out Operating system all about

Still a problem and you scratch your head Strip the hardware out instead Nothing wrong but still a prob

Turns you in to a screaming blob Wires, ribbons strips, and motherboard, In a heap in a hoard

Strewn across the floor

You scratch your head again once more,

And wonder why you done this all, and face defeat Hours gone by and all together now, and complete on it boots up, and still the same

Enough to drive a saint insane Rant and rave and threaten this you do

The neighbors wonder who you're shouting to Hit it with a sledge hammer is that secret voice Turning off rebooting you have no choice

The world record holder for rebooting is you

This damn thing is playing with you and you've got no clue

Then much later switching on the Pc again It boots up normally, it is the usual game

PUPPIES

Little puppies small and sweet Unsteady, slightly stumbling on their feet Coats so soft and dowdy and incomplete

Always playing, wagging tails to greet big eyes that make your heart melt Innocence of a child, and still in whelp

Antics they get into, funny things that they do Daily learning they go through Naughty Puppy peeing there

Of natural motions they are un a where Anything that they can chew

It may be something personal to you It's just their way of getting closer to They don't understand wrong or right Sometimes tries your patience it might but as they grow a personality does arise

As they grow and develop before your eyes Mans or woman's best friend

They always get there in the end Try to respect them, be patient and kind

They will treat you the same as you will find A member of your family, they will become Loving, affectionate, and lots of fun

Sensing emotions that you emit Being there and doing their comforting bit

As the saying goes, they are for life

They need you there please don't give them strife Enjoy them, watch them, love them, be as one with them

as they really care Regardless of anything they will be there

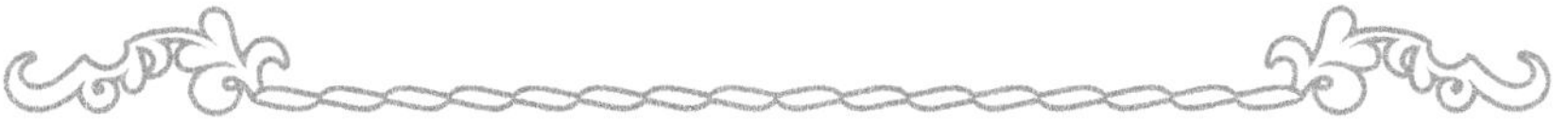

THE ROBIN

Little bird why did you die? Once you lived, and used to fly Now limp in my hand you lay You lived your life until this day Once you stood upright and Proud Your shrill singing Crisp and loud

Your Bright Red Breast Tattooed on your chest Lively with your cheek One of a species unique And as I dug the soil

I watched you search the spoil You had no fear, you became a friend

Time with me you did spend As I threw you crusts of bread

You sang a tune of gratitude as you fed Shrill you sang and true

I would have said you was saying thank you Each time I came to that place

You were there to greet me face to face

Singing your song with chirping sound as you cheekily hopped around

And now you've come to your end I will miss you my little friend

SCHOOL HOLIDAYS

Well Parents, Schools and Colleges are back in swing 6 weeks of hell, that prison thing

All those weeks of pressures Looking after your little treasures as those kids get bored

Extra cost and expenses you can't afford More meals supplied

Extra washing or laundry applied

The fighting amongst the kids gets more intense

The slightest thing becomes a major offence and you coping with the insanity day by day Wishing the turmoil would go away

Hoping the days would just whiz or fly

But as time draws nearer those days get longer and slower as they pass by

Then comes the final day

All the kids start Schools and colleges, off they go on their way

Pity we don't have Summer Camps here in the UK Like they do in the USA

It's us parents we need the break

Can't we have 6 weeks off instead? The change we would all love to make

16 to 20 years the ritual of what we have endure A long time that's for sure

96 weeks of summer holidays in our lives

But they the ones who bear the brunt of this, is Girlfriends, Partners, and wives

Well, it's all over and done

Getting back to normality seems to be the number 1 "Till next year"

HOUSE OF SWEETS

Somewhere in the realm of a dream of treats There's a house in a place of the land Sweets Where leaves on trees are made from paper rice Frosted with glistening sugar ice

And bark on the trunks encrusted with chocolate flake Paths made out of nut cluster toffee bake

A bed of lollipop flowers in a dark rich soil of fudge There a pond of creamy chocolate sludge

Candy striped columns, around liquorish doors Treacle toffee bricks, makes its walls Clear sugar pane windows of gloss

Curtains of wispy pink sugar candy floss Press the M&M chocolate bean button, of the bell as the door opens to an aroma of heavens smell Baked cakes from the entered confectioned hall into strips of colored Liquorish paper on a wall

As you gaze on black and white Bertie Bassett tiles on the floor

Pear drops and pineapple chunks mosaic held in store to a gaze of a ginger bread settee with jelly beans inset A crispy wafer coffee table is met

Up a flight coated chocolate pairs and walnut and dates of banister stairs

To a red and white candy striped four poster bed with pink soft marshmallow pillars to rest your head Falling asleep on a mattress of angel cake

Then suddenly realizing you're awake After drowning in a bath of coffee cream You realize it's only a dream

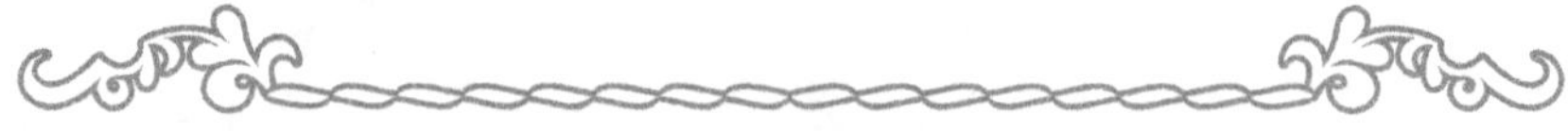

A TEAR

A single tear drop cascades from a glassy eyes that displays
One single pearl rolls down the cheek As inner emotions reach a peak
The light makes it glisten and gleam Crisp, Transparent, sterile, and clean A prism of rainbow color's reflects Of warm solution the eye rejects Softly it ascends on a downward trace Mapped on contours of the face Always on a downward flows
The direction a tear falls always goes

TEDDY BEAR

My old and little teddy bear
Has one eye, and missing bits of hair in places scuffed and worn
Pads on hands, snagged and torn Sticking out, bits of straw
But still loved, and has a place in store with that fixed smile upon his face My teddy has that special place
Teddy has been there through all my life The little button in his ear, says steiffe My Teddy may be old
He has a story to be told We will always be together
My cute and cuddly friend forever

TEENAGERS BEDROOM

The teen-agers bedroom the dreaded domain

A place of their own privacy and inner sanctum remain That dreaded bedroom door and what you find inside Heart thumping as your hand touches the handle, no place to hide

Opening the door and slowly walking in Knowing that you're about to enter the residential bin.

The room dark, sedate, and dim, trying not to trip or fall

With just the glint of light from the showing from the hall

Dark mountains and shapes all around

As you opened the curtains your heart falls to the ground. Standing in the light and in its true glory and now in shock Piles of dirty clothing and smell of sweaty sock

Ashtrays full and flowing and trash where the bin used to be

Where was the carpet the one we used to see?

Cans, bottles, crisp packets, sweet wrappers, yoghurt pots, things that look obscene

Makes the local garbage dump look quite tidy and clean but worst is yet to come when peering under the bed The sight that greet you, wishes you were dead

Cups, dinner plates, and side plates covered in alien culture, that fills you with dread,

Books, comics, paperwork and magazines swimming in your head

And all the hours of cleaning up the endless mess the teenager comes home and you can only guess

MOM! What have you done to my room? Its private I said Screaming, tantrums, and abuse going through your head After all the time you spent and the miracle, you have done

Another battle not quite won

TEENS

Isn't teenager's hard work?

Little wannabe adults, with a childlike quirk Hormonal bombs, which are actively fused

So, want to be independent, but easily confused "I want to do everything cause I'm grown"

But when it goes pair shaped, enraged and tantrums are thrown

How they perform in outrageous fits As things of lost patience end all up in bits

No matter how you try to please

You tend to walk on eggshells, with no ease And those fateful words that you dread That seems to swim around in your head

I want to try smoking, booze, sex, and drugs As they turn into impossible adolescent thugs From faze to craze, that seem to shock or amaze

As late nights turn to midafternoon bed ridden days Those once angels, you were once proud

Now Mange, Marilyn Manson, gothic makeup, they walk round in a shroud

Decibel breaking music that shakes the street Compiled pigsty bedroom hovels make it all complete

And the invasion of half the nation that traipse through the home

And the receiving of heart attack bills from the use of the phone

But as parents, we are old, and we don't understand As they scream I want it now, are the many expensive things they demand

Roll on twenty as you pray to the gods So that they can leave home, the little sods

THE COVER OF A BOOK

I am a book that sit upon the shelf
One of many, unique and a single one myself My cover looking
slightly rough and worn Inside my pages tattered and slightly torn
Covered with a coat of dust
with the smell of musk
My appearance leaves me on this shelf While younger, fresher,
newer ones radiate wealth
I once was popular and new Neat and tidy with an exciting view
years of reading me have made look misused Wear and tear of
being abused
But if you take the time to read me well, I still have a good story
to tell
Many covers have I worn to hide to attract others to read inside
but when the cover is removed, I am cast aside for looking used
So here I sit in my place Waiting for someone to show me grace
Take me off to be repaired Open my pages and make them aired
To love my story through to read again for pleasure new
So don't reject me by my cover Look inside and you'll discover

THE FOOD AND VEGGIE BALL

I dreamed that I was invited to a ball It was the strangest thing of all

All the guests were fruit, veg, cakes, and sweet I laughed so must it knocked me off my feet Food wearing clothes with faces stood around And me laughing on the ground

The host was Lord and Lady Parsnips

They stood there frowning with hands on their hips The duke of ring Doughnut was not amused

The Cucumbers asked to be excused As I made into the dance hall

I watched Mrs. Jelly and Mr. Ice cream trip while dancing, and fall

They bounced all over the place

And the Duchess of trifle was leaving in great haste Sir Cracker Biscuit and lady cheese melted into each other's arms

And there by the bar Mr. Turnip was wooing Miss Carrot with his charms

And further in the Room Lady Melons was flirting with Captain Avocado Pear

Lots of fruitiness and flirting going on there The Reverend Gurkin stood upright and erect

Mrs. Gurkin stood in the background with a feeling of neglect

The Cherries jumped in to the cream The strawberries let out a delightful scream

Mr. Cabbage laughed so much, that he was falling apart And Mr. Celery was exposing his heart

The Tomatoes as butlers serving drinks to all The Potato Orchestra played music at the ball As the Muffins danced around with glee

Baroness Mushroom was talking to Mr. Green pea and those Spanish dancing Onion rings

And doing the flamingo getting into the swing Sir Cream puff
stood nobly by

As Countess Von Strudel started to cry Those Macaroon Tarts
flaunted their stuff

And in the excitement one of the Eggs got cracked and went off
in a Huff

Apart from that a good time was had by all at the food and
veggie Ball

THE LITTLE PUZZLE BOX

I had a little wooden puzzle box from China it was made Took some working out as I played

All different symbols to line and match small dials with a faces to line up and catch Many, many hours to fiddle and move Occasionally too difficult to prove

Lots of combinations with lots of complications Frustrating and difficult Working to get the basic root

Trying to get them all lined up in order Sometimes took me to a mental border How I tried

It sometimes tested me and hurt my pride But I persevered I never gave in

Just to break the puzzle just to win Time after time twisting and turning Looking and learning

Memorizing all the ways

A Lot of time spending whole days and then one day just by accident I solved it That was the day I was happy every little bit

It just clicked and burred Twisted and turned

The little box chimed and rang a tune

A little dancer popped up with a golden moon and round and round it danced

To a tune of romance

Oh, that little box of great surprise That unfolded be before my eyes All that work for such a result Some clever Chinese man had built

It was the simplest way that was done you'll find Just to get there was really fun with your mind

THE MOTH

Oh, tender moth how you fly in the twig light of the sky Flying round and round

Above a distance of the ground Attracted to the lamp or light Shinning in the darkest night, is it light or is it heat?

That makes you determined to meet Your delicate wings pulse to a beat Your determination makes no defeat And yet no matter how you try

In the end you get burnt and die Sad what nature does intend the way your life seems to end Oh tender moth how you fly In the twilight of the sky

THE NAUGHTY CHILDREN MONSTER

A devious monster am I

Hiding in dark corners to make children cry Making myself disappear or reappear Making naughty children quake with fear

I can even enter their dreams

As I enjoy listening to their screams or even come in the dead of night

Causing imaginations to run wild with fright Every naughty child is my joy

My plaything, my emotional toy

I don't like good children, they are no fun with wicked ones, I can get things done

I am here, there, and everywhere So misbehave if you dare

I come in all disguises All shapes and sizes

So please all you naughty children, do your worst You will be the ones that will be cursed

I love to make those bad children suffer best Leaving my victims muddles and stressed Please all those children don't be good

Cause I want to visit you in your own neighborhood

THE RACING PEN

Those words keep rattling over, and over, in my mind Not made for this brain that's designed

Phrases, words that seems to rush Never giving a moments rest or hush Syllables spew forth, like a water fall Cascading never seeming to stall Twisting

Not resisting Always insisting

Clouding the mind and making it misting an inner struggle to find the words to slot the times, before they are forgot

And those thousands of subjects Most of the time my head rejects So much to put down on paper Before they disappear and vapor the quickness of the hurried pen

as words race down on paper then starting, never stopping

Like a typical list for shopping Always things to add

Is an insanity that drives one mad?

And the pen races on

Till chapter, and verse is done and there lays the finished creation

Of written words in anticipation, it's done at best

Time to rest

THE TOY BOX

A little one-legged soldier leant in the corner of the box Talking
to the worn face of a fluffy fox

The three-legged donkey stumbled to and FRO

As the doll with the broken eye asked "where do all the broken
toys go?"

I've no idea said the action man with one arm Maybe they go
to a special hospital away from harm Said the bear with the missing
nose

Well said Barbie I can't find my missing clothes They must be
amongst these bits and bobs at the bottom of

this box

Among these old jigsaw pieces and discarded building blocks

Said the jack in the box who has a broken spring and the old
Buzz light year held together with string Funny said the three wheeled
car

How those humans are

When new, they play with us for ages and never put us down

But when they are carless with us, drop and break us they leave
us on the ground

I do remember said the Game Boy with the cracked screen
Those grown-up humans pick the broken toys up and put them in a
black bag, This I've seen

But after that I have no idea

They never come back said raggy doll that's what it would
appear

Seems some don't have any care for us toys or appreciation

Said the clown with the big red nose and the missing carnation

VISIT TO THE DENTIST

The dentist gave me a filling When he started drilling Before that, he gave me a shot

The drill inside my mouth was getting hot

And all manner of utensils hanging from my lower lip Me now sweating, hoping he doesn't slip

Head now vibrating as the drill is grating

Screeeeeeeeee goes the sound as my heart starts to pound and the pipe sucks all the time Toothache was the crime

All the time I became a were

Me hanging on, and gripping the arms of the chair Thinking at the time, it's just not fair

All I could do is sit and stare Then the drilling ceased

Now the silence of the screaming beast Porcelain or metal filling?

Anything to get it over, I am willing Then the heater thingy stuck on the filled tooth

And the pink and rinse stuff

As I walked out, thinking it's not so bad All over, relieved, and glad

THE WEB

Oh, what splendored web you weave Intricate of design you precisive

Silk of splendor in glistening in morning dew Encrusted by gems of each day new

Soft but delicate, but deceivingly strong Always perfect but never wrong

....

Like vail of sail wafting in the breeze, Crisp, white, and crystallized in winter freeze

Soft and pleasing to the eye Made to trap morsels passing by

Of insects of all kinds of insects that come to rest on time and energy you invest

.....

A home, a source of food, A nursery for tender brood

Who could imagine a web with so much use the many tasks to produce

A web for one spider in the 4seasons of man from beginning to end of a short life span the architect of each one's design

of gentle threads that entwine

A lace of webbing of yours not mine

WHAT IF

What would the future bring?
If I could not sing What if I could not dance?
Or take a chance in love or romance See no works of art
Or if poetry has no heart No TV
No PC
No creativity No longevity
Not allowed to play and have fun
A sense of humor, that is over and done And yet they are all part of giving Makes one's life worth living
And if all these things are lost, what would we see You might as well lock yourself away, and throw away the
key
No stories to tell Wouldn't that be hell?
So, let's keep our heritage intact to teach our children how to act Teaching the value of these things
That fun, culture, and laughter brings and our world will be a better place
To make our life's more enriched in the human race Enjoy what life has to offer every day
To live life to the full in every way

WHAT'S IN A HUG?

A hug for some is warmth, and what we all need Expression without words to feed

Needed when some ones feeling down Help them feel better, and feel wanted around

Hugs for loving posture between couples, that intimate touch

That need for couples, partners, is a hug is wanted very much

A hug to warmly greet a friend

Bonding, making a person on what you can depend Lifts your day

In a lovely way

Makes you feel warm, safe from harm Makes those who give them a touch of charm

So, when you greeted with a hug Smile! Your wanted, be a little smug

And those who give it will make a person's day Given freely and without pay

WORDS

It's Ironic isn't it Putting words together to fit
Making smooth lines go Those bounces along to flow
Words that dance along
To the tune of a catchy song Moonlight sonata Vivaldi vibrato
All the magic that can be composed of verbal text of sweet reposed CIVIL WARClassic and swish
Yearning orations of a wish Syllables of tears Characters of fears Pens and pauses Comers and clauses
Rough notes and writing in fine Papers and line Jumbled text
Frustration and vexed Thoughts of how you feel Play with words that appeal Sadness and whit
That all fit together bit by bit Poems and odes
Fire the minds and goads All this for an inspired poem Just to get the verses going

YOUR SMILE

Your smile makes me feel eased
A welcoming feeling, that makes me pleased of gentle persuasion of being relaxed
Warm and relaxed
A slight tingling sensation inside Emotionally pacified
To me that means a million things of pleasantry brings
Almost to a state of tranquility Away from the world of hostility
I love to see you smile
That means you're happy for a while and if you are, then so am I Better to smile, rather than cry
And if you can stand and hold that smile on your face Then I know you have a touch of grace
And OK, I know you will always be the one to take it
and though life's tough deals you'll be the one to make it Please don't ever give your smile away
It helps everyone through their day I do love your smile
Makes me and others happy for a while

THE LITTLE ZOO

I once knew a woman with a hundred dogs.

Out in the yard she kept pigs and hog's Birds and parrots she kept in the loft Cats and kittens oh so soft

Fish and carp, she kept in a bath Frogs, newts, and toads at the end of the path

Hamsters, Guinea pigs and mice in a tank Insects and spiders kept in a bank

No waif no stray never turned away Not really a place for one to stay Goats and sheep kept in the shed

And a cow lying down on a straw bed A Horse in the garden and not in a field Sad looking Monkeys appealed Iguanas kept on a shelf

I wonder how she looks after herself Chipmunks, bats, and hedgehogs too All fitting in the little household Zoo Ducks and geese in a garden pond

of all pets and animals, she is fond Well I couldn't put up with it all

So, I left, escaped from natures call Pet free zone is where I reside

The peace and tranquility is now where I hide

A Book of Dark Poems

CONTENTS

ADDICTION

Disclaimer: I don't condone the use of drugs; this is an insight of into a typical user.

Her eyes flicker open after another heavy night as another day hit the dim room with light Shakily her hand reaches for a ready-made Joint,

She needs it now; it will help her to a point

As she takes her first puff, it will burn away all hope Just to tide her over, so she can cope Trapped and helpless in another day

Wishing deep down she could escape and get away Her only thought in her mind, is an amber white line That her body now yearns for, at this present time Relaxed now from the shakes

As drug addiction makes

She dresses in oversized clothes that used to fit They now hang loosely off her every little bit

The loss of appetite and for food she needed to feed Her habit is her only need

Losing all her self-respect that she needs to sell

on any street corner, as any curb crawler knows well

Just one more trick for another daily score to pay In the hope she gets her fix for another day

She used to have a life once, when she was free Thinking to herself, this is now me

She carries this heavy shame inside Something now she knows she cannot hide

Losing all family and friends that in time she ripped off one by one

Her need was greater, now it's done

Her only friends now is the dealer and the gear The only need in her life now, she holds dear A small packet in a wrap

Knowing the risk that it's cut with all kinds of crap Rushing back to her little hovel she calls a place

The excitement and the wanting, makes her heart race Oh the desperate need for that warm injection

She cannot fight that addictive infection Now the rush

She needed very much

As a thousand unconscious moments surge as she relaxes to a fulfilled urge

Her eyes slowly close gently Limp both physically and mentally

She draws a breath Taken now by death

As her lonely sole drifts off from its holds release, She, another statistic of an O/D in a report by the police She will not know pain anymore; she's left it all behind A family will now carry that pain in memory in mind

THE ALCOHOLIC

He wakes up and reaches for a cigarette

The dry acrid taste in his mouth is the taste of regret And the empty bottle on the floor, is the reminder of something he's trying to forget

As the shaking starts and he begins to sweat and he's sorry

But the vicious circle that he's in, is far beyond a worry Now he reaches for the half empty glass from the night before

A livener for the start of the day is what he's looking for the bruise on his face, from the fight he does barely remember

The scrape on his knuckles in the day light of September the bits and pieces in his mind he recalls

The fight, the drunken stupor, and the stumbling falls Now the only thing on his mind to find and open store to buy and drink more

To look upon his pitiful face

As his looks unkempt and a disgrace

As his life sunk into oblivion, lost the person he used to, be without trace

The drinking reaching an incredible pace His daily routine is just to drink

It helps him; it numbs his thoughts and helps him not to think

The last thing on his mind is any form of reconstruction as he obliterates and drinks himself into destruction

ALL HALLOWS DAY

Take time way back in the history of all hallows day
Back in Neolithic and pagan times they say
The one time of the year that spirits rise up from eons past
From earthly beds to walk the earth in mass
And as night drew near
Fires were lit to keep away fear
As groups gathered together round a fire
Safe around that warm bright pyre
To celebrate relatives and friends of long since passed times
That night retuned in spirits minds
Fires burning to keep evil spirits at bay
While sprites, witches, and daemons play
As those ancient people waited till morning light
Praying to the gods for safety through the night
Hoping to keep their souls safe and sound
Not stolen by spirits and taken to hallowed ground
When Morning came a feast and time to celebrate
That those survived from hells open gate
And all the old gods and spirits receive
Of Hallows day and hallows eve

ARMIES OF DEATH

The Mysterious shadow of a figure stands on the darken shore

Hands rose to the sky, as he cursed and swore Chanting his old commanding spell Beckoning the dead from the watery hell

I command you give up the dead from the depths of the sea

Release those soles they all belong to me Silence of the tide, in the dimness of the night skies One by one, figures of the dead soles walked out the

ocean, and began to rise

Then in hoards and armies marched from the deep on to sand

Silhouettes of lost souls, to the evils one's command Millions gathered on the cost

Ready to battle for the evil host

The shroud of mist covered those figures in the dark Glistening carcasses move and jostle to his hark And Eire moans of desperate soles cry out

Now stood in ranks all about Admirals and captains organize platoons

As the sailors played with flute and drum the deathly tunes Cannons dragged, musket, sword, cutlass, spears, and bow and arrows

Cannon balls carried in slime filled barrows The gathered columns now march inland

To the beating of the drum, as the evil one doe's demand

as they passed by graveyards, Soles rose up to join the call

To conquer every living thing so they die and fall

Now Hell has come back to reclaim

For the goal of the Evil ones aim

The battle of evil and good

As the world will now run with blood

Death will cover all the lands

To the gesture of the evil, one's hands So all you good soles sit there and wait

And if there's a knock at your door? It's too late

BAD NEWS

When the phone rang, you gave me bad news What you told me changed my views

And my friend, I'm so sorry

I guess as a parent you must be sick with worry,

I know in the same situation I would

Knowing your daughter is sick, your own flesh and blood and I, like you, feel so helpless

Liver failure, through a cry for help is not what I think of any less

A young child dealing with mixed and confused emotions the over dose of Co-proximal was taken in the turmoil of devotions

Her plea of parents splitting, the tablets washed and cleared

But Doctors didn't explain the damages and the after effects adhered

Now Months after, one so young lay in a critical state and they say it could be too late

God I really hope she makes it though My heart really goes out to you

I've met her you see, she so young and yet to grow This to you my friend, must be a crashing blow I'm here for you any time you need

Cause I'm hers, your family, and your friend indeed

CURRY ANYONE?

Oh god, oh god, what have I done? I killed the cat while having fun

I heard it let out a scream

When it was put in the mincer machine Still there's no hurry

Not when it joins its friends in a curry A rat, a cat and the rest of a dog

Even a piece of hedgehog Anything to make money

And all those people who have eaten it, it's funny But I have made an awful lot of money

My bank account is nice and sunny

I'll say I'm innocent as I'm caught on the hop The Owner of the local curry shop

DANCING LIGHT

I lay in the darkness of my room Shadows seen to stretch and loom the lightness taken away

Outlines of black and grey

Longing for the lightness of the day to the light my room I pray

Then something catches my sight A small prism of bright light

As beams radiate through the curtains onto the wall Slender it dances a dance so small

Flickering, shimmering bright to take a were-ness of the night and it gave me hope

For those seconds of my illness gone, so I could cope and while the light did remain

Forgotten was the pain Could this have been the sign?

For my own personal healing time? Dance oh light dance, take my attention Take me to another dimension

I breathe the air of relief Re constituted is my belief for my life is brief

But taken is the grief

Beads of sweat lifted from my brow I will survive my illness now

And the light does dance to restore life's balance Thank you small light

You helped me mend and took away my darkest night

THE DARK SHADOW

There are those who hide from a dark shadow of the past and bear the deep scars that never leave, and last

There are those who suffer from that dark shadow in their lives

"IT" has the power to possess and hold husbands or wife's "IT"s weapon of fear used like a tool

Constantly demeaning, those weaker, treating them as a fool

All Opportunities "IT" uses to grind you weak to make your desperate daily struggle oblique

"IT "Sometimes uses physical violence to imprison those in "IT"s hold

To have the ultimate power and make those who fear and have them controlled

Tyranny and oppression as "IT" use's force Pretending "IT" is the victim and feigning remorse Saying its love when they know really its possession Disbelieving its "IT" that's really at fault and denying confession

As "IT" takes cruel sadistic pleasure in inflicting misery and pain

As "IT"s disease repeats its self over and over again Emotional Black mail "IT" would use

As "IT" inflicts daily abuse

Convincing others that "IT" is the victim put in the frame and that it's really you to blame

As this dark shadow evolves and grows You that take those arduous blows

Making you doubt yourself and laying self-blame Putting yourself out to please to ease the pain

Bringing down yourself esteem making you doubt after so long

And "IT" feeds from that, making its self-strong The bully that uses Psychology for its own aims

As "IT" uses for demanding and demeaning games but, "IT"s weakness it fears and hides those fears inside the dread of you winning and "IT" losing you is what it

hides

The more you stand up the more punished you become the more "IT" fears, the more damage to you is done Possession, fear, Blackmail, and pain

Are what "IT" uses for you to remain

As long as "IT" has got that power over you

"IT" stands on its pinnacle on high on that towering view but "IT"s weakness is within yourself you know and when you're at your end, you leave and go

Making that powerful house of cards collapse and fall Bringing that "IT" weakening to Call

And "IT" does not accept defeat Chasing after you when you retreat

"IT" will trick you by begging forgiveness as you led to be told

Saying "IT" will change and a promise of a new start, as it lies to hold

Because "IT" knows it is losing its tyrannical rule of "IT"s way

And will try to repossess its lost possession of the day Because "IT" knows it's not love, just some tool to Blame For "IT" has to lay fault on someone in life's game

Walk away if you make that break Never look back a new life you must make You know in your mind you done your best

All that's time you wasted that time you did invest and if "IT" shows its ugly head

Send "IT" on its way use, the Authorities instead Wipe your hands clean of "IT" clean out your life Enjoy the freedom away from "IT"s strife

Because eventually "IT" will have been paid back in time

Left in its pain ridden world with this on its mind and time will pay "IT" back as they say

And you you'll have you day

DARKER DAYS

As darker days fill my empty day Somebody took my light away
And in the twilight of the evening light Days turned to night

You took me by the hand and guided me through As I knew
you would do

Crowds of doubt gathered all around

Lost in the land of no self-esteem on swamped ground A mist
of low feelings clouded and hung in the air Driving me into deeper
despair

You gave me a glimmer in hopes light to help me through my
fight

In the distance heard were my cries of a desperate plea They
heard, and came to rescued me

Oh, angel of mercy lifted my soul and helped my face my life as
a whole Softly held me and gave reassurance

Comfort and Insurance Gave me back the will to live to con-
tinue my life to give Helped me mend broken parts Put feeling back
into hearts

Lifted my recompense Encouraged my intelligence I thank you
with all my heart

For making my life, my feelings restart Thank you for not tak-
ing me for granted and for making me feel wanted

DARKER THOUGHTS

I am the dark force

I am in everyone's mind, of course Always there, waiting for my chance to take control for my influence Looking for my break

For someone to make a mistake I am the perpetrator of crime When my deeds are done

And I have had my fun Then I disappear

Leaving those to pick up the pieces, when my coast is clear

I am the perfect criminal, for the perfect escape I leave others in a scrape

I am always in the mind of everyone They always take the blame, for all I have done

Conscience is not my friend

And sometimes it gets the better of me in the end But I am patient, as I can wait

I strike without mercy, when it's too late and at times, I can be addictive

Rather cruel, and vindictive Sometimes inconclusive Devious, and elusive

The dark side of thought, in your mind I leave trouble and turmoil behind

And when there is nothing and you're diminished Then I am, with you finished

DEATH OF A POET

I saw the day the poet died

The agent of his work, with delight he cried All those poems written, when the writer was alive

Means others will benefit, profit, and thrive but the poet died a pauper, he died so poor Clever words from an agent's promising allure

For the love of poetry, the writer wrote and not for gain Recognition was all he wanted for his pain

Poems to be printed in a book

But written unfinished works was took

As the literary vulture's tear over pages and fight for a small piece of the action, they bicker and bite History talks of artist's insecurity

Those who die in obscurity Is this the price of fame?

Words in a book, a picture in a frame?

A legacy left behind Chapter and verse in a fancy bind

And a signature in a book For others to read and look

THE DOGS OF WAR

The dogs of war are on a leash that's strained as they struggle for release, but are restrained They have the scent of death and blood

Paused to strike and stalk the world's neighborhood Waiting for the command

For the loosening grip of their master's hand as the beast's howl and bay

Eager for release in the playground of war, which they hunt and prey

They thirst, they hunger

On the work of the war markers monger Foaming, snarling, gnashing, yellow teeth

To strip the soles of conflict, that lies beneath Pain, sorrow, and injury is their meal

No emotions for their quarry do they feel for them the master relies on its sport

To weed out the weaker sort

While those hide in safe bunkers. Who run the helm While Dogs of war run free to hunt in their realm It's the nature of the beast

To thrive on those victims as they feast Listen to the deathly Howling of those hounds

Of the beasts at your door, and in their hunting grounds And those Masters as they prepare

Of us they don't really care

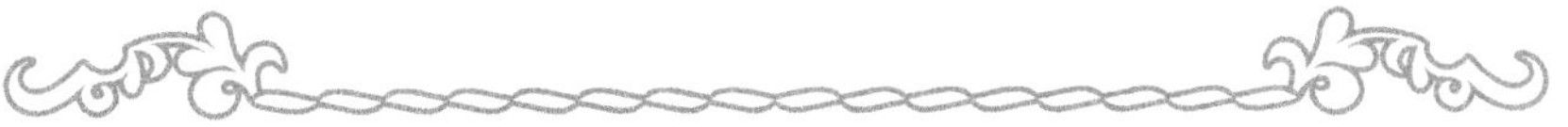

A GHOSTS TALE

In cold and dim lit room at night
A blood curdling scream let out with blight Floor boards creak and groan
Followed by a low and tuneless moan
A grey and veiled form across a room did float Like a gentle drifting boat
And there to whiteness, caught in time The lady in white, the victim of a crime She looks for her murderous host
The one who made her a ghost Centuries past and now and still
The scene played over and over at will A lost and aimless sole is she
Trapped in time for ever more to be Oh where are you she pleads Her betraying lover she needs Not knowing she once died
From one she loved and trusted, he lied and he at rest and passed on long ago As she doesn't realize or know
As she has not passed over to respective place The look of pity on her grey stone face
Her restless role in what she played Trapped in a situation and she can't be swayed
All this created by one who she trusted, loved in her past life
He the devious cheating lover, he the user of the Knife Does she crave for eternal rest?
Only she would know best So I'll let you decide her fate
From, she the lady in white, who's late

THE REALM OF THE BEAST

The gathering masses gathered round on fiery burning brimstone ground

The entire multitude in suffering in eternal pain as the beast that ruled rose up again

He stood on obelisk that reached the sky and looked on his minions with evil eye As he raised his hand

To order his command

I am the face of many you all know well Lord and sovereign over hell

Here in my domain

I inflict my pleasure of pain

I own your souls to do with what I please to amuse myself at my whim to tease Your very existences I do own

As he sat upon his throne Misery is my pleasure

To toy with you at my own leisure Stand against me you cannot win

For all those you are mine, those who committed sin and as for those in the future who are yet to do

A sin of any kind I will be waiting for you I have an eternity to wait for souls to receive

Those souls I will retrieve

The Vile beast rose to his feet and let out a vile laugh Rubbed his hands and his cruel eyes burned like a fiery hearth

Sin if you dare

Because in hell, I'll be waiting there

HOGARTH

The old Warlock stood there in his place.

Calling the old gods and forces of nature to his face I command you to appear

I stand protected and have no fear I HOGARTH do command
To help us mortals here at hand

. . . .

Rise up, rise up, I call on you as I have need Assist me with my mystical deed

I command you by all the gods that's I known Appear before me spirit of GOAN

For I have need of your services, from your grave I beckon you, my salve

. . . .

Wind, Storm, Torrent came Howling voices in moaning pain
HOGARTHS greying hair and beard tossed in winds that blew
Ghouls in a circle, Spirits flew with tempest all around
The warlock stood his ground
Once again, I shout GOAN I command thee to come You are in my power till my deed is done

. . . .

From darkest gates of hell Spawned a foul and ghastly smell

A dark silhouette writhing against his will Screaming a deathly howl in a deafening shrill I HOGATH command you not to resist

You are in my power I insist

As the creature rose on earth to full height His massive form swamped the night

. . . .

A creature with leather blue grey skin Like a crocodile covering with horns set in Tall and hunched

Face taught, twisted, and slightly bunched Deepest eyes or glowing yellow red

thick set brow and malformed head Protruding teeth yellowed
with age
Thick lower lip taught with rage

. . . .

GOAN roared "Who has summoned my here on this night
from where I dwell?"
Booming voice that shook the depths of hell
I HOGARTH warlock of the place of When lock, I have called
thee
I have the power over you to do my bidding for me For You
GOAN have a contract with me to fore fill the demon spoke "Hogarth
I am at your will" What is this quest you will have me do?
Name this deed I do for you

. . . .

I have an enemy that's cast on me his hex unto me, he has
angered and made me vex for this I seek revenge
I will not stop until avenged Go seek him out and take his soul
This your reward when the deed is whole for myself, I take his
powers to be mine Those skills and property I can combine

. . . .

His name is DYTHON in the vale of dean He's cruel, ruthless,
and branded mean
Go GOAN bring him to me here in this place So I can see the
terror on his face
Goan roared writhing, twisting with pleasure and pain
HOGARTH waited for them to return again

. . . .

Time passed throughout the night when GOAN returned
Dumped down a sack, inside screams and pleading was heard
Goan picked up the sack and shook it about DYTHON rolled
out of the sack unto the ground and out
Mercy, mercy, he did plead
Cuts and bruises his wounds did bleed Goan Picked Dython
up by his hands
Struggling foe went limp, helpless as he hangs

. . . .

I take your powers DYTHON for my own All your knowledge, properties, and your home

Spell now cast and all goods received DYTHON now stripped and cruelly relieved

GOAN takes the poor wretch in to the gapping ground HOGARTH listening to the screaming sound

Closed earth, now deed was done Warlock HOGATH victoriously won

THE HORSEMEN

On normal calm and reddened sky strange things occur on high the clouds suddenly tear apart

To the thunder of horse's hooves, that excites the heart Screaming of the sound of riders on horses

As they are set on their intended courses Three shapes from the heavens appear Striking into hearts, terror and fear

To look on these three faces you are already dead Your soles claimed, predicted it's said

Now is the beginning of the end

The world is helpless from these, no one can defend Pestilence, Decease, and Death are the riders Among the three are they the soul's dividers

The three horse men of apocalypse as they go to work and get to grips

The song of Pestilence sings his deathly sound Death gathers souls he's found

Decease spreads his seeds that's sown Across the planet they have blown

The scythe of death swings and reaps far and wide Gathering soles as the scythe smoothly glides Pray that death be swift

As mercy would be a gift

They sweep the lands to make them clean Eager for the work they are keen Destroying all in their path

In a devastating aftermath They will not stop till they succeed

And the reaping of tormented soles are done indeed They won't listen to pleas or reason

For a prayer or pleading mercy to them is treason Death and the gathering is their business, the goal is fixed

Souls are profit and they won't be tricked Pray you never see them for real

As Death will take your sole, I can reveal

I VAMPIRE

I vampire here in the darkness, I lay Skin cold to the touch, clammy and grey

Asleep and waiting for the day, to pass and go away

for the familiar shroud of darkness to show me the way I lay here in my coffin lined with motherland earth from my roots of the place, I was given birth

But that was in my mortal time, of now centuries past and in my mind of the memories, of eons past How I fear the light, which brings intense pain

The source of sunlight, which can extinguish my life or drive me insane

My kind so misunderstood

Just because I survive on drawing others blood I and my kind a very different race

The old nation, which occupied the night's space Our ways secret now, driven underground

Persecuted, driven to extinction, not many of us found A whole nation of us that existed long ago

Exposed by the writer Bram Stoker as history would show Stories exaggerated, stretched to create fear

The pen that's showed the wrong side, it would appear and how the day dwellers would react

For the wrong writings and misinterpretations of the fact Our whole nation lost

From the profit of a writer, we have paid the cost Our sacred book hidden away

Never to see the light of day at one time we co-existed

The day dwellers gave us life, they never resisted We lived in harmony, they sharing the day

And us sharing the night, we were all happy in every way but history breeds myths and lies

The tens of thousands of night dwellers soles die's and the few of us left now cries

The nights left empty of those that used to roam Empty now the place that we called home

We never took life, as lifeblood was given freely but now desperation has forced us dearly

I vampire here I lay

Waiting for the light of day to go away

and the familiar nights shroud to show the way

This the story I have told

Of a culture passed, gone and old

IMAGINATION

Vivid moonlight casts the shadows on the bedroom wall as darkness of dusk begins to fall

Those shadows seem to twist and dance Point and mock at every glance

The imagination runs away

It's time for fear and thoughts to play the branch of the tree outside, rattle and tap

Whilst under the quilt of the beds trap Doors slam and floor-boards creak

The wind whistles through keys holes seeming to speak Lunar light catches the glint of the knife

Reflecting the light on the ceiling of the taker of life Heart pounding on the chesty drum Feverish cold sweating, struck dumb

And the cupboard door in the corner, begins to slowly open wide

Is that the place where the monsters hide? I've come for you, imagination would say I've come to take you away

Frozen with terror, too scared to scream and suddenly waking from the haunting dream

The Child wakes

To witness the day that breaks Laying there relieved and at ease

And the reality of its not for real and feeling pleased It was all pretense

Of the Childs Imaginations unwitting defense

NO ONE BUT NO ONE

I awake in the dark, on a hard surface, that is flat Why I am here, I can't comprehend that

This is not my bed Where am I? Am I dead?

God I am so cold, so cold, I long to be warm again Trapped in this darkness is the way I'll remain Time passes, what seems like eons stretched so long I can't get up or move, what is wrong?

I can hear and I can see the cold is as bitter as can be

The door at the bottom of my feet is opened wide Flooding in with blinding light inside

I seem to slide forward into the room I feel the warmth-ness resume

All I see is a ceiling and lots of faces Different ceilings in different places

Still, I cannot move I am paralyzed with fear What am I doing here?

The sound of the cutter and vibrating pain I cannot speak or complain

The spattering blood and ripping flesh and spleen No one, but No one can hear my scream

PARANOIA

He sits in a darkened somber room, praying for a release from the mocking of a thousand voices of the beast

No one could ever understand the beast's demand

The tightening of the grip of the hand

At the beasts never ending, unmerciful command Wrestling with his conscience, between wrong and right Twenty-four times seven, day and night

Voices constantly taunt, mock, saying" they are all against you, you know"

There is no escape, nowhere to go

He stands up to full height, and screams Let me be Tormented soul that's twisted, longs to be free Bruised and bloodied hands, from the pounding on the wall

Are no redemption at all

The voices keep saying, Go On! Go On! Kill yourself and do us all a favor

They keep saying to him, the only escape, is death your savior

They, the voices have taken all control Weakening his punished and pitiful soul

He shouts above the constant droning of the angry crowd But no one wants to hear, his one small voice is not allowed

Drowned out by the babbling of countless chatter Ignored he feels, he doesn't matter

Help! Help! Screaming get me out of here Because the burden of paranoia is his fear

PAST GHOSTS

The ghost from the past Turns up quick and fast
A situation you can't get away Seems yet again your made in life
to pay
More pain and anguish to bear down Sent to test your renown
lies cover you in that shroud
Of those past things done that's made the ghost proud Though
being innocent of your reactions
To justify those actions
Of all those accusations that did make Makes me want to bend
and break Funny! how I can face with no remorse I have nothing to
hide of course
But You the ghost cannot
A sign of guilt by that party not forgot Something to hide? there
is no doubt
Excuses made to escape, by the ghost to get out Avoiding the
truth you will find
As self-guilt and consequence plays on those person's mind
The ghost has told so many lies to hide the truth
Acting like a guilty youth What do I need from you?
Nothing. For what you've put me through Just leave me alone
To carry on healing on my own Instead of having an affair with
my friend
And sending them round to haunt me to the end I do not want
to be teased
Not so your mind is justified and eased and after all I can say
I did nothing wrong in any way
So don't use my good name to hide behind
As others will know the real truth as you will find.

SELF-HARM

It's the tool, the instrument that cuts so deep That gives the pain to make me weep Being punished is my need

And doing this fulfills my deed No one seems to understand the need to meet this demand

I don't have any type of control

Hurting myself is my only goal

Others think I'm playing a game Punishing myself is my only aim I cut myself on any wrist or arm

I do self-Harm

Though self-blame, comes the guilt

In this never-ending loop that I have built I wish I could just stop, just halt

But I am still Insisting it's my fault This nightmare I put myself through Until I can fix myself it's all I can do

No matter what help is offered, or others say I can only get through this in my own way

THE BELL

Hear the solemn bell that tolls Across my life, the echo rolls
Vibrating in empty rooms and across halls Through brick walls, it calls
Come to me it constantly rings, it does insist Beckoning I cannot resist
Calling, calling
The deep tone never stalling in its tone it tells a story
Of the greatest tragedy and glory the urge of its call is so great
End of my life is now late; it's now a game of wait So great is the contemptuous force
I have to find the source
Oh God, Oh God, I cannot fight
As the distant bell tolls through the Day and Night It's my un-turning destiny, as I go with dignity
To lose myself into infinity
As the heavy hammer strikes the bell Do I go to heaven or hell?
I breathe my last
Recalling memories flashing of the past Ascending to the course, and the great tunnel of radiant
light
And to the end of the welcoming end, in sight the bell tolls on
As it sings its song Tolling on and on as it sings its song

THE EDGE OF LIFE

I stand on the edge of a precipice so high Paused, to throw myself of to fly

As I gaze into the swirling darkness of the mist into the welcoming abyss

I lean forward to the point of no return

Heart pulsating, thumping as I twist and turn Off the edge I fall

Leaving terra-firmer with no care at all My thoughts are of the life I once had

Tormented, abused, from when since I was a lad and still to very day, I pay the price Unhappiness and pain of all these years to suffice This the straw that broke my very soul

Tired of life, and snapped inside, No goal

As the exhilaration of the winds push through my face and hair

The force of the rush, As I leave a life too much to bear Saying good bye to all lost hope

How the hell did I cope?

As the ground meets and comes closer fast Impact as my body smashes and I breathe my last Splintered bones and flesh do rack

To the point of no going back

As the dark consciousness takes hold

My body dies and grows cold As My soul leaves its earthly bind

I feel at utter peace, all the rigors of a tortured soul left behind

Oh peace, oh rest; of this life I'm tired Escape away at best, this life now expired Not a fitting end of ends

I leave behind my family and friends This, an insignificant life is lost

To escape a tragic cost

I write this not to contemplate suicide but the end of one period of life. And the Start of a new Phase of life

THE EXECUTION

The dawn is yet to come When it does, I have to face the gun
The solitary post stands in the yard

And the gravel beneath my feet is hard the last and final yards
I walk

I hear the Priest in whispers talk the silence of the dawn

The place where my life will be torn Soldiers stand in a single
line

And the bullet will finish my time 1915 was not my year

And my crime was fear Nothing more

Those Safe Generals planned for me what is in store The post
is closer now

With pounding heart, and sweating brow A last cigarette for the
condemned

And the last words, do you with God amend Hands bound
behind my back

The Blind fold turns my vision black

I hear the words, aim, load, and I perspire Then silence and the
command fire

The firing of the rifles, I jump with surprise and pain racks
through my chest, and the pain dies

Then Nothingness

British soldiers were made an example of in the 1st world war,
because the French soldiers went on strike.

THE GIBBET

Oh, rotting carcass there you hang and fly Face contorted was hanged or did you die Did you dance on the rope and choke Then the final snap and you're neck broke

Now wrapped in a wrought Iron cage on show to deter those wrong doers so they might know

The hungry birds have eaten most of you, and had their meal

But because you're long since dead you didn't feel Flesh green and rancid falls off those bones

It doesn't become you those shades of blue and green tones and the smell now all too much to bear

You are given a wide berth of those who are passing there the once fine cloths you wore now torn to shreds

And the fine head of hair now mouse's beds Maggots eat away greedily with ease

Chrysalises store inside your body to mature when they please

Your bodily fluids drip down and refresh the earth The new growth of mandrake has given birth

So, my friend you have been useful after all You have given to others after your deaths call and there you are on show like an exhibit

On the cold and lonely Gibbet

THE HOUSE

On the hill stands a tall, old, forbidding house Alone it sits, as quite as a mouse

Wrapped in overgrown, and neglected ground Unkempt, threatening, as dusk draws all around Greeted by a slightly open front door

Entering in, and walking on an oil cloth Floor As you walk into Dark, and gloomy entrance hall

Wondering what of the fate that will befall Floor boards groan and creak

As you hesitate to speak "Hello is anyone there?"

Cold and wet you enter without care Glad of the shelter on offer inside Wondering what horrors reside

Darkness plays in the shadows, shapes twist and form and being there, makes you wish you had never been born

Screeching in the night Makes you jump with fright

But hesitating you ask yourself of what does hide Fear that seems to hurt your pride Nervous as you feel some doubt

Of what hides in the shadows, ready to jump out the smell of musk fills the air

Old dust and damp, makes your imagination scare Silence rises to a deafening sound Wondering what's waiting around

Heart beats to a fearful pace

The fear of the appearance of an unknown face Echo's in this empty place resound and bounce as courage takes every ounce

The flick of a light switch to get some light

But the light doesn't work and shadows stretch in the night Cobwebs brush against your face

In this eerie, forbidden place

Nervous finger tips brush against the wall Careful not to trip or fall

The dusty Mirror reflects the shape of the scary scape

As I venture in to the darkest room A white shape appears to loom

A voice rings out I scream and shout
With cold and sweating fear, I run
Racing my way out the door I'm out of here, I'm done Never
looking back behind
Fear that makes one blind
As the house behind me disappears
as moonlight shines and dark skies clears
The distant outline disappears from view
A sigh of relief I give out, phew

THE LOST HOPE BAR

Somewhere in the street of life, there's a flashing neon sign

Where lost souls visit from time to time The Lost Hope Bar, all are welcome there Broken hearted and all who carry despair Inside this bustling place

There's music for all those with sad taste Come drink a glass of humiliation Cocktails served of emancipation

Pints of sorrow, and agony snacks served in bowls Drinks and snacks to serve and suit all soles

As the bar tenders lends ears to sad tales of the down trodden over misery ales

on the dance floor is the dance of pain

The dance that others do over and over again the regulars come back for more

The way of things, they know the score There is the odd new face

Who visits this mournful place

To get intoxicated and drown their sorrows Looking for hope to fill those hollows Maybe to meet a new friend and be a pair to tell each other's sad tales and compare So if you're passing? Pop in and say hello and who you meet you'll never know Open 24 hours a day 7 days a week

Come in mix and speak at the lost soul's bar All are welcome from near and far

THE NAUGHTY CHILDREN MONSTER

A devious monster am I

Hiding in dark corners to make children cry Making myself disappear or reappear Making naughty children quake with fear

I can even enter their dreams

As I enjoy listening to their screams or even come in the dead of night

Causing imaginations to run wild with fright Every naughty child is my joy

My plaything, my imaginary toy

I don't like good children, they are no fun with wicked ones, I can get things done

I am here, there, and everywhere So misbehave if you dare

I come in all disguises All shapes and sizes

So please all you naughty children, do your worst You will be the ones that will be cursed

I love to make those bad children suffer best Leaving my victims muddles and stressed Please all those children don't be good

Cause I want to visit you in your own neighborhood

THE PSYCHIC VAMPIRE

I hide in the shadows, as I wait,
I have a date
I the psychic vampire Stealing thoughts, I aspire I don't steal much
Just a tiny touch
My victims hardly notice a thing Their thoughts on a platter to me they bring
I'm never greedy; I just take what I need in small proportions I feed
Leaving them Unnoticed, with their heads light Then I disappear into the night
Drunks are the ones that I like best As I stand with them and Joke and Jest
They never seem to notice the amount I take They think the hangover is their mistake So when you're out enjoying the drink
I might be waiting for you; doesn't it make you think?

THE SCAFFOLD

Three minutes, up those wooden steps I go to a fate, on that scaffold that I know There before me hangs the noose

Empty for the moment, loose I am scared my body shakes

My legs shiver and my insides quakes Heart pounding with growing fear

As the pending end of my life is near

the angry shouts from the jostling crowd As I stand before them, bound but proud the executioner places on the hood Darkness now surges my blood

The rope I feel around my neck

And the moment of the trapdoor opening through the deck Flashing images of my life, flash before

As I fall through the floor

The rope yanks hard as it tightens taught

With every breath to grasp for every moment fought the final agonizing snap of the neck, as I dance

Now I know I've lost my chance

And with my last conscious breath I am taken with death

My last thought of the innocence and the grave injustice is my last sense

Darkness, nothingness

and the final word "God Bless"

THE VAMPIRE

Twilight lights a beam, in a cellar that is dark Outside Wolves howl and bark

Night throws a shroud over the land in the darkness a coffin opens by a hand as it creaks and groans as it opens wide A silhouette looms, and climbs outside

That insatiable taste for blood

Would feed his hunger and make him feel good He makes his way across the cold damp floor in the musty smell, he opens a heavy door Outside in the open, cool, safe, and dim

His form, now changes his every limb as his wings flap as he takes flight into the moon lit night

His eternal hunting on his quest for virgin maiden blood is best

He needs to be safe back before the light of day Time is against him, he can't delay

Miles over land across the sky

His hunting ground is wide, as he drifts to fly the light from a bedroom window shows the way to a

meal

Open now he slips in, to quench the taste of bloods appeal He changes his form, and stands over his victim, tall

The female laying there doesn't stir at all red eyes glare, Ivory fangs bite

He sucks the blood from her jugular vein tight She lies there under his will

He won't stop till he's drunk his fill He then leaves in his other from

Now time fights, against the coming of dawn Now he's made it back to his resting place

As he climbs back into his coffin, blood upon his face Ascended from Vlad the Impaler

The vampire has become his own jailer Trapped by the light of day

His eternal prison in every way He lies there waiting for the night
The way of survival is now his plight So sleep and be a-were
Because he could be at your bedside standing right there

TWISTED THOUGHTS

Oh, does death makes me want to sleep Do I cry or do I weep?
Or does inside of me scream? In this never-ending living dream
My agonized sole is burning

But time and the world keep on turning in my mind comes the constant yearning of past thoughts that keep returning How can I keep suffering this fate?

As nagging thoughts turn to hate I struggle as my insides writhe in the search for lifting blithe

I try hard to resist Getting by to just exist

And to rest, but have to try No time to give up and just die to rise about this internal battle That monster I have to tackle

Long away from Harm To mental peace and calm and oh that somber rest

To familiar surroundings I like best

VLAD

Who would have thought Dracula? Your stories of old Of Vlad the impeller would be forever told
A Turkish Prince of nobility and station
Would throw a tyrannical rule over a Rumanian nation Cruelty was your name
To torture, inflict injury, and maim
Those you impaled in steaks, as they slowly slid down to agonizing pain
Some said you were insane
Heads of vanquished enemies' hand on spikes above you gate
A man with no respect and of sheer hate Rotting carcasses were put on show
those on steaks died long and slow
Pleasure you took amongst those exhibits, as you dined A sight for those poor peasants to remind
Your legend has become immortal
The name always to be remembered for those who are mortal
Carved in stone
The word "Vampire" stands alone

WHAT A WASTE

The way you left, everyone was so surprised Things were never as bad as everyone realized It was the way it was done, that shocked us all.

how it was done, without any stall

Silent depression was your friend

it got you in the end

Your life quietly fell apart in heaps of mess everyone around you felt so helpless

But didn't think? How you were so selfish

How things could have been different now, we wish the blood spatters on a white tile wall

Over the bath, the ceiling, and floor

The lingering odor of death and Sulphur fills the air Why did you have to kill yourself there?

The gun still in your mouth, the police at the door It's the young children now crying, I feel so sorry for They are now heart broken and blind

Now you've left them behind

to me you were a beautiful woman

With wonderful children and a loving man No consequences in committing suicide No dignity and certainly no pride

How could you have done this in such haste?

What a loss, and what a waste

The Come and Read Me Book of Poems

CONTENTS

A THOUSAND

I have lived a thousand life's on earth Since the thousand times, of my birth Felt a thousand sorrows

Of those thousand spans, of life that borrows Dreamed a thousand dreams in turn

And had a thousand nightmares in return Had a thousand hopes in time

And those thousand dashed, and left behind I have a thousand feelings kept inside

A thousand angry emotions, I have had to hide I have searched a thousand hearts for love Felt a thousand angels, from heaven above Championed a thousand causes, and lost

Won and lost a thousand at a cost

A thousand things of regret, I have said and a thousand sorry-s, screaming in my head

From my heart a thousand things, I gave on the thousand occasions I forgave

of the thousand People, I had saved

In the thousand times, I've became enslaved and the thousand kisses, for I have yearned Those thousand times, my heart was burned I have heard a thousand cheers

Shed a thousand tears

And of the thousand, welcomes with open arms There was a thousand, goodbyes with smiles and charms

All those thousand things, I could say

Of all these thoughts and feelings in one day

A BLANK PAGE

I stare at a blank space
A piece of paper in my face Empty, all the lines look the same
Borders set in a blank frame Seems I haven't got the will
For words to pour out and fill the pen lies on the page
As a sentence takes time to gage Thought's grind to a halt
It's not my fault White, square, on the sheet
I need to motivate, to make words complete Not sit here, and
face defeat
Isn't life sweet?
Seems words have no respect
The bin over flows with screwed up balls that I reject Papers in
piles of reams
Frustration lets out screams Just get the words rolling Get the
pen controlling Let's get the flow
Get those words on the go and there lays the lazy pen
I sit and stare at the empty page again

A SENSUAL MOMENT

Warm touch leads to sensation of dreamy, drifting elation
As hormones react to mingling Responding to the tingling
Glanced, by half open eyes
In the place where passion lies Gentle shivers
As tender body quivers and finger tips deliver
From the touches of the lover's giver How the moments drift
From that sensual gift to a heated writhe
Where immaculate feelings thrive Uncontrollable pleasure
The moment of the measure Deep, with moved mortal sole
with no control
And how the body aches Moment shakes, as flesh quakes to
sweet rapture
Of the instant that those seconds capture Relaxation
Of fired, but satisfied perspiration A happy lay to sleep
Of the physical sensation, so deep Taste of love, now satisfied
No tenderness denied

A SLAVE TO LIFE

A slave to life, from the day we are born
as we ride the wave of an unpredictable storm
Our mortal spans, of miniature seconds is the time Survive the strokes of moments in line
As the eternal clock rolls on Eons have been and gone No beginning and no end
As the finger points on an ever-turning bend Each second, each hour, each day
Too large the time to comprehend that way and yet, we live in our minute allotted space on the ticking course in the constant race When our time has come
Life, expelled and done Do we start all over again?
Rebirth in another life, do we regain Tick tock goes the life as if taking stock as a heartbeats as ticking clock
We leave behind our spent remains and the mere pang of mortal pains

ADDICTION

Disclaimer: I don't condone the use of drugs; this is an insight of into a typical user.

Her eyes flicker open after another heavy night as another day hit the dim room with light Shakily her hand reaches for a ready-made Joint,

She needs it now; it will help her to a point

As she takes her first puff, it will burn away all hope Just to tide her over, so she can cope Trapped and helpless in another day

Wishing deep down she could escape and get away Her only thought in her mind, is an amber white line That her body now yearns for, at this present time Relaxed now from the shakes

As drug addiction makes

She dresses in oversized clothes that used to fit They now hang loosely off her every little bit

The loss of appetite and for food she needed to feed Her habit is her only need

Losing all her self-respect that she needs to sell

on a street corner, as any curb crawler knows well Just one more trick for another daily score to pay In the hope she gets her fix for another day

She used to have a life once, when she was free Thinking to herself, this is now me

She carries this heavy shame inside Something now she knows she cannot hide

Losing all family and friends that in time she ripped off one by one

Her need was greater, now it's done

Her only friends now, is the dealer and the gear The only need in her life now, she holds dear

A small packet in a wrap

Knowing the risk that it's cut with all kinds of crap

Rushing back to her little hovel she calls a place The excitement and the wanting, makes her heart race

Oh, the desperate need for that warm injection She cannot fight that addictive infection

Now the rush

She needed very much

As a thousand unconscious moments surge as she relaxes to a fulfilled urge

Her eyes slowly close gently Limp both physically and mentally

She draws a breath Taken now by death

As her lonely sole drifts off from its holds release, she another statistic of an O/D in a report by the police She will not know pain any more, she's left it all behind A family will now carry that pain in memory in mind

BREATHLESS WONDER

On granite stone, on slated land
Past souls that carved out, and shaped by hand Blood of Celtic ancestors stained the soil

with heavy, straining, agonizing toil
Hands calloused, and blistered
While the beauty of the mountains whispered the force of life's where they belong

In proud ballads of singing song Lifted are the heavy hearts now proud from the heavy deluging cloud Rugged in all its wondrous sight

As the sky burns red with the dragon's flight Myths of Hero's tales

Of sacrifices made down in the vales The call of the valley of the Rhonda All this fills a child's head with wonder

As the little ffestiniog train winds up the track Past green grass and trees, where once stood slack Those of Celtic tongue forlorn

Into proud heritage born Sing of hero Owen in a song

Speak Thomas Dillon in poetical long Castles, valleys, hills, mountains and sea Welsh in traditional dress, now they are free Stand on the high, breath god's air

And give thanks to natures creation, if your ever there to purvey all around that splendor prevails Breathless wonder in the land of Wales

BROKEN PROMISES

It seems Promises can be broken

From those words of pretense that are spoken

And those who make them, can't comprehend

Of those who are hurt, who never have the time to mend I wonder if they would feel the same

If someone played them at their own game Wouldn't be a neat trick

If they were the receivers on the other end of the stick,

I don't think they would like it one little bit

I would imagine they would throw a right fit How would they like the bad news?

If they were in your shoes

There are those who are honest in the promises they give There are those who use promises to live

and those who use promises to inflict pain and there are those who use promises to gain Is promise just a word?

Is a promise of a contract verbally heard?

If a promise cannot be made

Or kept, then it should not be displayed Not a word to be used as fond

But a pledge of a bond If a promise is to steep

Then it's a promise you cannot keep Don't make those promises, I say

And respect would always come your way

ACCENTS

Where we Come from round the globe, the language spoken Plain or bold.

From where we live the Twangs still hold, take mine for instance, Centuries old.

IT GOES LIKE THIS:

Ello ow au ya or yow oroite (as we say), in our friendly greeting way.

I'm from bemingum yow ok? put wood in the ole, Meaning close the door.

Yow cun ave sum tae and sum more, We talk like this, and without a miss,

that's why you all take the (****) the micky.

Slightly slow in speech or very fast,

The sounds and Vowels from our inherited past.

South of BRUM is not so bad, the north of BRUM is really Mad.

Interpreter needed for the broad of speech, in our Helsowen street.

Where I live is very mild,

Not like the north and Black country very wild.

Odd sayings for young and old, and phrases that we Brummies hold. Confuses others the things we say, but we are used to it in our own way.

But the world over is the same, but written text is universal and plain.

Apologies for the spelling mistakes, but it's to express the local dialect.

CHOCOLATE

The word "Chocolate" makes the most passionate woman let
out a delightful scream

Cocoa butter, milk and sugar dream Soft pink jelly, of Turkish
delight Bourneville as dark as night Almonds, fruits and raisin

Honey, and honey comb, amazing Runny fondant coffee cream
Coated by a covering of cocoa bean Liquors tantalize

Exotic shapes of all sorts set before the eye's

Hazel nuts, coconut desecrated Lemon and orange zest grated

Cherries glazed created Taste buds elated

Brazil nuts sank in caramel The urge of chocolate does compel

Mint the bitter cool Creamy strawberry fool

Thin, crisp, wafers just melt away

of the senses of delicious, tend to play

No wonder some get the chocolate urge

To treat themselves to a chocolate splurge

COMPLEXITIES

I've seen the roof of the top of the earth Seen volcano's give lands new birth Swam the deepest of the ocean floor Opened heaven's door

Felt the rains pour Surprises held in store

Witnessed the birth of a child Felt the wilderness in the wild Held the warm sun on my face

Been welcomed to a friendly place Explored the realms of space Watched an angel fall from grace Saw battles fought and won Constructed wonders, built and done Technology in its wonder's breath Saw relatives at their loss, grieve Tricks pulled from a sleeve

None believers, believe Knowledge in its infinite wisdom sought

Thinkers pondered deep in thought Writers create the word

Music and images, seen and heard All these things witnessed and seen the actions of a human being

The gentle flight of the dove

But who can understand the complexities of love?

CONFLICT

I am a young soldier in this foreign land

I spit out the dust of the blowing desert sand in the heat of the day and the cold of the night My orders are to fight

I fight for those who are weak

Who have no voice, and are unable to speak

I have not yet met those, who I would give my life for But I hope I do, if I survive this war

Bullets whiz and fly Fear makes me think I'll die

Bombs, missiles, and mortar quake the ground There is confusion all around

But out of all this, shouts a steady command

Of the officer we trust, as the fighting is now hand to hand I, like others are so scared inside

But with all going on around, I put those feelings aside Winning the battle is all that matters

Another step more, of driving those out, which leave lives in tatters

I hope this is going to be well worth all the effort, for a lesson taught

As we soldiers, for a principle of others are being fought May God keep us all safe, till we return home

And watch over those who feel alone till this fight is done

And the conflict of war is won

DANCING LIGHT

I lay in the darkness of my room Shadows seen to stretch and loom the lightness taken away

Outlines of black and grey

Longing for the lightness of the day to the light my room I pray

Then something catches my sight A small prism of bright light

As beams radiate through the curtains onto the wall Slender it dances a dance so small

Flickering, shimmering bright

to take a where ness of the night It gave me hope

For those seconds of my illness gone, so I could cope while the light did remain

Forgotten was the pain Could this have been the sign?

For my own personal healing time? Dance oh light dance, take my attention Take me to another dimension

I breathe the air of relief Re constituted is my belief for my life is brief

But taken is the grief

Beads of sweat lifted from my brow I will survive my illness now

And the light does dance to restore life's balance Thank you small light

You helped me mend and took away my darkest night

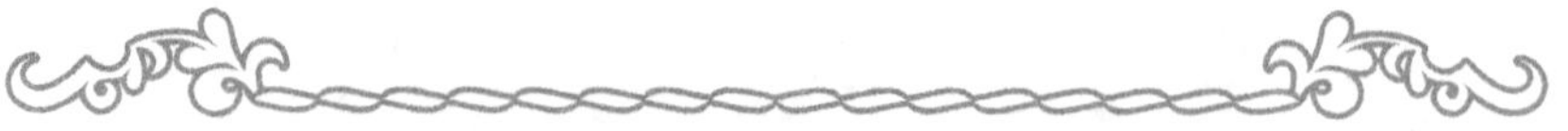

DARKER THOUGHTS

I am the dark force

I am in everyone's mind, of course Always there, waiting for my chance to take control for my influence Looking for my break

For someone to make a mistake I am the perpetrator of crime When my deeds are done

And I have had my fun Then I disappear

Leaving those to pick up the pieces, when my coast is clear

I am the perfect criminal, for the perfect escape I leave others in a scrape

I am always in the mind of everyone They always take the blame, for all I have done

Conscience is not my friend

And sometimes it gets the better of me in the end But I am patient, as I can wait

I strike without mercy, when it's too late

at times, I can be addictive

Rather cruel, and vindictive Sometimes inconclusive Devious, and elusive

The dark side of thought, in your mind I leave trouble and turmoil behind

And when there is nothing and you're diminished Then I am, with you finished

EASTERN LADY

Oh, Lady of the East What thoughts do feast?

Your personality of ginger spice Made from all delights that's nice Hair as dark as shiny night

Eyes of crystal burning bright Your delicate Pale coffee skin Makes others excite within

A mix of coffee and cream Swirling together like a dream A mix of burning ember fire the colors of your attire

All bright of rainbow silk Blended with ruby red and warm milk

And as the tiger and the Cobra cannot be one Forbidden love is lost and gone

So Mystic lady of the East All One can do at least

Is Ponder of those thoughts that Hide And keep ones feeling inside

EPITAPH FOR A SAILOR

A silhouetted figure stands alone upon the darkened shore Her love, her love, gone and lost forever more

A solitary tear cascades down her cheek How could she have ever lost one so meek?

As the moonlight caresses her face Here in the very spot, the very place

Where promises of a pledge between them were spoken She now stands in the twilight and is heart broken

Her prayer never answered, for her pleas gently on the soft sand, she falls to her knees

All she wanted, was for her fiancé sailor to be brought home safe

Now his life tragically ended by a bullets strafe only a memory came back

In the color of and armband of black the flag of honor, in a fold His hat and medals left to hold

She slips off the ring on her third finger of her left hand She nimbly tosses into the sea, from the land

Both hands cover a pitiful weep for a promise they could not keep

She utters the words; may my love be at rest Sleep forever as the oceans guest

I will always carry your love in my heart till the sea does part And she surrenders her dead

Then on that day we will meet, and wed as she slowly stood upright

A white dove passed in flight True love gave her the sign Forever Love will be thine

EVENING BRUSH STROKES

Brush strokes paint a pinky, reddened, Turkish sky of delight
The gigantic blood orange moon, hangs in flight Against the black foreground of twisted fingered trees Silhouette of the dark church spire lays in ease
Silver half lit cows, float in dusky light, against the silvered grass
In the soft yellowed amber pass
Water colored grey clouds paint a tint of heavens romance with tinsel spattered stars shine in prevalence
Together with a wash of indigo blue Pictures of an evening's wondrous view
Dusted with soft white mist in a dimmed light and the playing shadows paint a pictured sight The Easel paints each different view
The paper of the skyline a new

HEARTS

Take your hearts and keep them warm Keep them safe to weather the storm Protect in times of trial

Give them space, to rest a while if it's all too much to bear

A gentle touch of love will care

Hold them in both hands and make them strong So they can cope, and get along

And if the times that they get broke

Hope and time, will mend in tender words spoke two hearts begin to share

And feelings become aware in time they will bond

Tender rare moments, of growing fond as the heart yeans for hope

The need to share, so it can cope Beating in its constant life's span

In the chest of woman, child, and man if all can stand the test of time

Those beating hearts will be fine

To rise and stand against a fall conquer pain, love, trial, and all Then in one single heart does beat

To face what trials, and not admit defeat Then yours is the true, living part The strongest and the tender heart

HOLOCAUST

60 years ago, today 6 million souls led away to die No one could hear them plead or cry

There only crime was to be of different creed Disabled, out casts, infirm, homosexuals,

or from a so-called different breed

Not only one race, but any person with a outsiders face All who didn't meet the needs of a purified so-called master race

Those that didn't fit in to a Master plan

The ideals of a bullying, lying, cheating, scheming, Austrian man

He led those to believe they were off to a new way of life Taking those out of poverty and inner-city strife

To a new camp of luxury where they would "work to be free"

And above the Camps entrances the deceiving signs " Arbite macht fre"

As those horded form all over Europe into unknown elimination

Fooled mislead as they sang and was full of calibration

But little did they know the fate

That behind the mask of those who tricked them was a Race of pure hate

And as the air rained white ash and the furnaces burned white hot

Were those millions at that time, to be burned and lost forever and forgot

That Arrogant Man who thought he could win the world Through greed and ignorance watched his plans fall apart, become unfurled

Panic as he lost his grip of tyranny and fear and lost the war

To hide the biggest secret of all but as most things it came to light

The World now heard the voice of those victims' plight Something the human race should never allow to happen again

And there to this very day stands the Epitaphs of those remains

Those concentration camps there to remind us of this all as those 6 million voices call

Not one tear shed Not one voice heard Not one plea accepted Not one soul forgotten

Not one life wasted Not one death

Not one lost heart Not one belief

Not one individual

But one of 6 million all as one Now my remembrance is done

HOW CAN I

How could I fix the world, the way I am? For I, am a small and insignificant man Can I shape it delicately in my hands?

Change the shape of foreign lands Blow gently away hate of race Change the color of a face

Take away man's mistrust Like the fashioning of a clay bust Do away with Profit and greed

Make a trustworthy breed

Where marriages promise, means for life for loyal husbands and wife

Where children are safe from harm No mass paranoia or alarm

Anger, rage, and murder would not be thought in its place peace, harmony, sought

A world where people do really care Where equality and justice would be fair

Art, music, and culture would be open to all Freedom to debate, and prophesied would be at call Bountiful and plenty for all to feed

A place where there would never be need but my hands are too small

So, I could never change things at all

I VAMPIRE

I vampire here in the darkness, I lay Skin cold to the touch, clammy and grey

Asleep and waiting for the day, to pass and go away

for the familiar shroud of darkness to show me the way I lay here in my coffin lined with motherland earth from my roots of the place, I was given birth

But that was in my mortal time, of now centuries past and in my mind of the memories, of eons past How I fear the light, which brings intense pain

The source of sunlight, which can extinguish my life or drive me insane

My kind so misunderstood

Just because I survive on drawing others blood I and my kind a very different race

The old nation, which occupied the night's space Our ways secret now, driven underground

Persecuted, driven to extinction, not many of us found A whole nation of us that existed long ago

Exposed by the writer Bram Stoker as history would show Stories exaggerated, stretched to create fear

The pen that's showed the wrong side, it would appear and how the day dwellers would react

For the wrong writings and misinterpretations of the fact Our whole nation lost

From the profit of a writer, we have paid the cost Our sacred book hidden away

Never to see the light of day at one time we co-existed

The day dwellers gave us life, they never resisted We lived in harmony, they sharing the day

And us sharing the night, we were all happy in every way but history breeds myths and lies

The tens of thousands of night dwellers soles die's and the few of us left, now cries

The nights left empty of those that used to roam Empty now the place that we called home

We never took life, as lifeblood was given freely but now desperation has forced us dearly

I vampire here I lay

Waiting for the light of day to go away

and the familiar nights shroud to show the way

This the story I have told

Of a culture passed, gone and old

IMAGINATION

Vivid moonlight casts the shadows on the bedroom wall as darkness of dusk begins to fall

Those shadows seem to twist and dance Point and mock at every glance

The imagination runs away

It's time for fear and thoughts to play the branch of the tree outside, rattle and tap

Whilst under the quilt of the beds trap Doors slam and floorboards creak

The wind whistles through keys holes seeming to speak Lunar light catches the glint of the knife

Reflecting the light on the ceiling of the taker of life Heart pounding on the chesty drum

Feverish cold sweating, struck dumb

And the cupboard door in the corner, begins to slowly open wide

Is that the place where the monsters hide? I've come for you, imagination would say I've come to take you away

Frozen with terror, too scared to scream and suddenly waking from the haunting dream

The Child wakes

To witness the day that breaks Laying there relieved and at ease

And the reality of its not for real and feeling pleased Its was all pretense

Of the child's Imaginations unwitting defense

MAKING LOVE

Our lips gently met and locked together Slightly parting massaging and yet

I saw your eyes close, you seemed to drift That sensuous bonding of that gift

My hand touched the nape of your neck as I gently caressed

I kissed your neck and shoulders, as you undressed

I felt your warm hands respond, as you touched the back of my head

Our bodies pushed closer together, in loves thread Feeling those hard nipples pushing through your dress Against my body, they did press

Excitement rose inside us both, sweet raptures did rise As I lifted you dress, I gently stroked and caressed your thighs

My hand cupped your most intimate part You quivered I felt your heart

I felt you shudder and tremble, as I manipulated that wanton part

Your kisses became more intense

Your eyes shut closed, as you lost your sense Hot and moist and wanting very much

As I removed the barrier for a better touch Nothing mattered, we didn't care

That elated moment there Hard and erect

Your body responded, I could detect

I felt your hands shaking as you hurriedly did undo and down dropped my jeans, off they flew

There in all its glory I stood proud as we both was utterly aroused You guided me to the goal

As I parted that tender fold I slowly pushed

Your breath held for a moment you hushed Then you gently pushed to meet

Our kisses hard and sweet Pushing, pushing, together deep the
pulsating rhythm that we keep
Tensions coming to bear
nothing could stop us we didn't care I saw the pain of pleasure
on you face
As I pleasured your erotic place On, and on we drive
as our passions thrive
Those cries as you tighten you grip as you are sent on a hor-
monal trip Driving passions burn
To the point of no return
Then exploding deep inside tense moments, we press together
Locked in time for what seems forever Then as we slide away
We collapse into each other's arms exhausted in every way
As you tremored, and shook uncontrollably, not able to move
our rendered moment, as each other's love was proved

MY LITTLE ANGEL

My little angel so small and sweet perfectly formed and neat
The look of innocence in her eyes No deceit to tell no lies
Uncorrupted, honest and true Giving unconditional love to you

.

Unknowing with an honest view
the want of learning, the need to do She is the apple of my eye
To defend her I would die I would give her my all Respond to
her every call

.

My little angel she brings love Sent to me from heaven above
the little gift to me
I will be there for her every need to do my parental deed

.

I would be there for every part of her life Though her happy
times, fear, pain, or strife to guide her through the life's path
I ask for nothing in return back as I will get it returned in kind
with no other thought in mind My little angel

QUESTIONS, QUESTIONS

Tell me, what do you see?
Chrystal clear? as things are meant to be?
Is the road straight and sure?
Or twisted and winding, unsafe and insecure?
Does the heart yearn or burn?
And does love play tricks as we live and learn?
How do you feel inside?
Or do you have deep moments in your sole you hide?
Can happiness come in short spells?
Are the roses given from guilt, hold sweet but bitter smells?
Can tears stop falling down a cheek?
Does the monster become compassionate and meek?
Can the gentle child hold out its hand and give? Would a self-made prisoner break out and live?
Can we ever find the time to be free? Could those devout enemies agree?
Can worlds governments be honest, just for once in time?
Would poverty break the bonds of crime? Can Races learn to accept and live together?
Can War and pestilence be wiped out forever? Could all religions live to the book of word?
Not listen to the lies and rumors, that they have heard?
Is there a time of honesty and fair?
Are there those out there, who really care?
Can there ever be true commitment to marriages course?
Is it too easy to walk away and get a divorcee?
Can youth be taught respect?
Or be told by do good-ers to reject? Questions, questions, all to ask
These many inquisitive posers of a heavy task All this and much, much, more to debate
Life has all these meanings for one to relate So tell me?
What do you see?

SOLDIER BOY

Oh, soldier boy keep on walking Drive out those Terrorists out, that's stalking

You fight for freedom, and the right to make your country safe and tight to oust out evil to make purity

To reassure the insecurity

At what price your life will pay? I wouldn't want you to, I pray

You and others, we hope God is by your side

We know you carry fear in your hearts, but feelings you have to hide

It's Now a matter of National Pride Saving face I can confide

Being proud and standing tall Fighting hard and fighting for all for what you fight for is, right You, and others with all you might

America and our UK could never fall One unity, One people, One Call

For stars and stripes, red, white, and blue the ensign for freedom for all of you What price will you have to pay?

For others, I cannot say

A SOLDIER'S SONG

young soldier your off to war You've been called to your countries call

A job to protect Liberty, and freedom for all Vengeance is mine sayeth the lord

A threat from a fanatical hoard for God and country you must fight

The fight against fanaticism and tyranny is right Drive on boys Drive on

Fight on till you have won

Don't stop till the battle is over and Done And every terrorist has been eradicated and gone

Enough We've had enough Let's call those murderer's bluff

Go boys Go do your stuff

They have played their game and pushed too far We stand, we retaliate, now angry we are

We tried piece, we tried, we gave

Now it's time to take the aggressors to their grave Push on boys push on

Until the battles over and won

TENDERNESS

I look into your wonderful face Excitement, Nervous, Trembling, as we embrace Your soft sensual lips slightly quiver as we kiss

Softly caressing in gentle bliss

A warm emotion as we both drift inside Bringing the moment together as our feelings entwine

Gentle hands stroke with pleasure Fondling neck and back bringing emotional treasure

Two delicate bodies locked in heavenly embrace

As heart and pulses start to race Sensual fingers cause the body to tingle as our Entities run deep and mingle Rising perceptions rush inside our souls

Like the burning embers of igniting coals

Your eyes close as your threshold reaches the point of no return

This moment of strong intensive Passions burns the height of ecstasy reaches a peak

Locked into unconsciousness unable to speak Two life souls united as one in hormonal instance

And a million experiences surge though our very existence Then peace as gently falls elevation

To a wonderful relaxation Together in each other's arms

Appreciating each other's tender moments and charms Looking into soft and dreamy eyes

That tender moment that never lies

THE LILLY GIRL

Was I asleep Deep in dream or awake?

A soft and gentle form does take Lulled in soft mist and gentle light She appeared from the night

Small, Delicate, flowing long brown hair with deep brown eyes and skin so fair Dressed in somber, flowing lacey white Like swaying lilies in nimble flight

She gently raised my sleepy head helped me rise gently up out of bed

Pulled me softly in to her arms

Placed my head on her shoulder, bathed warm with charms She spoke softly in whispered sound

I will lift the pain in what your bound I offer warmth I freely give to you

I will make you whole and feel new

Gently kissing me with her soft tender lips on mine sweet ecstasy our love entwine

The sweet smell of lilies perfume

My swimming head intoxicated and consumed As I awoke, she drifted distantly away

Leaving me there in the grey light of day Was it a dream of what could have been?

Or wishful thinking yet to be seen Who Knows?

THE ASSENT

Fingers grip, hands reach and clasp To hold in sinewed grasp Muscles twist and strain Taught and tense with pain Sweat and breathless climb

Mixed with dust and reckless grime Arms and shoulders heave and stretch

While hips and stomach tense and wretch Feet searching, not to slip or breach Delicately find the way, in difficult reach the climber starts to ascend

The body, the tool starts to bend

the cruel rockface throws up its wall

Teasing, tempting to slip and fall Limbs begin to falter

To the gigantic alter Ropes lay heavy on the back hooks jingle on the sack

The hard load gets heavy with all the weight it can Levey

And how the face of the climb does mock the worn-out climber, beats the rock

To see the pinnacle in sight

And defeat the mountains daunting Hight Looking on the tiny world below, look down Standing on the mighty mountain crown Feeling you're the winner that's applied

Elated with a sense of pride Knowing what you have done victorious, you have won

THE CLIMB

As I climbed the craggy mountain face Rocks and boulders barred and slowed my pace

Grey and misty clouds hung high aloft

As purple blue heather swayed in the breeze so soft Hands blistered, aching limbs, and feet tired and worn Clothes snagged, scuffed, and torn

Muscle and tendon stretched and broke Stress and fatigue beyond a joke Breathless as I battled against heavy defeat

On, and on, with utter determination to win and beat the summit slowly appearing in view

Worth all the effort for that I've been through As I stood victorious, on the mountains throne Aghast, insignificant, and all alone

Lady wind brushed her fingers against my sole with grace to witness this pinnacle of a vast and never-ending space Heaven's song whispered a tune into my ears

To the scene of vale, field, veined rivers, the heart reveres Lifted ecstasy to the heavens high

Touched deep within I began to cry

This edge of the world laid before my very sole Completing my conquest and making it whole exhilaration moved me deep within

That I had succeeded in the will to win

At bated breath I paused and stood in wonder

Of the misty view set asunder

THE COUNTRYSIDE

How I love the countryside Fields of space so far and wide Trees of leafy bloom

Air to breath, and loads of room The pace of life is calm and slow Time that seems to gently flow Cattle spread they seem to laze Laid back as they graze

Leafy lanes that twist and turn

Past woodlands of bluebells and green fern

as you climb the crested hill and see the view What is seen, takes your breath form you Quilted color's as far as the eye can define

The tiny church spires, like needles on the sky line Clouds of cotton wool gently drift

As the brightness of the sun gives a lift an old stone cottage topped with thatch

Hamlett and village wrapped around does match Down to the little rustic stone bridge

That spans the babbling brook and ridge in the distant the train crosses the marsh Rugged brushland that looks so harsh

But the wild fowl flies, to the of that trains sound A sense of freedom that is found

The echo of gaggling geese across the farm the open countryside that has its charm

THE FOOD AND VEGGIE BALL

I dreamed that I was invited to a ball It was the strangest thing of all

All the guests were fruit, veg, cakes, and sweet I laughed so must it knocked me off my feet Food wearing clothes with faces stood around and me laughing on the ground

The host was Lord and Lady Parsnips

They stood there Frowning with hands on their hips The duke of ring Doughnut was not amused

The Cucumbers asked to be excused As I made into the dance hall

I watched Mrs. Jelly and Mr. Ice cream trip while dancing, and fall

They bounced all over the place

And the Duchess of trifle was leaving in great haste Sir Cracker Biscuit and lady cheese melted into each other's arms

And there by the bar Mr. Turnip was wooing miss Carrot with his charms

And further in the Room Lady Melons was flirting with Captain avocado Pear

Lots of fruitiness and flirting going on there The Reverend gherkin stood upright and erect

Mrs. gherkin stood in the background with a feeling of neglect

The Cherries jumped in to the cream The strawberries let out a delightful scream

Mr. cabbage laughed so much, that he was falling apart And Mr. Celery was exposing his heart

The Tomatoes as butlers serving drinks to all The Potato Orchestra played music at the ball As the Muffins danced around with glee Baroness Mushroom was talking to Mr. green pea

And those Spanish dancing Onion rings

And doing the flamingo getting into the swing Sir Cream puff stood Nobel-y by

As Countess Von Strudel started to cry Those Macaroon Tarts flaunted their stuff

And in the excitement one of the Eggs got cracked and went off in a Huff

Apart from that a good time was had by all

At the food and veggie Ball

THE LOST HOPE BAR

Somewhere in the street of life, there's a flashing neon sign
Where lost souls visit from time to time
The Lost Hope Bar, all are welcome there Broken hearted and all who carry despair Inside this bustling place
There's music for all those with sad taste Come drink a glass of humiliation Cocktails served of emancipation
Pints of sorrow, and agony snacks served in bowls Drinks and snacks to serve and suit all soles
As the bar tenders lends ears to sad tales of the down trodden over misery ales
on the dance floor is the dance of pain
The dance that others do over and over again the regulars come back for more
The way of things, they know the score There is the odd new face
Who visits this mournful place
To get intoxicated and drown their sorrows Looking for hope to fill those hollows Maybe to meet a new friend and be a pair to tell each other's sad tales and compare So if your passing? pop in and say hello and who you meet you'll never know
Open 24 hours a day 7 days a week
Come in mix and speak at the lost soul's bar All are welcome from near and far

THE MORNING

The reddened sun and sky kissed in the dawns early rising mist
Lulled fields of early morn Another day is being born Silence dulled,
across acres
To wake the early morning wake-r's The glorious dawn calls
As dusk vanishes and falls
Comes the dawn chorus of the singing birds in the field of gathering herds
Cows walk in rows, to milking time
The farmer breaths the fresh air, and feels fine Bleating sheep
echo's, in the dullness
As the sun rises to its fullness The cockerel crows, as if to wake
to announce, day break
And the world stretches its arms to the ringing of clocks alarms
Once again, the morning sleep does spoil Starting the task of
daily toil
Then comes the groaning traffic, set in lines Beating to the railway times
Hustle and bustle of a working day begins as workers earn their
wages for their sins The city wakes, and drones
Traffic honks, and moans Crowds rush around in amok the day
started in a shock Comes that busy day
Work, earn, eat and pay

THE RACING PEN

Those words keep rattling over, and over, in my mind Not made for this brain that's designed

Phrases, words that seems to rush Never giving a moments rest or hush Syllables spew forth, like a water fall Cascading never seeming to stall Twisting

Not resisting Always insisting

Clouding the mind and making it misting an inner struggle to find the words to slot the times, before they are forgot

And those thousands of subjects Most of the time my head rejects So much to put down on paper Before they disappear and vapor the quickness of the hurried pen

as words race down on paper then starting, never stopping

Like a typical list for shopping Always things to add

Is an insanity that drives one mad and the pen races on

Till chapter, and verse is done there lays the finished creation

Of written words in anticipation, it's done at best

Time to rest

THE SHIP

The Tall Ship majestic Mary Marion sailed across the stormy seas

To choppy waves and blustering breeze her sails bellowed wide and full

the sky grew gloomy, dark, and dull Dark thunderous clouds hung over cast

Whistling winds blow hard and sheeted rain lashed the mast

As she the splendored cutter began to climb Crash down to that cruel storm torrent time Masts strained and groaned in a low moan

As the gale force wind and blinding rain are driving home Ropes snap and wildly become unfurled

Rigging flaying, sail ripping, as the ship churned and hurled

Waves like thousands of hands lashed across her wooden bow

As the captain stood on her poop deck as she was dragged down low

Cut the sails he commanded, and screamed the bosun to the crew

As they responded without question as they knew what to do

Mountains of water crashed against her Keel and starboard side

Flinging her like match wood as if to hurt her pride Ghouls screamed and howled as she drove to the storm lashed shore

Uncontrolled and as if adhering to the sirens call to her final moor

Lost and driven without control

As head long She surges to her reluctant goal Those rocks now vibrating to thunderous sound as on she rides storm ward bound

Abandon ship the crew hears the captain shout

As the life boats are cut free and the crew dive out Every man for him self

As she hits the oceans shelf Screaming timbers break and smash

As if to cry her last against the rocks she does crash Shouts and screams sound distant on her crumpled desk she lists to her side that doomed wreck

Her back broken as she cries her last of all she gave That merciless sea sent her to her grave

Taking 58 poor wretches with her down to rest Oh sweet Mary Marion you done your best

THE TAKING OF INNOCENCE

I saw a little child pass away and die

A small innocent soul float to heaven and fly I saw the parents break down and cry

At that very moment on the child's face, I saw peace and a smile

Now you're at rest for a while

The pain and anguish of one so small Tears of grief brought to all

As God takes a gentle hold to bring you back into his fold

There the angles rested you on a celestial bed Kissed and gently stroked your head

You're welcome here

All that are friends are near

Don't be afraid now, your safe in this place God has put a smile on your face

Here in this place, there is no hate, no pian, no fear All now to you is very clear

Although your life was taken short

And this situation been brought God gently took your hand

And took you to his heavenly land So Parents don't you cry I say

You will see your lost child one day So lift your pain

You're not the ones really to blame

Until that time, that child will watch over you. you were good parents more than you knew

THE VAMPIRE

A twilight lights a beam, in a cellar that is dark Outside Wolves howl and bark

Night throws a shroud over the land in the darkness a coffin opens by a hand as it creaks and groans as it opens wide A silhouette looms, and climbs outside

That insatiable taste for blood

Would feed his hunger and make him feel good He makes his way across the cold damp floor in the musty smell, he opens a heavy door Outside in the open, cool, safe, and dim

His form, now changes his every limb as his wings flap as he takes flight into the moon lit night

His eternal hunting on his quest for virgin maiden blood is best

He needs to be safe back before the light of day Time is against him, he can't delay

Miles over land across the sky

His hunting ground is wide, as he drifts to fly

the light from a bedroom window shows the way to a meal

Open now he slips in, to quench the taste of bloods appeal He changes his form, and stands over his victim, tall

The female laying there doesn't stir at all red eyes glare, Ivory fangs bite

He sucks the blood from her jugular vein tight She lies there under his will

He won't stop till he's drunk his fill He then leaves in his other from

Now time fights, against the coming of dawn Now he's made it back to his resting place

as he climbs back into his coffin, blood upon his face Ascended from Vlad the Impaler

The vampire has become his own jailer Trapped by the light of day

His eternal prison in every way He lies there waiting for the night
The way of survival is now his plight So sleep and be a were
Because he could be at your bedside standing right there

THE WHITE PALACE

On soft and gentle scenic view,
The sky hangs in clear blue
Against the texture of warm and golden beach As the Tropical Sea brushes against the shores reach
On the land stands a regal palace in glimmering white Statues of beauty stand either side and greet stairs flight As I climb the easy stair
I am greeted by a Garden of Eden there Walking bare foot on tepid marble floor I go through into the garden door
A long courtyard stands before me with a fountain and pool
Shade and coulombs stand in rows, shadows fresh and cool
The sweet perfume of honey suckle fills my nose and flora and foliage fills my eyes with sweet repose Birds of color sing their song
Insects and bees go about their business and buzz along And as I wonder at this marvel
Walking on black veined and crisp white marble Music in the distance greets my ear
The sound of flute, harp, and mandolin as I draw near Laughter and song fills the air
Those inside this palace without care I draw closer to the sound
I see through the curtain's young ladies dance around As I brush away the silky colored hanging freeze That seems to be dancing to the breeze
There she stood Like a goddess in chiffon white Her dress flowing soft and transparent in the light A jewel (a Bindi) on her forehead shinning bright Dazzling as caught by sunlight
Her hair, long, and shiny black
That flowed down her long and slender back
Her coffee skin of radiated complexion Dark brown eyes burns to meet perfection
And the silhouette of her perfect body seen through the dress
Took my breath away I must confess

She turned and smiled, and with a gesture beckoned me Held her arms out to greet and welcome so sweetly

and took both my hands to gently dance

As if to know me by chance We talked, Laughed, and ate

Had many things in common to relate as the day turned to twig light

I told her I had to go as its nearly night She turned and we kissed

Told me I would be missed to come another day

But inside I think I really wanted to stay we walked across that marble floor

Our last kiss on the sandy shore

We bid good night as I walked away,

I retuned the following day

There was no palace on that plot of land No stairs to greet me at hand

Just an empty space

And an expression of shock on my face

TIREDNESS

It's been a long day
Tiredness has heavily rested upon me in every way My eyelids fight
With the starting of the night Worn out too tired to write Exhausted to get things right My bed calls
Down along dim lit halls Rest and sleep beckons, so away
To a place that dreams play
and where thoughts gently rest to where tired bones know best
A good mattress and a warm quilt wait And yet I still hesitate
I have this poem to complete Sitting here, resting feet Much too tired to move Getting up, difficult to prove
I'll smoke this cigarette and go I now feel lethargic and slow
So sweet slumber I hear you call good night to you all

TOUCH THE SKY

One minute grain of sand are we are Against the countless numbers of the nearest Star

Tiny, insignificant among the measureless heavens of space

And yet the dark unknown touches each curious individuals face

It fills us with the thirst to explore

to push and seek just that little bit more

Trapped in our limited gravity in the small time of our longevity A quest to look into the unknown

As ancient symbols are carved in stone Point the finger, touch the sky

Groups of stars, in god's names they cry Solar systems like snow flakes

Who is the creator? Of this wonder makes We are infants, who have time still to evolve Leaving precious time to solve

To touch the outer layer of our little earth Standing on terra-firmma our place of birth Philosophers, predicted

Of a time to come, where there are no barriers depicted Until then we can only stare with open Jaw

At the Heavens marvel, creation with awe How we work at our persistent labor's

To touch the hand of our distant neighbors

How Lucky we are to witness this wonderful site

as the stars light up our darkest night

The Come and Read Me Book of Poems 2

CONTENTS

A DAY OUT IN WALES

Llanelli how I dream

Stood on the shore and survey your scene The green cove that surrounds the sea Sandy beaches pleases me

As the four of us play Frisbee Laugh and joke as we keep busy

It's quite amazing, stood there in Wales As hilly green mountains, avails

Into rolling beaches

As the estuary swings round and breeches in the warm summer breeze

Distance tiny villages, hide in the trees Cockles in the bay, makes me pleased Houses stream down the green hills All this inside with wonder fills Coffee on the sea front cafe

Talking to a local chap

How we four friends had a real good time Will always be remembered in my mind

A DAY

This topsey, Turvey Life it goes That keeps us on our toes
But if every day was the same
Life would be so boring, and so mundane Each day to run the test
Stops us stagnating into rest
It makes us laugh, joke, and Jest Makes of minds confused at best It forces us to try
Sometimes makes us cry
As we tread on that upward path that never ends Twisting and turning on those hazardous bends in our constant daily struggle
As if trying not to burst our safety bubble Not knowing what's in store another day brings
For its destiny that pulls the strings or of what would be the next surprise That unfolds before our very eyes
What comes next? Of that the day does borrow We will have to wait and see, tomorrow

A LIFE IN A HOSTEL

A life in a hostel is not much fun
to those who are lost, spent, and done
Those once useful members of what society cast out That no one wants those who are full of doubt Drinkers who have ended at the bottom of the pile
Drug users and loners, that's stop there for a short while Then because of a feeling of not belonging move on
A stable life is not for this one
Then there are those who of escaped from being abused the lowest ebb in life and who feel used
And those who cannot and do not know how to cope Lost and wandering for those who have no hope
For the few who strive to make things better those who follow the system to the letter Most cannot help the way they are
Some from near and some from far
All in their own individual ways trying to fit in those who have lost a battle and fail to win
The system lets them down
And in all the confusion and the bustle they drown Others have the will to get up and get about Hence the Name of Down and Out

AFRAID TO

If my heart had been broke a thousand times for so called relented crimes

Then surely, I have paid the price

And therefore, the wage has been settled to suffice Tormented in solemn pain

In what does endlessly remain and looking for the break

Say a niche, to force open, widens and make Looking for that open door

Slightly ajar to begin with, we are all looking for and finding goals slightly out of grasp Losing a grip of a loosely held clasp

And in the end losing it all, watching it all slip away in the reality of the cold light of day

Isn't life like that?

Almost deep within, afraid

Of getting to close, only to be rejected, and dismayed Even when true feelings are displayed

Then cast aside, feeling used and betrayed and others ask the question why?

Told that you don't even try

To me it's really safer not to get too involved That way it's easier to be resolved

It really is hard to trust

When your heart on more than one occasion has been bust Any way it's safer to just have friends that you can believe Not lovers who want to deceive

ARMIES OF DEATH

The Mysterious shadow of a figure stands on the darken shore

Hands rose to the sky, as he cursed and swore Chanting his, commanding spell

Beckoning the dead from the watery hell

I command you give up the dead from the depths of the sea

Release those soles they all belong to me Silence of the tide, in the dimness of the night skies One by one, figures of the dead soles walked out the

ocean, and began to rise

Then in hoards and armies marched from the deep on to sand

Silhouettes of lost souls, to the evils one's command Millions gathered on the cost

Ready to battle for the evil host

The shroud of mist covered those figures in the dark Glistening carcasses move and jostle to his hark And Eire moans of desperate soles cry out

Now stood in ranks all about Admirals and captains organize platoons

As the sailors played with flute and drum the deathly tunes Cannons dragged, musket, sword, cutlass, spears, and bow and arrows

Cannon balls carried in slime filled barrows The gathered columns now march inland

To the beating of the drum, as the evil one does demand and as they passed by graveyards, Soles rose up to join the call

To conquer every living thing so they die and fall Now Hell has come back to reclaim

For the goal of the Evil ones aim the battle of evil and good

As the world will now run with blood

Death will cover all the lands

To the gesture, of the evil one's hands So all you good soles. sit there and wait

And if there's a knock at your door? It's too late

BAD NEWS

When the phone rang, you gave me bad news What you told
me changed my views

And my friend, I'm so sorry

I guess as a parent you must be sick with worry,

I know in the same situation I would

Knowing your daughter is sick, your own flesh and blood and
I, like yourself, I feel so helpless

Liver failure, through a cry for help is not what I think of any
less

A young child dealing with mixed and confused emotions the
over dose of Co-proximal was taken in the turmoil of devotions

Her plea of parents splitting, the tablets washed and cleared

But Doctors didn't explain the damages and the after effects
adhered

Now Months after, one so young does lie in a critical state

And they say it could be too late

God I really hope she makes it though My heart really goes out
to you

I've met her you see, she so young and yet to grow This to you
my friend, must be a crashing blow I'm here for you any time you
need

Cause I'm hers, your family, and your friend indeed

WRITERS BLOCK

Writer's block is a funny thing Thousand words in your head does sing Sentences you want to say

Jumbled and confused in a strange way Subjects and lines running through your head Getting them organized is what you dread Paragraphs and verse you cannot say

Endless wrestling with word play

I think at one time we've all been there Tends to throw you off somewhere Wondering what to say

Empty paper and pen does lay Well you think, it's time to do Not an easy thing to go through Inspiration is what you need to motivate the deed

But somehow you get there in the end Good old you, you can depend

Keep plodding is the thing you do Something will eventually come to you Another poem in another way

You've made a difference to some one's day

THE NAUGHTY CHILD

Out when shopping you take your child You enter the store and off, they run wild

Bad enough trying to remember the shopping list but a disappearing child can be missed Wondering where and what they have done?

Being brought back by store detective is no Fun "Now child stand and walk by my side"

All red and embarrassed you want to hide Then it comes. The question you dread

"Mummy can I have?" running through your head "Because you've been Naughty!" I say NO Then the tantrums and screaming off they go

"I want it I want it" is bawled in a cry

And all in the store looking round, you want to die Tempers and tantrums screaming and fits Bringing to the end of your whit's

Trapped and no escape in the queue Nowhere to run and nothing you can do You're the OGRE parent, Mean and tight

As you battle with shopping and child full of fight The EXIT you headlong rush is the goal

Escaping the embarrassment from on lookers on the whole Then you make it outside the screaming gets worse

As parents we know the routine chapter and verse Then as you travel away from the store Child now calmed and saying no more

Getting home the child runs inside

As though nothing has happened with smile beaming wide Oh well Parents, we have all been there

Situations like this make you pull out your hair but little darlings they are, and where would we be as part of them growing as we can see

BEHIND THE FACE OF A CLOWN

Circus comes but once a year Bringing Joy and Happiness, from far to near

All manner of fun and laughs, do bring Entertainment in a Circus ring

We always remember the things we see Those Funny Clowns so clearly

But what has a clown got to hide?

His big red nose Those black, crossed eyes

That white completion Those funny smiles

Outward appearance does he deceive? An observer of life Does he preserve? Makes others laugh and what great fun Leaves others happy, till his work is done but what is his real feelings?

In life's complicated dealings Does he really run and hide?

Or keeps his tragedy hidden inside Covering it all up to create a laugh No short measures not by half

Behind the mask what does he really hide? Knowing to only himself those feelings inside So who knows? And when you see

That wonderful Clown could be me

CRICKET

Cricket season comes again in the field of green the game A team of men dressed in white

To joust opponents in the field of fight the weapon a willow bat a leather ball The need to win comes to call

Course laid out and wicket set the gauntlet thrown to win the bet

to gain the honored prize

The ashes cup for the team of size and play on hallowed ground Crowds gather clap and cheer

Stood wicket keeper and overseer

With team opponents here to face

In Lords ground the cricket heroes place the batsman challenges the ball

Defending wicket, as not to let the bale fall the bowler reels the throw

The sound of leather hitting willow the crowd roars and cheers
To the Game of peers
The ball hits the boundary wall Hit for six but scored for four the game is done
Those the victors have won
The champions hold the cup up high
As pride is held to the sky yet again
Those who played and won that revered game

DO YOU?

You are of flesh, blood, and bone? Do you really have a heart of stone? Does the blood surge in your veins?

Or do you get pleasure from giving pains?

Have you any reason to understand? Do you shape hearts with your hand?

Does love or hate in your human reveal? Is it so hard to show how you really feel?

Are your thoughts so crystal clear? Or are you as cold as you appear?

Do you give in one hand and with the other take? Are you so perfect you never make a mistake?

Does pride come before a fall? Is it so hard to admit wrong to all?

Can you raise a hearty smile?

Or does the fixed cold expression make you vile?

Can you be read like an open Book? Or have the pages torn out and took?

Has life treated you so bad?

You've lost the feelings you once had?

Can you ever love or feel again?

Or the way you are now, will remain?

All this is down to you It's up to you what you do

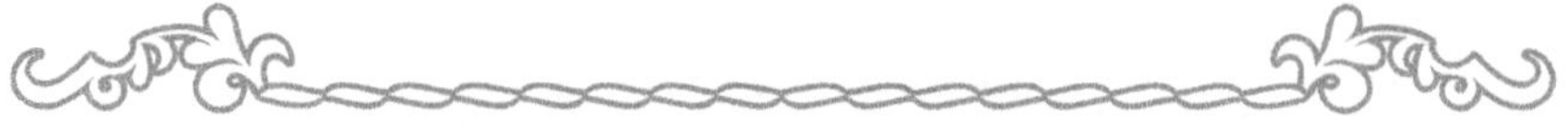

DOWN THE TRACK

Going down life's rocky track Down and down, never looking back

Always sinking lower

To a sea of turmoil, drowning slower Never stopping till I'm there

Can't stop now, no time to care They just seem to stop and stare Sir have you any change to spare

Need to make a phone call, cause life aint fair how I try

To hold back the tears, and not cry Doesn't time fly?

Inside I just want to die the bottom is getting nearer

And the cost of life is getting dearer Looming bottom of the abyss is bigger

As the shovel carves out the hole with a digger Looks just my size

to the judgment of my eyes

all is getting Chrystal clear

Like the stabbing of a burning spear Down that rocky track

Never looking back

Just nudge me when I get there

Cause the path of life unstable, tread forward if you dare when I get to the bottom, I will know

Maybe there's a sign on show Pointing the way to a rocky climb

And maybe I'll get back up there in time

EMBARRASSMENT

The embarrassing Mistakes sometimes we make Sometimes the silly chances we take

This really happened to me one day Whilst walking through my town on my way

Eyeing the females as we males do play on the hunt as we say

All sizes slim and perfect to be found with eyes wide open and mouth to the ground

Saw a blond with long silky hair

Small rounded backside and thought she's fair Thinking I of the things I'd like to do

Some things I can't divulge to you I made the usual chat up line

Said excuse me LOVE you got the time Thinking I have succeeded right

She turned around and got a fright There was greeted with a smile Hairy Lip with moustache pile

"OH MY GOD ITS a GUY " !!!, I replied

Wanted to run away and hide He said 2.45 and just smiled

Me just standing there feeling small and defiled I apologized and quickly went

Getting away I seemed hell bent

So please don't make the same mistake Look before you speak for god's sake

Making sure it's of the opposite sex when you use the chat up line

Then you'll be ok with no embarrassment you'll doing fine Never chat up someone from behind

And you will never be put in this situation you'll find

EMPTY HEARTS

What happens when a heart becomes an empty husk? Hollow, light, that blows around in the desert dust No course, No direction

Aimlessly lost without detection All hopes and dreams dashed away Loneliness and self-pity here to stay

Feeling it has nothing to offer in return Knocked back at every turn

If there was one small glimmer of hope A tiny chance inside to cope

Then why does it, yearn and beat? For a special person's warmth and heat

Wanting something you can't hold

As you're gently cast aside, and left cold All that desperate pain you feel

You know you seemed to have lost your appeal Rejection of more than friendship, seems to burden hard Thrown away like a devastated retard

Is this the game of life's play? Just to exist for another day

What course should a lost heart take?

In what direction shall it make? Moving on to a destined search yet again left in the lurch Who knows what life will bring? Thrown into life's daily thing

EYES

Eyes the windows of your soul

Tells you what is deep inside a person as a whole Sadness inside their life they hide

Inner fears and feeling that are hidden inside Happy or sad Healthy or bad

As we meet someone familiar or new, we tend to check at a glance that optic view

Love from them can be seen and felt deeper feelings in them can be held Reactions to the eyes can be seen

Even lies told that have been Deep emotions they do hold for untold stories they behold

Recorders of life events that have unfold in history of one's life untold

So, when you meet a friend or someone new Look into their eyes; it could be useful to you

FIRST LOVE

I think of you, and you remind
Of the past things, long ago I left behind
Like the first time, I looked into the eyes of innocence Kissed those lips of naïve sense
Held your hand and gently led
As music of the day, flowed through my head Sun shone through the trees
In the warmth of that summer breeze Together into the fields of dancing yellow corn
A boy to a man, a girl to a woman, that day was born My first love, but not my last
Through the swirling times of the past,
It all sped by now fast and so
It seems so long ago
But many hearts have been broken now, on the way Games of minds been put to play
And yet no matter what Your First love cannot be forgot
I can always remember in great detail
Our first innocent loving moments that did prevail Our childhoods we gave away and lost Never to be returned at sacrificed cost
In my heart, I will always for you carry a place and to this day I see you face Something special in my mind
First Love can never be put behind

MY LITTLE FLAT (APARTMENT)

My little flat is small but neat A quiet place to rest one's feet The lounge dressed all in red

A ruffled net curtain hangs over the bed All the comforts of home

To ponder with friends or on one's own tiny kitchen to fix a meal

Small bathroom and shower to appeal Friends who visit feel relaxed They unwind and feel untaxed How I love your place they say

So warm and intimate they want to stay This flat is part of me

As anyone can see

I've worked hard to get it right Dim light and cozy at night

I welcome all my visitors and give them space and don't push them and give them haste

My little pit as I call it, they love it every little bit

GROWING OLD

Why do shiny days, now seen dull And once hectic days go into a somber lull

Once the in the youth of life, the sun shone hot and those busy times now, seem long forgot

to slow and easy days

Have now established permanent ways Once times fiery and full of vigor Seems strained and hard to figure

Do these things come with age? As years, and decades turn the page

Company was compulsory, and always wanted Funny how we take all these things for granted Now it's all been blown away

To every normal single day Partner, wife, husband, children, and friends

All those things that company depends Lost and now gone

Who now is the lonely one?

In self-company, time is all that's left behind and thoughts of past things left to mind Once life's experiences from the past

Loving memories seem to be present, in a remembered cast

Comes to one who's growing old

Still warm youthfulness inside, but never cold Out there, is a yearned hope somewhere?

One day, just one day if you dare

HISTORY AND TIME

Born in the late 1950s, how time has flown
As in history and I have watched, Learnt, and grown as time and, I evolved
Conflicts of wars tragically rose and resolved the first man to walk on the moon
Concord aircraft breaking the sound barriers boom the invention of a Texas Instruments LED watch and calculator
Fantastic changes for an aircraft aviator
Black and white TV, to color remote TV with digital surround
Mono to stereo to Digital sound
From a Vinyl record to tape and CD to DVD to MP3 To technological advances form a mechanical binary machine to ever growing PC?
From Alexander Graeme Bell, to text sent on a mobile phone
From Pesticide uses, to Cell developed Clone Cooking on a stove, to Micro wave Energy efficient devices that save
A Letter put in the post email sent through a Network Host
All these things in my short life I've seen Past through History have come and been
What more marvels does History hold in store?
In the future opening its door

THE HUNTERS

Why do these people play mental games?
Just to suit their own aims Fooling others just to get their way
All the charming, deceiving things they say Like a hunter looking for its pray
A weak but honest victim for the offering to the slaughters lay
Building on the weak and venerable as they give them some hope
Pretending to be their friend so that they can cope A prize of conquest is their only goal
To take advantage of that person as a whole and as the victims build up their hopes and dreams
Listening to the smooth talker it seems the hunter or huntress promises the earth
For a wonderful relationship to be given birth Lies and subterfuge is their tool
Deceit and Manipulation set to make them cruel and when the deeds are done
Knowing that they have their fun They drop you like a hot stone
Leaving you the victim destroyed and alone Devastated and hurt, mistrusting
While the hunters move on lusting
To the next victim, for one more amusing fool
as they collect their trophies and think their cool but what of honest folk
They are the ones who are treated like a joke Those who want real love and romance Those are the ones who don't stand a chance

HOW DO I FEEL?

I sit alone here at night

Lost in a world full of fear and fright I used to have a purpose in life to abide

A love, a reason

Waking up was once, by your side and all my love I had to give and show

Where I went wrong,

I do not know I wanted us to be together for life You for me, the wanted wife

Now cast me out without a word The nasty rumors that I have heard and you ask me how I feel?

Thanks for making me insecure But I am now working on a cure Thanks for changing my life

Filling it full of hurt, confusion, and strife But I am on the mend

At least it's just myself that I can depend and still you ask me how I feel?

I don't think it's any of your concern in life we tend to live and learn That web of lies you had built

Just to hide your actions, and justify your guilt So ask me how I feel

Now to your conscious does it now appeal?

THE PC

The things I notice about my PC It's the stupid things it does to me

All the wrong things that you don't want it to do It does. Annoys, and plays games with you.

It does not work; you check it inside and out Operating system all about

Still a problem and you scratch your head Strip the hardware out instead Nothing wrong but still a prob

Turns you in to a screaming blob Wires, ribbons strips, and motherboard, a heap in a hoard

Strewn across the floor

You scratch your head again once more,

And wonder why you done this all, and face defeat Hours gone by and all together now, and complete on it boots up, and still the same

Enough to drive a saint insane Rant and rave and threaten this you do

The neighbors wonder who you're shouting too

Hit it with a sledge hammer is that secret voice Turning off rebooting you have no choice

The world record holder for rebooting is you

This damn thing is playing with you and you've got no clue

Then much later switching on the Pc again It boots up normally, it is the usual game

POEMS AND POETS

Poets and poetesses there you sit Paused for words waiting to be writ Words expressed in Verse and line Events and happenings set in time Tragic syllables on a page

Emitting happiness or rage Feelings put in to word Waiting to be read and heard

Each poem done in its own particular style Opening as is written, as it does compile A story made

In a role of life that's played

To touch the heart stings as it brings A tale of many things

Some bounce along Just like a lifting song Others a tale of woe

With sadness that echoes so or words that leave an impression Powerful, and full of expression

Ones that make you laugh and dance and some that are full of love and romance

Those ones that tend to touch Poems that we love very much Hard, at times to write

That sometimes flows fast, and light Words written on a score Poems, Words, lines, verse and all

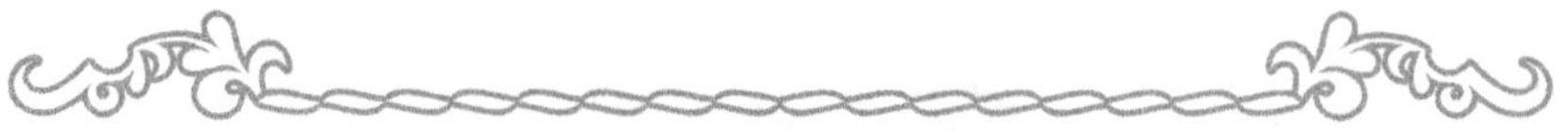

PROMISES

If I could have a penny for every promise made and for those broken promises, be paid

I would be rich it seems

for all those broken dreams

And every promise I have do make I keep make no mistake

Why do others make promises that cannot be kept?

Not very honorable or adept Playing on others' emotions Toying with devotions

Not a game I like to play

I don't think others do either in any way After all impressions bleed

When broken words tend to mislead Honesty is the finest quality that one can hold

Respected when the truth is told and if those who do deceive

Life will pay them back in kind as they receive That's the way of things

To those individuals it brings Promises that you can deliver Makes you the truthful giver You can hold your head up high

Knowing your proud, you never lie as for those who play these games

Self-denial and disrespect are their aims We will find out in the end

On that you can depend

SMOKERS

As a smoker, don't you feel your rights have been infringed?
Your ousted habit has now singed
Not being allowed to smoke in a public place Because the smell of stale nicotine offends, it's a disgrace Outlawed, condemned, outside to brave all elements of the
weather
Smokers, like lepers all huddled together Those reformed smokers have laid down their laws
Complaining of used butt ends stubbed out on the floors The stale smell of tobacco in the air
Saying to the condemned it's just not fair Passive smoking is now to blame
And we the addicted is the target of aim
I must have killed over a thousand in my living room at home
And five hundred more over the phone Funny how a small minority
Can change the habits of a majority And Ok I do understand
I smoke openly, and not underhand for this I'm not really proud
But I am part of the smoking social crowd and if it offends, then move away
You don't have to stand next to me, I say it's my choice, my body, to do with as I please
And if I die, then it's you I don't have to appease from your cigarette loving friend

SOME POEMS

Some poems easy or are hard to write Others you can do in a day or even a night and some take no time at all

The challenge of others requests that call

But the hardest one to do is this flipping Robbie Burns Like a foreign language of twists and turns

Tae this and och that

Makes me feel like some demented prat Don't get me wrong the Scots are nice folk

But head and tongue round this Scottish language can be a joke

Gees how I wrote and tried

But spending hours on that poem has made me die inside A fact I don't want to hide

I know that Robbie was a respected Bloke Loved by all his Scottish folk

I must admit I like him too

But to write and speak like him I could never do and like Shakespeare that's another quest

Maybe cause I'm English and it's easier to invest

Something I like to do Is Elizabethan script

But writing in Scottish has my Intelligence stripped Oh well practice makes perfect as they say

And who knows I might get my head round Burns one day Until then I'll just keep on doing what I do best in verse and stick to what I'm writing and something not quite adverse

My pen run-eth out as they say Another poem, another day

THE LINE

Oh nations, this a thing we all go through A common cause we all have to do Patiently in line we stand

At post offices, shops, and Banks across the land Front to back in a line

Waiting for our turn in time Hated,

but we have no choice

Stood there silent and without voice or in traffic jam

Stuck in a queue in a car or a van as your patience reaches an end

This breaking point makes one go round the bend as you stand there thinking this is wrong

Being forced and jostled along Labelled as a number

Bored in mental slumber Annoyed when someone pushes in

Or jumps the queue, a battle you just can't win Whose idea was it anyway?

To invent queues or this system as we say Like cattle or herded sheep

Rows of People in lines we keep from super market to traffic queue This indignant thing we do

By the way I wrote this in a line, you know My numbers called and I have to go

THE LITTLE PUZZLE BOX

I had a little wooden puzzle box from China it was made Took some working out as I played

All different symbols to line and match small dials with a face to line up and catch Many, many hours to fiddle and move Occasionally too difficult to prove

Lots of combinations with lots of complications Frustrating and difficult Working to get the basic root

Trying to get them all lined up in order Sometimes took me to a mental border How I tried

It sometimes tested me and hurt my pride But I persevered I never gave in

Just to break the puzzle just to win Time after time twisting and turning Looking and learning

Memorizing all the ways

A Lot of time spending whole days

and then one day just by accident I solved it That was the day I was happy every little bit

It just clicked and burred Twisted and turned

The little box chimed and rang a tune

A little dancer popped up with a golden moon round and round it danced

To a tune of romance

Oh, that little box of great surprise That unfolded be before my eyes All that work for such a result Some clever Chinese man had built

It was the simplest way that was done you'll find Just to get there was really fun with your mind

THE LOVE AND WAR

How you stand over me, and gloat over what you've done
Another fine example in the battle you have won
A broken glass candlestick lies on the floor
The blood on your hands is mine; again, you've won the war
Once more I didn't react Against the act of violence you did enact
One more cut, another scar, and more bruises to hide and the feeling of humility that a battered guy against honest pride
I took you and your children on, because I loved you, as honest love would do
I never knew how I took it for ten years, that I cared willingly, and gave to you
And yet from the start you taught your children to disrespect me at every turn
How you made me trapped, humiliated, and made my heart burn
But in spite of all, I loved you and how I tried too hard Thinking that things would change with every regard The abuse became so intense
Six against one, became so immense Was this how it was supposed to be?
Was this how your love was meant for me?
The shame of this man, who was mentally and physically abused
Then cast out on the street after being used I feel so undermined and weak
But was brought up to be honest, loyal in love, true and meek
I don't think I could ever change It the way that this life does arrange

THE LUSTY SELLER

She stood on her market stall, shouting all her wares and in her hands, she held the juiciest of pairs

Nice I thought

As a guy stood in front, his face strained and taught I asked what's up with him.

It's Ok lovely, she said an all the din He's bruised his banana

And caused a major drama

The other Lady stood there showing off her melons She said these were once Helens

Go on lovely, she said, have a nice good feel They are big and firm and make a lovely meal Gees I said that's a whopping marrow

It's so large it fills most of the barrow The lady said my tomatoes reach a peak And I've got apple so clean they squeak I got carrots to make your eyes water

And fat and juicy turnips from the farmer's daughter Cabbages with massive a heart

And collies that will make you **** (pass wind) Cocoa nuts so hairy

And flowers from the garden of Mary Passion fruit to open your eyes

And Monkey nuts from the three wise So gather round she said and feel me wares

My gooseberries smooth with hardly any hairs Cucumbers so long and straight

One glance it would make the ladies faint Come buy my Lusty, Honest gear Cause every week I will be here

THE MAN

There before you, stand's a man that's proud Who's head stands above the crowd

Who greets you with a smile Makes you want to stay a while Listens to all you have to say Who helps if he can in any way Lifts your burdens if he can Some say that he's the man

Treats how he expects to be treated Fights on, even if he's defeated Never gives in

Always tries to succeed and win Never puts himself above others To him you all sisters and brothers His motives are always good

He never argues and is never out for blood Always puts others before himself

He owns no riches or wealth

He holds all things precious in life dear Keeps his friends close and near

Treats all with respect

From him that's what you would expect for every day is special to him

He trod his path without sin

And at any time, he stumbles and does fall He is only human after all

Perfect he's not Himself is all what he's got

He is just what feels, hears, and does see I know him well believe me

Rich in life, from when his birth began How I think he's a lucky man

In this university of life's quest

Right up till the time of death he does invest

He really does bleed A breed apart indeed

THE NAUGHTY CHILDREN MONSTER

A devious monster am I

Hiding in dark corners to make children cry Making myself disappear or reappear Making naughty children quake with fear

I can even enter their dreams

As I enjoy listening to their screams or even come in the dead of night

Causing imaginations to run wild with fright Every naughty child is my joy

My imaginary plaything, my toy

I don't like good children, they are no fun with wicked ones, I can get things done

I am here, there, and everywhere So misbehave if you dare

I come in all disguises All shapes and sizes

So please all you naughty children, do your worst You will be the ones that will be cursed

I love to make those bad children suffer best Leaving my victims muddles and stressed Please all those children don't be good

Cause I want to visit you in your own neighborhood

THE OFFICE HITLER

Be where; be where, of the office sneak He or she turns up as you speak

Scoring points, to climb up the bosses Bottle and glass (slang for backside)

Career advancement their prepared to grass Turning up at the most unexpected places Just to put gossip to faces

And they are the ones as miserable as sin Creating an atmosphere so thick, you need a sword to cut

it thin

They are the ones in a position of control Making the work place a drudgery as a whole Striking terror and fear

As they suddenly out of nowhere appear There can never be a big enough scooper to shovel up this party pooper

A Hitler on constant patrol

To go running to the boss, tale telling is their goal and this is the beauty

They never ever take time off, always on duty Ready to have anything to report

I'm sure they do it just for sport I've got to go

I've just seen the snoop lurking, and not quite on show OK you've caught me, you can tell the boss

Because personally I don't give a toss

THE OLD VETERAN

The old veteran soldier the last of his breed Who helped change the course of history in the 1930s
indeed
Without him our world would have been a totally different place
This world would wear a different face Many of us would not be alive to day
If a certain Austrian German would have got his way Those heroes, unlike others are not around
As each year passes, they are getting thinner on the ground Great grandfathers slipping into histories tide
To once again to be written in the annuals of the past to hide
Most now carved on epitaphs on memorial stones Those memories of past heroic deeds all lie in bones Heroes should be respected
It's only to be expected
Those who gave up their lives for us all to be free Freed from hate and tyranny
In those immortal words once spoken and set
****"Lest we forget"****

THE PLANE

Flight on a plane listening to the engine sound from a vacation I am homeward bound Twenty Thousand feet in height

Smooth and easy flight Touching the breath of heavens scene Above cotton wool clouds I've been Clear Sky of royal blue, drifting by Into Sun set of orange fiery red sky

Drifting on the wind

As the plane spreads it wings Gently passing over sea and land

Panoramic view, that display that's grand Me up there, and them so tiny down below Hard to really believe it so

That inner feeling that seems odd Brings you closer to God

Felling the motion of a downward draft of the landing craft

The screech of wheels hitting the runway Landing safely you almost in relief pray and as the engine reaches a rising pitch You know your home without a hitch and as the plane taxi's round

You know you're on home ground Home, Home, that's place you know

And yet returning back you didn't want to go but the calling of your roots brings you back to normal life on track

THE PSYCHIC VAMPIRE

I hide in the shadows, as I wait,
I have a date
I the psychic vampire Stealing thoughts, I aspire I don't steal much
Just a tiny touch
My victims hardly notice a thing Their thoughts on a platter to me they bring
I'm never greedy; I just take what I need in small proportions I feed
Leaving them Unnoticed, with their heads light Then I disappear into the night
Drunks are the ones that I like best As I stand with them and Joke and Jest
They never seem to notice the amount I take They think the hangover is their mistake So when you're out enjoying the drink
I might be waiting for you; doesn't it make you think?

THE SCAFFOLD

Three minutes, up those wooden steps I go to a fate, on that scaffold that I know There before me hangs the noose

Empty for the moment, loose I am scared my body shakes

My legs shiver and my insides quakes Heart pounding with growing fear

As the pending end of my life is near

the angry shouts from the jostling crowd As I stand before them, bound but proud the executioner places on the hood Darkness now surges my blood

The rope I feel around my neck

And the moment of the trapdoor opening through the deck Flashing images of my life, flash before

As I fall through the floor

The rope yanks hard as it tightens taught

With every breath to grasp for every moment fought the final agonizing snap of the neck, as I dance

Now I know I've lost my chance

And with my last conscious breath I am taken with death

My last thought of the innocence and the grave injustice is my last sense

Darkness, nothingness
and the final word
"God Bless"

THE SERMON

The gentle priest stepped on to the alter His speech memorized so he does not falter and the service sits and quietly waits

As the priest stands up and orates Starting off in gentle sound

As he feels to get his verbal ground Eyes peer at the congregation

As they sit there in anticipation Then the voice that raises to a shout Now there's no escape and no way-out Fire and damnation, Hell and brimstone

Excommunication to all those sinners known the hand that will strike you down

Hell's fire will burn all around

Repent, Repent sayeth the lord, screams the priest and you will be forgiven at least

The congregation sits there paralyzed with fear

As their retribution is upon them and very near A fist bangs heavily on the pulpit

His teeth now gnash and grit

As many sits frozen and stiff as the priest delivers for all those god-fearing forgivers

Stunned and sat in silence now in shock as they sit in judgement in god's dock

the priest says in a quiet tone

We shall now sing 126 Lord Take me home

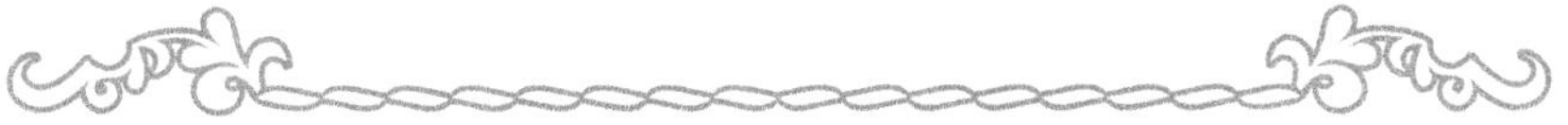

THE TINY VOICE

In the night a tiny voice cries out Insecure and full of doubt

But in the busy bustle of life that voice is lost Forgotten in that hectic cost

For ignorance is bliss and that small cry is missed

Others too busy to care on that fast track

Always pushing forward and never looking back No can hear that desperate plea

Left abandoned, just left be Alone and scared Confused and impaired Desperate and alone

Its very existence threatened on its own That tiny voice now silent and gone Singular and just one

Insignificant and so small Now silent to all

What did tragedy lay? On the night of that day Not a voice but a sole

That passed on to a different role

THERE WAS PRIDE

There once was a man of pride, once tall he stood for partner and her children, he gave his blood They couldn't have been happier in life

Wanted the woman to be his wife

Proud of the home he sweated for, that she displayed Was it ignorance? Or just wrapped up in bliss?

Or was it something important he did miss?

To lose everything so fast, so swift Cut loose to drift

Lost in brain racking thought

Or was it a cruel lesson been taught

Where? He thought did he go wrong

to be ousted from a family he did belong

How could he have been so misled?

Heart truly broken and bled Picking up the broken remains Bewildered with cruel pains The aching of the heart

That makes the strongest fall apart Trying to reason and feel

Is this nightmare for real?

Of the insecurity of a living hell Doubt and mistrust in time can only tell

THIS LIFE

This life we lead
That drains our soles and makes us bleed Wears us down in every way
Persistent struggle of each new day Pressures down on us, we have to bear Who says life isn't fair
Those arduous riggers of daily toil Just to earn our piece of spoil
Our small moments of happiness taken away and our personal feelings on display
How hard we try to prove Just to stay in the groove Yet we show no remorse Set on our daily course We don't question why Just grateful for getting by
Some unknown surprise that seems to spring Of Unexpected news each day will bring News brought to the door
Or from a phone call of what's in store on this trek we seem to go
Of what's waiting round the corner you'll never know Getting by the best way we can
For woman, child, and man from birth until death each day we try
On right up till the day we die Never ceasing to the end
Surviving, Living, in all this life we spend

Another Come and Read Me Book of Poems

CONTENTS

A FOOTBALL WIDOW

A football widow, there you sit Can't stand football one little bit Empty cans, and snacks in bowls

To the shouting of those scoring goals Attention half time, you're not elated

22 blokes kicking a pig's bladder round a field, to you is not rated

Pretending your enjoying the game, oh you must be so frustrated

David Beckham is the only thing worth the view and every football season, this you have to do Don't suppose your partner would really care

Him being so enthralled in the game, you might as well not be there

Your purpose is just to keep up the supplies Make sure the beer and snacks, that never dies

I bet your praying for the football season to be over That day you'll be rolling in clover

Soon it's the start of another sports fanatic's widow's reason

It's now the start of the cricket season

A GAME

Looks like you have a game to play but now I see through your way Your feeling hurt

As you have took another Knock in life and your feeling inert

But take one good hard look at yourself for one moment Stop and take stock and lament

You just can't see it can you? Treating others, the way you do

I can understand your past abuse the way you put it to use

Why do you think I took a step back? Is it true compassion that you lack? I'm not the one you should attack

After all I helped you get back on track Was, I so wrong in this thing I do?

Helping and healing you?

Is this the way I'm to be Paid?

To live this life of a so-called masquerade?

You must realize your hurt is self-imposed the true motive? its only you who knows A pattern in your life revolves

And finding it harder to get off, as it evolves, I haven't bothered you. I have just stayed away Not used others as a tool, just to have your say

Me the Villain You the heroine

Well, you know the truth and the treason and by now others know the reason

I hope you are Happy now, and you have your day Looks like you have a game to play

A TALE OF SADNESS

I saw a tear fall and trickle gently from your eye as you began to cry

I felt the hurt and pain in your heart Your shaken voice as you told your part

As your heart rendering story started to unfold Shaking as your past was told

How you managed to stay alive I wondered how you did survive Those dreadful things life put you through

And how you didn't deserve those things that person Done you

How did you stand it those things that was done I know for you it couldn't have been much fun I felt you agonizing pain

As you have to lift your life again

How I wanted to hold you, and ease your sad distress

I know that anger and hate is a thing you have to address But I sit here and listen to your sad tale

And in the end, you will prevail

You blame yourself you thought you have failed Not you, you tried, you availed

I'm deeply touched inside

In my tender heart my feelings I hide as you brush away that tear

Eased now, I hope I've took away that fear Gave you hope and heart

To make a fresh new start

A VALENTINE CARD

I received your valentine card All tiny hearts on a floral facade As I opened, and read inside

The moving verse written, tears I cried Those words written, touched my heart Reached my intimate my tender souls' part and now I know your love is meant for me Moving words, made me see

I felt the movement of the verse Those lines of emotion disperse Each word echoes in my mind

Right down to your hand that signed All those words of love displayed Those feelings portrayed

True love never needs a word

Even spoken, never needs an ear to be heard Deep feelings tell it all

No matter how insignificant or small

ACTORS

The actors stand upon on the stage Each event turns the page
Of characters, that they portray in the roles of a script they play Actions mimic deliberate moves and words of a story proves Costumes play historic parts

To respond to the players hearts Lights, curtains, and act the scene

To tell a part of history past that's been Romance from lover's tales

To end in tragedy that prevails Comedy played form a cast Long ago moments from the past as dramatic scenes unfold

There is a story to be told These moments of an age

As the Actors stand upon the stage The final curtain falls

To a rapturous applause and encored calls

AUTUMN SEASON

Rusty red, golden carpet adorns of brilliant orange yellow morns
Bare branches, twist and reach the sky Somber grey days, mock the eye Shadows stretch and loom
To the fullness of the silver moon and the heavens paint a crisp deep blue
Where the prisms of the stars shine through A nip of a chill in the air
The calling of winter fare Summers fallen asleep
Out are the hunter gatherers collecting, Nuts and Kernels to keep
Builders of the straw homes
and the falling of pine nut cones Dry and grassy straw
The hold of the winter's store Man tends the field
Plough and harrow, for next year's yield
the black speckles of the birds, migrate
A warmer climate they go to emigrate Comes the cold autumn air to blow
And waiting for the winter snow Another season passes by
How the seasons fly

THE TOE IN THE TAP BLUES

I was lay there soaking in the bath Resting from the day's aftermath

Steam and heat a comfortable atmosphere Suddenly gripped with fear

You know you fiddle with feet into the tap Well I fell right into that trap

TOE stuck fast and jammed right in Started shouting made a din

Now neighbors banging at my door dreading what actions would befall

Heard them shouting up my hall with 911 or 999 call

Sirens screaming to and FRO and door caved within Let them all the Police, fire, Ambulance and multitude in

Bathroom door pushed open wide There was nowhere else for me to hide Like an exhibit at a show

Men, Women, and child were there to know A crowd of faces eyes open wide

Grinning teeth, guffaws and laughs to hide I lay there, hands cupped over my manhood Otherwise it would float like wood

Was I red just with heat?

Or was it embarrassment with all to meet Drain the water someone said now it's getting cold

Now with shock and shrinking and not so bold GUYS YOU KNOW THE STORY TOLD

A kind fireman covered me with his coat by now I couldn't face the neighbors, how?

After being on show for all to see Like a comedy on TV

Hands of plenty all around, Questions and riddles to answers found

They pushed and they tugged with all their might

My toe still stuck there tight with manhood now shrinking in hand

It all became rather bland

Cold and wrinkly, white and chapped Lying still there with hands capped Time running out and passing fast All resources running to the last

One fire woman said let's get the saw I screamed what for?

They chuckled and said just to cut the tap and get you out this dreaded trap

One-woman said use butter I said what for?

To lubricate your toe some more Funny thing it just fell out

Must have been the cold no doubt Not the only thing to shrink

But doesn't it make you really think Well all the drama over and all gone Wasn't I the embarrassed one?

So be warned and watch out too Otherwise it could be you

BED

Oh, it's time for bed
My brain is worn out and dead the rigors of the day
Have worn me out in every way Time seems to be steep
Now all I think about is sleep Eye lids start to fight
It's the end of another night
I hear the call of my slumber pit
To where my head to the pillar does fit
It's that time I know Off to bed I go

BONFIRE NIGHT

November the 5th when fires are burning bright Fireworks light up the sky at night

Whistles, bangs, and explosions fill the air The smell of brimstone and fire everywhere Kids excited jump around

As they watch and listen to fireworks sound Hot dogs, baked potatoes, and sausage rolls Fill the need for hungry holes

Hand held sparklers that's are waved Shapes and signatures in the dark are made

Spent and smoking fireworks lay on the ground Burning embers in charred heaps are found Eerie smoke that's lays a veil

Morning light looking pale Guy Fawkes comes to mind He, That History left behind

CHANGES

I see the changes in your face The way you've changed your place

The rose wilted that I gave you, that you wore Now you don't want me anymore

Those dinner stains upon the wall

Tells it all

Am I blind to what I see, or was I mistaken?

For my love that you had taken Was it the hurt from your past? Means love to you will never last You talked about him all the time Couldn't get him of your mind He treated you so bad Sometimes made you mad

The phone and texts you received Was to you, that disbelieved

I watched you sinking

Every moment of him, you were thinking I thought I'd had a chance

To give you genuine love and romance but how I was wrong

It didn't take long You've taken him back Things are on track

And nothing has changed Well, you did arrange

So, I won't bother you anymore I know the score

Your situation that you're bound good luck and I'll see you around

CHARACTER ASSASSINATION

Character assignation isn't a joke
When a coward or cowards insult the good name of a bloke
Unfounded accusations point the finger
Leaving a bad taste in the mouth that does linger
What gives this person or persons the right?
That involves a good and respected name, to be involved in their fight
Are they so insecure?
Are they so afraid? So unsure? How they hide behind a user name
Laying unfounded accusations, as they lay the blame Edited false text
Is what from a blamer? You can only expect Someone jealous of popularity and artistic value Is the kind of underhanded things they would do?
Hide go tell your lies
You're the one whose personality dies
I hope you read this poem, I have written by my own hand and like every poem I've written is in popular demand original copy writes and hand drafts I've kept as proof
I don't need to hide behind user names, to stay hidden and aloof
My user's name is known to all and is the only name I've used
My word is my bond, and I'm no bigot is the word you freely abuse
So, point your finger, tell your lies I'm not the one hiding from eyes

CHAT UP LINE

I just sit there and stare Should I care?

Or do I dare?

I see her, but she is not aware Do I get up out of this chair? Be brave enough to ask?

Or hide behind this mask Do I decline?

Wait and bide my time as the beer glass drains

Another glass of Dutch courage dulls my brains She still sits alone at the bar

So near and yet so far

I'm sure I can make some excuse

By smiling and saying, they let me loose Can I use my time?

By using some cheesy chat up line

As I bravely rise, look over, and think great but some guys beat me to it, I'm too late

CHRISTMAS

What is the meaning of Christmas to us all today?

Over the decades we have drifted away Not the old excuse of Christmas is for giving

But for Commercial Profiteers to make their living All dressed up with bells of holly

Decorations and cries of noel and jolly Blackmailed by companies for our children's emotions

Urged to buy based on our parental devotions That yearly theme we spend to buy Tempting expensive fads pass by

And each year gets financially harder to cope All in the name of Christmas hope Psychologists, economists, hired to exploit us for commercial gain

Those usual pressures that still remain All in the name of Christmas noel

Families, Parents, Partners put through hell The time of year when couples fall apart

The final financial straw that breaks your heart Designer clothes, Toys, and gifts

That causes families to argue and creates rifts Christmas comes but once a year

That time of year that many fear So what is Christmas all about?

Time to look back and sort future finances out We have all been forced to move away from the real

Christmas time

The real true giving of Christmas kind

CONFIDENCE

When confidence is lost inside

And self-esteem wants to run away to hide and all that life is a never-ending knock as life passes in that ticking clock

Trapped and helpless in a deep rut

There's nowhere left to strut

It's got to the stage where you can't say hello There's nowhere left to go

Locking yourself away safe and sound Preferring to stay on safe ground Oh God! How so ugly you feel

And to the opposite sex you think that there's no appeal Almost sorry now, and so afraid to commit

Feeling there's no place left to fit with all the friends that you know

Alone so alone inside is the only place to go That constant feeling of reject

Is the daily thing to expect? The feeling of self-eject Losing one's self respect

Loneliness becomes a constant threat Something carried heavily around, that's a sure bet

Is this the path that's does induce

to become short of becoming a recluse,

But you have to stop and smile You still have your life, just for a while

THE DATE

I went to meet a person on a date Something we have all done and can relate Worn the roses on our chests

Carried books and papers and signs of interests Organized where to meet

Excited and nervous on the way to greet

Not knowing what you'll find there at arranged meeting place

Heart thumping arriving there wondering what you face There you wait lost and forlorn

And wishing you'd never been born People passing to and FRO Backwards and forwards they do go there she stands Rose in hand

6FT 8 and 20 stone not what you planned OH MY GOD you think, is she the one? The rose I carry screwed up and gone and she reaches for her mobile phone She dials; you're on your own

Waiting for yours to ring

Wanting deep inside you Want to smash the thing If it rings there nowhere to hide

Excuses needed you scream inside It can't be me

Please it can't be me

But it's not my phone ringing you see there's the victim on his phone They meet shake hands and off they go

Breathing a sigh of relief now they have gone Thinking that was close, thanking GOD I was the Lucky one

What about my date you ask, and how did it go?

As per usual they didn't show

ELEMENTS OF THE STORM

Dark clouds roll over each other up on high Black horses Rear up to ride the sky

The winds moan in a low pitch drone, as they pass by And Shards of lightening fly

How the mighty unseen titans clash they're colossal weapons crash

The gigantic swords in the sky that flash

To the tears and sweat pour down in rains that thrash vibrating thunder shakes the earth

To the battling of the tempest giving birth Torrent waves of the confused sea rise and roar to the

shore

Smashing down heavily to the rocks does pour As the Gods battle in the struggling fight

The raging confusion in the night Ride the winds and sail the storm

The tempest shows its tormented form Horses writhe and scream with foaming bit The gods fight on in demented fit Shattering sheets of icy hail

Blinding elements of confusion prevail All thrown in to nature's battle

To be unraveled in torrented tackle Screaming howling winds call to the land The Storm stands firmly in command

Lightning throws its sparking, cracking prisms that blind That leaves dark shadows to the eyes behind

How the mighty opponent falls To Natures eternal calls

The weathers Performance gave

To tribute the fallen and the victors brave all calms to the quieting sound

To softening fresh airy ground

As the battle of the elements move on into the distance it's now gone

ENDLESS LINE

I'm in a queue as far as the eye can see I don't want to be here, believe me

One step forward in this never-ending wait Time ticking by, making me more and more late Children screaming as they run about

As they swing off the line ropes, running in and out

The old lady in front bangs your shin with her shopping trolley

And someone from behind stabs you with their brolly Jolted forward and papers dropped

Leaning forward to retrieve them elbow in the eye is copped

Staggered back tripped and fell

Landed on your backside, not a funny thing I can tell you pick yourself up and brush yourself down

Looking round and feeling like a clown

With a feeling of disgrace Looks like of lost my place

So now my place is to the back, as I start all over again,

I just can't take the strain

There in a line to hear my number called Dazed, lost, and totally appalled

when you standing in a queue

Spare a thought and be careful what you do

FOUND OUT

Don't you stand there wide-eyed, with an innocent look on your face?

You know what you done and what took place It's no good acting, or starting to cry

I can hear it in your voice that you lie Sometimes I wonder if you're my child Sometimes unruly, sometimes wild

At times you wear my patience thin

The antics you've got up to and the places you have bin But, now you have been found out

It's the truth I want, without any doubt Turning on those tears don't really work with me

I've been there many times you see

I know all the tricks, and fibs that you will ever tell all the excuses yet to come, I know very well

As adults we know all the score

We've done them all before So dry those tears and come clean

To lie to us, is just obscene So tell the truth and be true

People will respect, and look up to you

And besides it less painful, less punishing on that guilty mind

And will ease the consequences you will find Always remember tell the truth

It's all part and parcel of your growing youth

FRIENDS

Seems friends are important indeed for those being in need

How, at times they are taken for granted at times, that's never what is wanted Sometimes it suits their aims

To play their emotional games but a friend is a friend

No matter what happens in the end Support, advice, and a crutch

And at times, that diplomatic touch

Tea and sympathy as they say, time to listen Tarnished gold does not glisten Seeing good friends come and go

For reasons why, only they know So what is a true friend?

Someone to help mend Loyalty and understanding Not controlling or demanding Just someone to be there Strong enough to be aware

to be objective

Put things into perspective

So, if you're a friend, when in need Then you are a true friend indeed

FULL OF IT

There is he, the man who likes to brag About those escapes he likes to bag You think you're so fit

In reality, you're so full of it You treat all, like a door mat

And there you stand with tipped and tilted hat Truth is you're a low life, so vile

King of the heap, Lord and master of the pile There will be a day we watch you sink

Then we will really smell the stink with defecation you're stuffed so full There's seepage, with all the bull

Talk and it trickles from the corner of your mouth Want good advice, go head south

Well, my tarnished knight

to the man who's always right

One day your reign will end You will be the loser, friend When it all comes to a stop

We will all be there to watch you drop Enjoy your day while you can

For the moment, you are the man

GRACE

Tender is that gentle touch of grace That strokes softly against your face Warm petaled lips do purse

As I watch your mouth move as you converse Eyes opaque, that flicker and gaze

As pupils react in many ways Lashes with a simple curve

Long and curvaceous as I observe as the light shines across your cheek

Changing shape as you speak Small but perfect nose Compliments your face it shows Down to your soft and delicate skin All set in a perfect profile within

I could sit here and stare at you all day Watching your face in awe all in every way

And that hair so dark and soft with every perfect strand as you brush it through your hand

Those ears so nicely set Listening to every word that's met

And as you speak, I hang on every word Softly spoken, Chrystal clear and heard as your mouth does softly smile

I'm taken, lost, and breathless for a while All these things that I do see

Is what your face means to me? So, in my mind I keep your face Your gentle touch of grace

ALL HALLOWS DAY

Take time way back in the history of all hallows day Back in Neolithic and pagan times they say

The one time of the year that spirits rise up from eons past from earthly beds to walk the earth in mass

And as night drew near Fires were lit to keep away fear

As groups gathered together round a fire Safe around that warm bright pyre

To celebrate relatives and friends of long since passed times

That night retuned in spirits minds Fires burning to keep evil spirits at bay While sprites, witches, and daemons play

As those ancient people waited till morning light Praying to the gods for safety through the night Hoping to keep their souls safe and sound

Not stolen by spirits and taken to hallowed ground When Morning came a feast and time to celebrate That those survived from hells open gate

And all the old gods and spirits receive Of Hallows day and hallows eve

HEATED WORDS

Some say "nothing like a good argument" or a blazing row It releases tension and clears the air some how

Heated words in an exchange Ending up in a violent rage Two sides with an aimless view

Building up in frustration in everything they do A game of verbal winning

As nerves fray from the beginning Hurtful comments passed to and FRO Losing tempers as they go

That game of verbal tennis Discord becomes a menace What's the point in this escapade?

No one wins in this masquerade After all you never get to agree

A waste of time, effort, and energy All those nasty things that was said Running through each other's head

Making up in the end, to relinquish guilt Not the way life should be built

For some not easy Just to sit and calmly talk If it starts its best to walk

Wait till things calm down Then nicely talk each other round

Solutions solved better to a gentle sound Together closer you are bound

Better to talk things over in this way Serves no purpose just to blaze away No wedge to drive between

More sense to keep it clean

If this is a thing, we all can do

Then the world will be a better place for me and you

THE HORSE

You the Noble beast stands from 11 to 40 Hands

The steed of regal stance Free in the fields to dance Sport of kings you participate

Both friends to master and mate You with majestic strut Who ploughs a fields Rut Hunters that peruse a fox One who rides in a box

Dray horses that pull Brewery Dray Just for another working day

Beast of burden to pleasure ride Excites riders deep inside Loved and adored

Groomed and adorned

the finest saddle on you back

You wear bright and shiny tack Reigns, stirrups, and bit

Canter to gallop to make you fit One of the animals that's supreme You, one of every little girls dream You of high intelligence amount For the rider on your mount

With flowing main and splendid tail,

The need to win and not to fail

You the Regal Horse Set upon your daily course

IF

There's a hollow in the pillar, where you used to lay Another day, another night, of loneliness and dismay Where are those gentle hands in the morning that used to stroke?

Where are the morning tender words you spoke? Those eyes that used to give that loving greet the morning kiss that used to meet

That perfume smell that filled the air I lost you, you are not there

Oh god I feel so lonely IF only

But the word IF is a cliché

That means the start of an empty day Half empty shelves and draws Emotionally I'm clutching at straws Half my life gone

Lying here with tears in my eyes Deceived, mislead, with lies

And yet for one second, I would have you back You are the missing thing I lack

At a drop of a hat, I would forgive Just to get our lives back and live but now I lay in a half empty bed to face another day I dread

LADY ASIA

Lady of Asia you are the glittering shinning jewel The beauty of the stone, to the touch that's cool You are the slender movement of the tigers walk the soothing chatter of the monkeys talk

Swift in thought of the cobra's strike

Astuteness of the mongooses like Wit as sharp as the scorpion's sting Gentle as the songbirds sing Nimble of the prey mantis dance Strong as the elephant's stance

You stand above the noble ox Cunning as the bushy tail fox

Dark as the leopard who stalks at night Bright as the ruby's stunning light You are the touch of silk

You are the mother of milk You are adorned on palace walls

Displayed in Khans halls Kings utter your name Child givers in births pain

The empress who wears the crown Held in high esteem, away from renown Lady Asia you stand above your crowd

History says you should be proud One small glimpse of you face Says you are the one with grace

All these things they do all men say and for once this is your day

MY LOVE

Where my love, my sweetheart, where will you be?
Far across lands, and over the sea green cliffs of the kissed shore
Cry out, for you forever more
Hills and trees of our homeland weep for the love inside I keep
I wait for you in the misty glen My heart is there, waiting for
you then
My love, my love, I miss you so
More than the warm breezes in the valleys blow May you hurry
on the tide?
From O the sea and ocean wide When that ship is on the sky
line Then I'll know your home and mine May my love find you on
the air?
Hurry home my love, may the winds be fair till my arms hold
you firm
The heart inside me, for you love does burn May our kisses be
firm?
My love, my love, till you return

NEGOTIATIONS

Police cars screaming in the streets Sirens, blue lights, come in fleets Armed police rush about

Bark their orders in a shout The pounding on a door

The place of murder, blood, and gore This crime committed minutes before Who knows what's in store

A scream, the ring of a shot They surround the spot

Rifles and pistols held at the ready

The commander shouting steady boys steady A crack, a flash

A ricochet, a window smash Who is the guilty perpetrator?

Who is the life taker? Then a call for calm The plea to do no harm

Steady is the voice of the negotiator To relax the nerves of the instigator Throw down you gun

Make it easier on yourself to come Then silence and paws

Breath draws

Out walks the condemned man Ended now, from when it all began

I'M NOT A POET

I'm just a writer of line and verse

Of sights, feelings and life, in words that I converse Just words written on a page defines

A collective of syllables grouped in lines an expression of emotions written down

Adjectives and characters Jumbled with noun but all put together in line

To narrate those stories of Life, in rhyme One skillful word can say it all When inspiration comes to call

But if wrongly put down it can fail When it comes to make a rhyming tale All done in a different style

In many different ways to compile at times not an easy thing to do Inspiration plays a big part too

However, I do my best Competing with the rest others work I have to admire

In their own individual works as they aspire Touching and caressing to sensitive ears and hearts They preach

Tender moments as their words do reach Each one a Bard in their own right

As they struggle and word play with what they write I am not a poet

Just a simple man of word

And glad that others appreciate what is written and heard

ONE OF THOSE DAYS

Is it one of those days?
Everything goes wrong in many ways Not as things appears
A day to scream, and burst into tears All the troubles of Nations
Rest on your shoulders with no reasonable explanations
Burdened with your heavy sole
A down in the dump's day, takes its toll Almost afraid
Tempers displayed
And to cap it all, you feel you're to blame Knowing you're not,
is just not the same Gets to a point you can't take the strain Feeling
like you're going insane
There you are, in the thick of the scrape Hands clasped on both
ears, can you escape?
Filling that already full head Empty, weakened, and fully bled
Can't get those things, sorted in a hurry Maxed head ready to
explode with worry Don't you want to run and hide?
Chill out and unwind?
In time things will sort itself out Keeping cool, no need to shout
at the end of that day Things will work out, I can say

RACE

So, you never lose your way in the race or never want to lose face

In the never-ending human-race and after all it's no disgrace
If you fall behind and lose your place This normally is the case
And easy to for steps to retrace It's a goal to act with grace to interact and interface

So don't feel so glum, just watch this space and you'll be the one who's ace

ROSE IN TIME

A small green bud grows Evolving colors glows Petals in the warm sun, form A rose is born

Beauty to the eyes does please

it gently sways in summer breeze

Picked and kept in treasured hold for an instant in a moment told

Rigid is the stem, and thorns so strong Can this creation last so long?

Petal's curl and wither Fall off and shiver Helplessness as it slowly starts to die Elusiveness the rose does tell a lie

It doesn't last for ever

To possess this treasure, never

The impression leaves a fond moment in mind an image and epitaph left behind

Remember, remember, and do not forget the time held, is no regret

Yours for those small seconds in time Appreciated, yours not mine

You held the rose

You smelt the perfume of its repose It was yours and yours alone
Something borrowed, you could never own

SHE SLEEPS

She sits on the edge of the bed Betrayal and lies, rang through her head

Her hands cover the tears on her face Trust turned to mistrust, gave her disgrace She had the right

When the truth came to light All this time

The one she loved, committed the crime She could not believe

How one so trusted, came to deceive Now it's all come out

Her shattered life in pieces, all now in doubt the pain now weighted, and pushed

Her heart crushed Driven to despair

She feels life has not been fair

She gave it all; she gave more than her share Seems He didn't care

Alone now she has to brave the fight

No one there to help her share her plight She pitifully weeps

Till her weary sobbing closes her eyes and she sleeps

HOUSE OF SWEETS

Somewhere in the realm of a dream of treats There's a house in a place of the land Sweets Where leaves on trees are made from paper rice Frosted with glistening sugar ice

And bark on the trunks encrusted with chocolate flake Paths made out of nut cluster toffee bake

A bed of lollipop flowers in a dark rich soil of fudge There a pond of creamy chocolate sludge

Candy striped columns, around liquorish doors Treacle toffee bricks, makes its walls Clear sugar pane windows of gloss

Curtains of wispy pink sugar candy floss Press the M&M chocolate bean button, of the bell the door opens to an aroma of heavens smell Baked cakes from the entered confectioned hall into strips of colored Liquorish paper on a wall

As you gaze on black and white Bertie Bassett tiles on the floor

Pear drops and pineapple chunks mosaic held in store to a gaze of a ginger bread settee with jelly beans inset A crispy wafer coffee table is met

Up a flight coated chocolate pairs walnut and dates of banister stairs

To a red and white candy striped four poster bed with pink soft marshmallow pillars to rest your head Falling asleep on a mattress of angel cake

Then suddenly realizing you're awake After drowning in a bath of coffee cream You realize it's only a dream

TEDDY BEAR

My old and little teddy bear
Has one eye, and missing bits of hair in places scuffed and worn
Pads on hands, snagged and torn Sticking out, bits of straw
But still loved, and has a place in store with that fixed smile upon his face My teddy has that special place
Teddy has been there through all my life The little button in his ear, says steiffe My Teddy may be old
He has a story to be told We will always be together
My cute and cuddly friend forever

THE CALL FOR HOME

I hear the haunting pipes down along bogs and mountain sides
The flute in green valleys and wilds the beat of the drum, like the Celtic heart
The plucked strings of the Irish harp Music in my head, to the lands of Low
As the breeze of peat flowers sway and flow the shamrock trembles as it does a dance To Limerick words of Irish romance
Loch carries the Carrack down to the seas Past grassy green, and leafy trees History sang in words of a song
Of a tradition of a sacred heart so strong in the music tells a story
Of hope, loss, and glory And yet there's a beckoning call
Back home to the emerald isle would befall Where ever in the world, an Irish heart does roam T 'is the call for home
Where the heart is tied
For the true sense of Irish pride

THE GUN SLINGER

The saddle and the horse is my Friend On both I ride and depend

The gun and holster hangs at my side the open rage, from town to town I ride A blanket is my home

Campfires mark where I roam from burning sun, rain, frost, and snow I travel through the seasons, where I go

Earning a living when I can the so-called saddle tramp, I am

I live by the gun

Moving on when my work is done the taker of life, the romancer

A gambler, a chancer I've seen the fear in man's eye

As I have shot them, and seen them die the law of the gun, says it's them or you Its survival is the thing to do

My name and reputations best

I am known throughout the West

Gunslinger is my craft and code

A career where you'll never grow old,

I am the cowboy with no home

In History books I will be known

THE THISTLE

The thistle, stands strong and tall Green, thorny stem, sharp spines and all

Blue purple flower of a gentle part

Unmoving as a man, and flower soft as a woman's heart There stands a symbol to the brave

This the Scottish emblem gave

Among the wild moorlands, of the highland peak Gave Scotland a voice to speak

Proud of the tartan clan

For every Scottish woman, child, and man You the thistle are the sign of the free

Spoken pride of Celtic tongues to be

You sway in the field

Hardy, stern, steadfast to never yield

To the sound of the pipes, of bonny lads and lass N'er the moments of history pass

Wear the Thistle with pride Scotland forever and tradition never died

THROUGH THE EYES

I sit on the side walk, and watch them pass by They don't care if I live or die

To them, I'm and object of fear They don't see the person I appear Looks can be deceiving

Loose change they drop, is relieving

My rag worn clothes, makes me a different sight Ignorance is just their way of being polite the system has not been a friend of mine

And I guess no one has the time

I used to be like them, but it's not what they perceive I don't think for one minute, they would believe They are too busy getting on

Things, Places, to do or be done I am un-noticed and forgotten Beguiled, and begotten

Now all I have is time on my hands While they rush to beat daily demands See then rushing to and FRO

But I sit; I've got nowhere to go Seen through the eyes, of doubt Me the down and out

VLAD

Who would have thought Dracul? Your stories of old Of Vlad the impeller would be forever told

A Turkish Prince of nobility and station

Would throw a tyrannical rule over a Rumanian nation Cruelty was your name

To torture, inflict injury, and maim

Those you impaled in steaks, as they slowly slid to Agonizing pain

Some said you were insane

Heads of vanquished enemies' hand on spikes above your gate

A man with no respect and of sheer hate Rotting carcasses were put on show

And those on steaks died long and slow Pleasure you took amongst those exhibits, as you dined

A sight for those poor peasants to remind Your legend has become immortal

The name always to be remembered for those who are mortal

Carved in stone

The word "Vampire" stands alone

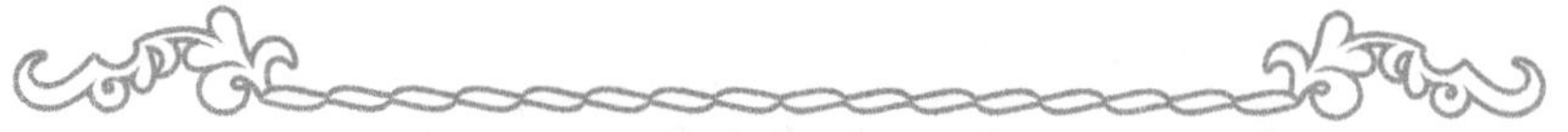

YOU ARE THE FLOWERS

You are the delicate Orchid, I hold in my hand The purple Sweet Peas, that grows in fertile land You are the blushing rose of infinite red

The swaying virgin Lilies in its bed You are the somber Sun flower in the field

The Tiger Lilly in full yield

You are the Tulip that makes you mine The Yellow Daffodils that shine

The pink Mission Bells

the Blue Snap Dragon that tells

You are the clover beneath my feet Nasturtium petals that is peppery and sweet You are the garden of my sole

Repose of bloom that makes me whole the garden of love, which I tend Delicately taking time to mend

Like most things that need tender loving care to see the color of beauty share

You are my Garden of elation Together we make creation

GROWING OLD

Why do shiny days, now seen dull And once hectic days go into a somber lull

Once the in the youth of life, the sun shone hot and those busy times now, seem long forgot

to slow and easy days

Have now established permanent ways Once times fiery and full of vigor Seems strained and hard to figure

Do these things come with age? As years, and decades turn the page

Company was compulsory, and always wanted Funny how we take all these things for granted Now it's all been blown away

To every normal single day Partner, wife, husband, children, and friends

All those things that company depends Lost and now gone

Who now is the lonely one?

In self-company, time is all that's left behind thoughts of past things left to mind

Once life's experiences from the past

HISTORY AND TIME

Born in the late 1950s, how time has flown

As in history and I have watched, Learnt, and grown as time and, I evolved

Conflicts of wars tragically rose and resolved the first man to walk on the moon

Concord aircraft breaking the sound barriers boom the invention of a Texas Instruments LED watch and calculator

Fantastic changes for an aircraft aviator

Black and white TV, to color remote TV with digital surround

Mono to stereo to Digital sound

From a Vinyl record to tape and CD to DVD to MP3 To technological advances form a mechanical binary machine to ever growing PC?

From Alexander Graeme Bell, to text sent on a mobile phone

From Pesticide uses, to Cell developed Clone Cooking on a stove, to Micro wave Energy efficient devices that save

A Letter put in the post email sent through a Network Host

All these things in my short life I've seen Past through History have come and been

What more marvels does History hold in store?

In the future opening its door

THE HUNTERS

Why do these people play mental games?

Just to suit their own aims Fooling others just to get their way

All the charming, deceiving things they say Like a hunter looking for its pray

A weak but honest victim for the offering to the slaughters lay

Building on the weak and venerable as they give them some hope

Pretending to be their friend so that they can cope A prize of conquest is their only goal

To take advantage of that person as a whole

as the victims build up their hopes and dreams

Listening to the smooth talker it seems the hunter or huntress promises the earth

For a wonderful relationship to be given birth Lies and subterfuge is their tool

Deceit and Manipulation set to make them cruel when the deeds are done

Knowing that they have their fun They drop you like a hot stone

Leaving you the victim destroyed and alone Devastated and hurt, mistrusting While the hunters move on lusting

To the next victim, for one more amusing fool they collect their trophies and think their cool but what of honest folk

They are the ones who are treated like a joke Those who want real love and romance Those are the ones who don't stand a chance

HOW DO I FEEL?

I sit alone here at night

Lost in a world full of fear and fright I used to have a purpose in life to abide

A love, a reason

Waking up was once, by your side and all my love I had to give and show

Where I went wrong, I do not know I wanted us to be together for life You for me, the wanted wife

Now cast me out without a word The nasty rumors that I have heard

And you ask me how I feel?

Thanks for making me insecure But I am now working on a cure Thanks for changing my life

Filling it full of hurt, confusion, and strife But I am on the mend

At least it's just myself that I can depend and still you ask me how I feel?

I don't think it's any of your concern in life we tend to live and learn That web of lies you had built

Just to hide your actions, and justify your guilt

So, ask me how I feel

Now to your conscious does it now appeal?

THE PC

The things I notice about my PC It's the stupid things it does to me

All the wrong things that you don't want it to do It does. Annoys, and plays games with you.

It does not work; you check it inside and out Operating system all about

Still a problem and you scratch your head Strip the hardware out instead Nothing wrong but still a prob

Turns you in to a screaming blob Wires, ribbons strips, and motherboard, In a heap in a hoard

Strewn across the floor

You scratch your head again once more,

And wonder why you done this all, and face defeat Hours gone by and all together now, and complete on it boots up, and still the same

Enough to drive a saint insane Rant and rave and threaten this you do

The neighbors wonder who your shouting too Hit it with a sledge hammer is that secret voice Turning off rebooting you have no choice

The world record holder for rebooting is you

This damn thing is playing with you and you've got no clue

Then much later switching on the Pc again It boots up normally, it is the usual game

POEMS AND POETS

Poets and poetesses there you sit Paused for words waiting to be writ Words expressed in Verse and line Events and happenings set in time Tragic syllables on a page

Emitting happiness or rage Feelings put in to word Waiting to be read and heard

Each poem done in its own particular style Opening as is written, as it does compile A story made

In a role of life that's played

To touch the heart stings as it brings A tale of many things

Some bounce along Just like a lifting song Others a tale of woe With sadness that echoes so

or words that leave an impression Powerful, and full of expression

Ones that make you laugh and dance some that are full of love and romance

Those ones that tend to touch Poems that we love very much Hard, at times to write

That sometimes flows fast, and light Words written on a score Poems, Words, lines, verse and all

PROMISES

If I could have a penny for every promise made for those broken promises, be paid

I would be rich it seems for all those broken dreams

And every promise I have do make I keep make no mistake

Why do others make promises that cannot be kept?

Not very honorable or adept Playing on others emotions Toying with devotions

Not a game I like to play

I don't think others do either in any way After all impressions bleed

When broken words tend to mislead Honesty is the finest quality that one can hold

Respected when the truth is told if those who do deceive

Life will pay them back in kind as they receive That's the way of things

To those individuals it brings Promises that you can deliver Makes you the truthful giver You can hold your head up high

Knowing your proud, you never lie as for those who play these games

Self-denial and disrespect are their aims We will find out in the end

On that you can depend

SMOKERS

As a smoker, don't you feel your rights have been infringed?
Your ousted habit has now singed
Not being allowed to smoke in a public place Because the smell
of stale nicotine offends, it's a disgrace Outlawed, condemned, out-
side to brave all elements of the
weather
Smokers, like lepers all huddled together Those reformed smok-
ers have laid down their laws
Complaining of used butt ends stubbed out on the floors The
stale smell of tobacco in the air
Saying to the condemned it's just not fair Passive smoking is
now to blame
And we the addicted is the target of aim
I must have killed over a thousand in my living room at home
And five hundred more over the phone Funny how a small
minority
Can change the habits of a majority And Ok I do understand
I smoke openly, and not underhand for this I'm not really proud
But I am part of the smoking social crowd if it offends, then
move away
You don't have to stand next to me, I say it's my choice, my
body, to do with as I please
And if I die, then it's you I don't have to appease from your
cigarette loving friend

SOME POEMS

Some poems easy or are hard to write Others you can do in a day or even a night some take no time at all

The challenge of others requests that call

But the hardest one to do is this flipping Robbie Burns Like a foreign language of twists and turns

Tae this and och that

Makes me feel like some demented prat Don't get me wrong the Scots are nice folk

But head and tongue round this Scottish language can be a joke Gees how I wrote and tried

But spending hours on that poem has made me die inside A fact I don't want to hide

I know that Robbie was a respected Bloke Loved by all his Scottish folk

I must admit I like him too

But to write and speak like him I could never do like Shakespeare that's another quest Maybe cause I'm English and it's easier to invest Something I like to do Is Elizabethan script

But writing in Scottish has my Intelligence stripped Oh well practice makes perfect as they say

And who knows I might get my head round Burns one day Until then I'll just keep on doing what I do best in verse and stick to what I'm writing and something not quite adverse

My pen run-eth out as they say Another poem, another day

THE LINE

Oh nations, this a thing we all go through A common cause we all have to do Patiently in line we stand

At post offices, shops, and Banks across the land Front to back in a line

Waiting for our turn in time Hated, but we have no choice

Stood there silent and without voice or in traffic jam

Stuck in a queue in a car or a van your patience reaches an end

This breaking point makes one go round the bend you stand there thinking this is wrong

Being forced and jostled along Labelled as a number

Bored in mental slumber Annoyed when someone pushes in

Or jumps the queue, a battle you just can't win Whose idea was it anyway?

To invent queues or this system as we say Like cattle or herded sheep

Rows of People in lines we keep from super market to traffic queue This indignant thing we do

By the way I wrote this in a line, you know My numbers called and I have to go

THE LITTLE PUZZLE BOX

I had a little wooden puzzle box from China it was made Took some working out as I played

All different symbols to line and match small dials with a face to line up and catch Many, many hours to fiddle and move Occasionally too difficult to prove

Lots of combinations with lots of complications Frustrating and difficult Working to get the basic root

Trying to get them all lined up in order Sometimes took me to a mental border How I tried

It sometimes tested me and hurt my pride But I persevered I never gave in

Just to break the puzzle just to win Time after time twisting and turning Looking and learning

Memorizing all the ways

A Lot of time spending whole days then one day just by accident I solved it That was the day I was happy every little bit

It just clicked and burred Twisted and turned

The little box chimed and rang a tune

A little dancer popped up with a golden moon round and round it danced

To a tune of romance

Oh, that little box of great surprise That unfolded be before my eyes All that work for such a result Some clever Chinese man had built

It was the simplest way that was done you'll find Just to get there was really fun with your mind

THE LOVE AND WAR

How you stand over me, and gloat over what you've done Another fine example in the battle you have won

A broken glass candlestick lies on the floor

The blood on your hands is mine; again, you've won the war

Once more I didn't react Against the act of violence you did enact

One more cut, another scar, and more bruises to hide the feeling of humility that a battered guy against honest pride

I took you and your children on, because I loved you, as honest love would do

I never knew how I took it for ten years, that I cared willingly, and gave to you

And yet from the start you taught your children to disrespect me at every turn

How you made me trapped, humiliated, and made my heart burn

But in spite of all, I loved you and how I tried too hard Thinking that things would change with every regard The abuse became so intense

Six against one, became so immense Was this how it was supposed to be?

Was this how your love was meant for me?

The shame of this man, who was mentally and physically abused

Then cast out on the street after being used I feel so undermined and weak

But was brought up to be honest, loyal in love, true and meek

I don't think I could ever change It the way that this life does arrange

THE LUSTY SELLER

She stood on her market stall, shouting all her wares in her hands she held the juiciest of pairs

Nice I thought

As a guy stood in front, his face strained and taught I asked what's up with him.

It's Ok lovely, she said an all the din He's bruised his banana

And caused a major drama

The other Lady stood there showing off her melons She said these were once Helens

Go on lovely, she said, have a nice good feel They are big and firm and make a lovely meal Gees I said that's a whopping marrow

It's so large it fills most of the barrow The lady said my tomatoes reach a peak And I've got apple so clean they squeak I got carrots to make your eyes water

And fat and juicy turnips from the farmer's daughter Cabbages with massive a heart

And collies that will make you **** (pass wind) Cocoa nuts so hairy

And flowers from the garden of Mary Passion fruit to open your eyes

And Monkey nuts from the three wise So gather round she said and feel me wares

My gooseberries smooth with hardly any hairs Cucumbers so long and straight

One glance it would make the ladies faint Come buy my Lusty, Honest gear Cause every week I will be here

THE MAN

There before you stand's a man that's proud Who's head stands above the crowd

Who greets you with a smile Makes you want to stay a while Listens to all you have to say Who helps if he can in any way Lifts your burdens if he can Some say that he's the man

Treats how he expects to be treated Fights on, even if he's defeated Never gives in

Always tries to succeed and win Never puts himself above others to him you all sisters and brothers His motives are always good

He never argues and is never out for blood Always puts others before himself

He owns no riches or wealth

He holds all things precious in life dear Keeps his friends close and near

Treats all with respect

From him that's what you would expect for every day is special to him

He trod his path without sin

And at any time, he stumbles and does fall He is only human after all

Perfect he's not Himself is all what he's got

He is just what feels, hears, and does see I know him well believe me

Rich in life, from when his birth began How I think he's a lucky man

In this university of life's quest

Right up till the time of death he does invest

He really does bleed A breed apart indeed

THE NAUGHTY CHILDREN MONSTER

A devious monster am I

Hiding in dark corners to make children cry Making myself disappear or reappear Making naughty children quake with fear

I can even enter their dreams

As I enjoy listening to their screams or even come in the dead of night

Causing imaginations to run wild with fright Every naughty child is my joy

My plaything, my imaginary toy

I don't like good children, they are no fun with wicked ones, I can get things done

I am here, there, and everywhere So misbehave if you dare

I come in all disguises All shapes and sizes

So please all you naughty children, do your worst You will be the ones that will be cursed

I love to make those bad children suffer best Leaving my victims muddles and stressed Please all those children don't be good

Cause I want to visit you in your own neighborhood

THE OFFICE HITLER

Be where; be where, of the office sneak He or she turns up as you speak

Scoring points, to climb up the bosses Bottle and glass (slang for backside)

Career advancement their prepared to grass Turning up at the most unexpected places Just to put gossip to faces

And they are the ones as miserable as sin Creating an atmosphere so thick, you need a sword to cut

it thin

They are the ones in a position of control Making the work place a drudgery as a whole Striking terror and fear

As they suddenly out of nowhere appear There can never be a big enough scooper to shovel up this party pooper

A Hitler on constant patrol

To go running to the boss, tale telling is their goal and this is the beauty

They never ever take time off, always on duty Ready to have anything to report

I'm sure they do it just for sport I've got to go

I've just seen the snoop lurking, and not quite on show OK you've caught me, you can tell the boss

Because personally I don't give a toss

THE OLD VETERAN

The old veteran soldier the last of his breed Who helped change the course of history in the 1930s

indeed

Without him our world would have been a totally different place

This world would wear a different face Many of us would not be alive to day

If a certain Austrian German would have got his way Those heroes, unlike others are not around

As each year passes, they are getting thinner on the ground Great grandfathers slipping into histories tide

To once again to be written in the annuals of the past to hide

Most now carved on epitaphs on memorial stones Those memories of past heroic deeds all lie in bones Heroes should be respected

It's only to be expected

Those who gave up their lives for us all to be free Freed from hate and tyranny

In those immortal words once spoken and set

****"Lest we forget"****

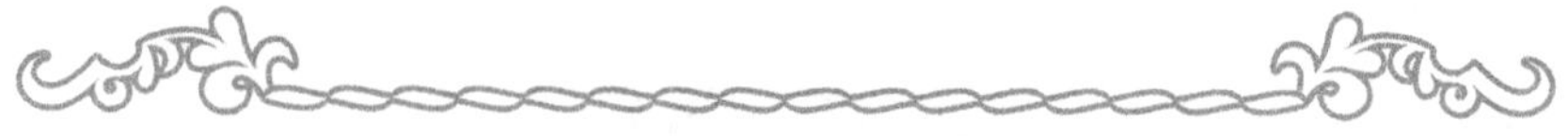

THE PLANE

Flight on a plane listening to the engine sound From a vacation I am homeward bound Twenty Thousand feet in height

Smooth and easy flight Touching the breath of heavens scene Above cotton wool clouds I've been Clear Sky of royal blue, drifting by Into Sun set of orange fiery red sky

Drifting on the wind

As the plane spreads it wings Gently passing over sea and land

Panoramic view, that display that's grand Me up there, and them so tiny down below Hard to really believe it so

That inner feeling that seems odd Brings you closer to God

Felling the motion of a downward draft of the landing craft

The screech of wheels hitting the runway Landing safely you almost in relief pray as the engine reaches a rising pitch

You know your home without a hitch

as the plane taxi's round

You know you're on home ground Home, Home, that's place you know

And yet returning back you didn't want to go but the calling of your roots brings you back to normal life on track

THE PSYCHIC VAMPIRE

I hide in the shadows, as I wait,

I have a date

I the psychic vampire Stealing thoughts, I aspire I don't steal much

Just a tiny touch

My victims hardly notice a thing Their thoughts on a platter to me they bring

I'm never greedy; I just take what I need in small proportions I feed

Leaving them Unnoticed, with their heads light Then I disappear into the night

Drunks are the ones that I like best As I stand with them and Joke and Jest

They never seem to notice the amount I take They think the hangover is their mistake So when you're out enjoying the drink

I might be waiting for you; doesn't it make you think?

THE SCAFFOLD

Three minutes, up those wooden steps I go to a fate, on that scaffold that I know There before me hangs the noose

Empty for the moment, loose I am scared my body shakes

My legs shiver and my insides quakes Heart pounding with growing fear

As the pending end of my life is near

the angry shouts from the jostling crowd As I stand before them, bound but proud the executioner places on the hood Darkness now surges my blood

The rope I feel around my neck

And the moment of the trapdoor opening through the deck Flashing images of my life, flash before

As I fall through the floor

The rope yanks hard as it tightens taught

With every breath to grasp for every moment fought the final agonizing snap of the neck, as I dance

Now I know I've lost my chance

And with my last conscious breath I am taken with death

My last thought of the innocence the grave injustice is my last sense

Darkness, nothingness

the final word "God Bless"

THE SERMON

The gentle priest stepped on to the alter His speech memorized so he does not falter And the service sits and quietly waits

As the priest stands up and orates Starting off in gentle sound

As he feels to get his verbal ground Eyes peer at the congregation

As they sit there in anticipation Then the voice that raises to a shout Now there's no escape and no way-out Fire and damnation, Hell and brimstone

Excommunication to all those sinners known the hand that will strike you down

Hell's fire will burn all around

Repent, Repent sayeth the lord, screams the priest and you will be forgiven at least

The congregation sits there paralyzed with fear

As their retribution is upon them and very near A fist bangs heavily on the pulpit

His teeth now gnash and grit

As many sits frozen and stiff as the priest delivers for all those god-fearing forgivers

Stunned and sat in silence now in shock as they sit in judgement in gods dock the priest says in a quiet tone

We shall now sing 126 Lord Take me home

THE TINY VOICE

In the night a tiny voice cries out Insecure and full of doubt

But in the busy bustle of life that voice is lost Forgotten in that hectic cost

For ignorance is bliss that small cry is missed

Others too busy to care on that fast track

Always pushing forward and never looking back

No can hear that desperate plea

Left abandoned, just left be Alone and scared Confused and impaired Desperate and alone

Its very existence threatened on its own That tiny voice now silent and gone Singular and just one

Insignificant and so small Now silent to all

What did tragedy lay? On the night of that day Not a voice but a sole

That passed on to a different role

THERE WAS PRIDE

There once was a man of pride, once tall he stood for partner and her children, he gave his blood They couldn't have been happier in life

Wanted the woman to be his wife

Proud of the home he sweated for, that she displayed Was it ignorance? Or just wrapped up in bliss?

Or was it something important he did miss?

To lose everything so fast, so swift Cut loose to drift

Lost in brain racking thought

Or was it a cruel lesson been taught

Where? He thought did he go wrong to be ousted from a family he did belong

How could he have been so misled?

Heart truly broken and bled Picking up the broken remains Bewildered with cruel pains The aching of the heart

That makes the strongest fall apart Trying to reason and feel

Is this nightmare for real?

Of the insecurity of a living hell Doubt and mistrust in time can only tell

THIS LIFE

This life we lead

That drains our soles and makes us bleed Wears us down in every way

Persistent struggle of each new day Pressures down on us, we have to bear Who says life isn't fair

Those arduous riggers of daily toil Just to earn our piece of spoil

Our small moments of happiness taken away our personal feelings on display

How hard we try to prove Just to stay in the groove Yet we show no remorse Set on our daily course We don't question why Just grateful for getting by

Some unknown surprise that seems to spring Of Unexpected news each day will bring News brought to the door

Or from a phone call of what's in store on this trek we seem to go

Of what's waiting round the corner you'll never know Getting by the best way we can

For woman, child, and man

from birth until death each day we try

On right up till the day we die Never ceasing to the end

Surviving, Living, in all this life we spend

Loving memories seem to be present, in a remembered cast

Comes to one who's growing old

Still warm youthfulness inside, but never cold

Out there, is a yearned hope somewhere?

One day, just one day if you dare

A FOOTBALL WIDOW

A football widow, there you sit
Can't stand football one little bit
Empty cans, and snacks in bowls
To the shouting of those scoring goals
Attention half time, you're not elated
22 blokes kicking a pig's bladder round a field,
to you is not rated
Pretending you're enjoying the game,
oh you must be so frustrated
David Beckham is the only thing worth the view
and every football season, this you have to do
Don't suppose your partner would really care
Him being so enthralled in the game, you might as well not be
there
Your purpose is just to keep up the supplies
Make sure the beer and snacks, that never dies
I bet your praying for the football season to be over
That day you'll be rolling in clover
Soon it's the start of another sports fanatic's widow's reason
It's now the start of the cricket season

A GAME

Looks like you have a game to play
But now I see through your way
Your feeling hurt
As you have took another Knock in life and your feeling inert
But take one good hard look at yourself for one moment Stop and take stock and lament
You just can't see it can you? Treating others, the way you do
I can understand your past abuse
The way you put it to use
Why do you think I took a step back?
Is it true compassion that you lack?
I'm not the one you should attack
After all I helped you get back on track
Was I so wrong in this thing I do?
Helping and healing you?
Is this the way I'm to be Paid?
To live this life of a so-called masquerade?
You must realize your hurt is self-imposed
The true motive? its only you who knows
A pattern in your life revolves
And finding it harder to get off, as it evolves
I haven't bothered you. I have just stayed away
Not used others as a tool, just to have your say
Me the Villain You the heroine
Well, you know the truth and the treason
And by now others know the reason
I hope you are Happy now, and you have your day
Looks like you have a game to play

A TALE OF SADNESS

I saw a tear fall and trickle gently from your eye
as you began to cry
I felt the hurt and pain in your heart
Your shaken voice as you told your part
As your heart rendering story started to unfold
Shaking as your past was told
How you managed to stay alive
I wondered how you did survive
Those dreadful things life put you through
And how you didn't deserve those things that person done you
How did you stand it those things that was done
I know for you it couldn't have been much fun
I felt you agonizing pain
As you have to lift your life again
How I wanted to hold you, and ease your sad distress I know
that anger and hate is a thing you have to address
But I sit here and listen to your sad tale in the end you will
prevail
You blame yourself you thought you have failed Not you, you
tried, you availed
I'm deeply touched inside
In my tender heart my feelings I hide
As you brush away that tear
Eased now, I hope I've took away that fear
Gave you hope and heart
To make a fresh new start

A VALENTINE CARD

I received your valentine card
All tiny hearts on a floral facade
As I opened, and read inside
The moving verse written, tears I cried
Those words written, touched my heart
Reached my intimate my tender souls' part
And now I know your love is meant for me
Moving words, made me see
I felt the movement of the verse
Those lines of emotion disperse
Each word echoes in my mind
Right down to your hand that signed
All those words of love displayed
Those feelings portrayed
True love never needs a word
Even spoken, never needs an ear to be heard
Deep feelings tell it all
No matter how insignificant or small

ACTORS

The actors stand upon on the stage
Each event turns the page
Of characters, that they portray
In the roles of a script, they play
Actions mimic deliberate moves
And words of a story proves
Costumes play historic parts
To respond to the players hearts
Lights, curtains, and act the scene
To tell a part of history past that's been
Romance from lover's tales
To end in tragedy that prevails
Comedy played form a cast
Long ago moments from the past
As dramatic scenes unfold
There is a story to be told
These moments of an age
As the Actors stand upon the stage
The final curtain falls
To a rapturous applause and encored calls

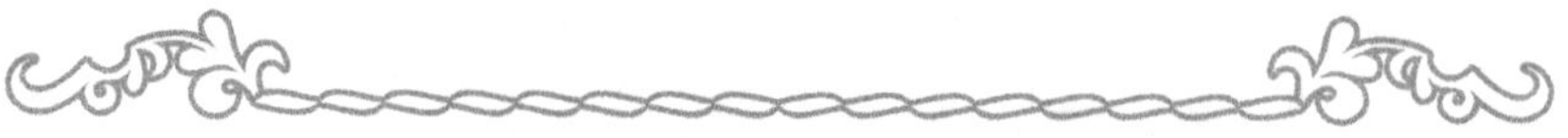

AUTUMN SEASON

Rusty red, golden carpet adorns
Of brilliant orange yellow morns
Bare branches, twist and reach the sky Somber grey days, mock
the eye
Shadows stretch and loom
To the fullness of the silver moon
And the heavens paint a crisp deep blue
Where the prisms of the stars shine through
A nip of a chill in the air
The calling of winter fare
Summers fallen asleep
Out are the hunter gatherers collecting, Nuts and Kernels to
keep
Builders of the straw homes and the falling of pine nut cones
Dry and grassy straw
The hold of the winter's store Man tends the field Plough and
harrow, for next year's yield
And the black speckles of the birds, migrate A warmer climate
they go to
emigrate Comes the cold autumn air to blow
And waiting for the winter snow
Another season passes by How the seasons fly

THE TOE IN THE TAP BLUES

I was lay there soaking in the bath Resting from the day's aftermath

Steam and heat a comfortable atmosphere Suddenly gripped with fear

You know you fiddle with feet into the tap Well I fell right into that trap

TOE stuck fast and jammed right in Started shouting made a din

Now neighbors banging at my door dreading what actions would befall Heard them shouting up my hall with 911 or 999 call

Sirens screaming to and FRO and door caved within Let them all the Police, fire, Ambulance and multitude in

Bathroom door pushed open wide

There was nowhere else for me to hide Like an exhibit at a show

Men, Women, and child were there to know A crowd of faces eyes open wide

Grinning teeth, guffaws and laughs to hide

I lay there, hands cupped over my manhood Otherwise it would float like wood

Was I red just with heat?

Or was it embarrassment with all to meet

Drain the water someone said now it's getting cold Now with shock and shrinking and not so bold GUYS YOU KNOW THE STORY TOLD

A kind fireman covered me with his coat by now I couldn't face the neighbors, how?

After being on show for all to see Like a comedy on TV Hands of plenty all around,

Questions and riddles to answers found

They pushed and they tugged with all their might My toe still stuck there tight

With manhood now shrinking in hand It all became rather
bland
Cold and wrinkly, white and chapped
Lying still there with hands capped
Time running out and passing fast
All resources running to the last
One fire woman said let's get the saw
I screamed what for?
They chuckled and said just to cut the tap
And get you out this dreaded trap
One-woman said use butter I said what for?
To lubricate your toe some more
Funny thing it just fell out
Must have been the cold no doubt
Not the only thing to shrink
But doesn't it make you really think
all the drama over and all gone
Wasn't I the embarrassed one?
So be warned and watch out too
Otherwise, it could be you

BED

Oh, it's time for bed
My brain is worn out and dead
The rigors of the day
Have worn me out in every way
Time seems to be steep
Now all I think about is sleep
Eye lids start to fight
It's the end of another night
I hear the call of my slumber pit
To where my head to the pillar does fit It's that time I know
Off to bed I go

BONFIRE NIGHT

November the 5th when fires are burning bright
Fireworks light up the sky at night
Whistles, bangs, and explosions fill the air
The smell of brimstone and fire everywhere
Kids excited jump around
As they watch and listen to fireworks sound
Hot dogs, baked potatoes, and sausage rolls
Fill the need for hungry holes
Hand held sparklers that's are waved Shapes and signatures in the dark are made
Spent and smoking fireworks lay on the ground
Burning embers in charred heaps are found
Eerie smoke that's lays a veil
Morning light looking pale
Guy Fawkes comes to mind
He, That History left behind

CHANGES

I see the changes in your face The way you've changed your place
The rose wilted that I gave you, that you wore
Now you don't want me any more
Those dinner stains upon the wall
Tells it all
Am I blind to what I see, or was I mistaken?
For my love that you had taken
Was it the hurt from your past?
Means love to you will never last
You talked about him all the time
Couldn't get him of your mind
He treated you so bad
Sometimes made you mad
The phone and texts you received
Was to you, that disbelieved
I watched you sinking
Every moment of him, you were thinking
I thought I'd had a chance
To give you genuine love and romance
But how I was wrong
It didn't take long
You've taken him back
Things are on track
And nothing has changed
Well, you did arrange
I won't bother you anymore
I know the score
Your situation that you're bound
Good luck and I'll see you around

CHARACTER ASSASSINATION

Character assignation isn't a joke
When a coward or cowards insult the good name of a bloke
Unfounded accusations point the finger
Leaving a bad taste in the mouth that does linger What gives this person or persons the right?
That involves a good and respected name, to be involved in their fight
Are they so insecure?
Are they so afraid?
So unsure?
How they hide behind a user name
Laying unfounded accusations, as they lay the blame Edited false text
Is what from a blamer?
You can only expect Someone jealous of popularity and artistic value
Is the kind of underhanded things they would do?
Hide go tell your lies
You're the one whose personality dies
I hope you read this poem; I have written by my own hand like every poem I've written is in popular demand
Original copy writes and hand drafts I've kept as proof
I don't need to hide behind user names, to stay hidden and aloof
My user's name is known to all and is the only name I've used
My word is my bond, and I'm no bigot is the word you freely abuse
Point your finger, tell your lies
I'm not the one hiding from eyes

CHAT UP LINE

I just sit there and stare Should I care?
Or do I dare?
I see her, but she is not aware Do I get up out of this chair?
Be brave enough to ask? Or hide behind this mask Do I decline?
Wait and bide my time as the beer glass drains Another glass of
Dutch courage dulls my brains
She still sits alone at the bar
So near and yet so far
I'm sure I can make some excuse
By smiling and saying, they let me loose
Can I use my time?
By using some cheesy chat up line
As I bravely rise, look over, and think great
But some guys beat me to it, I'm too late

CHRISTMAS

What is the meaning of Christmas to us all today?
Over the decades we have drifted away
Not the old excuse of Christmas is for giving
But for Commercial Profiteers to make their living
All dressed up with bells of holly
Decorations and cries of noel and jolly Blackmailed by companies for our children's emotions
Urged to buy based on our parental devotions
That yearly theme we spend to buy
Tempting expensive fads pass by
And each year gets financially harder to cope
All in the name of Christmas hope
Psychologists, economists, hired to exploit us for commercial gain
Those usual pressures that still remain
All in the name of Christmas noel
Families, Parents, Partners put through hell The time of year when couples fall apart
The final financial straw that breaks your heart
Designer clothes, Toys, and gifts
That causes families to argue and creates rifts
Christmas comes but once a year
That time of year that many fear
what is Christmas all about?
Time to look back and sort future finances out We have all been forced to move away from the real
Christmas time
The real true giving of Christmas kind

CONFIDENCE

When confidence is lost inside
And self-esteem wants to run away to hide
all that life is a never-ending knock
As life passes in that ticking clock
Trapped and helpless in a deep rut
There's nowhere left to strut
It's got to the stage where you can't say hello
There's nowhere left to go
Locking yourself away safe and sound
Preferring to stay on safe ground
Oh God! How so ugly you feel
And to the opposite sex you think that there's no appeal Almost
sorry now, and so afraid to commit
Feeling there's no place left to fit with all the friends that you
know
Alone so alone inside is the only place to go
That constant feeling of reject
Is the daily thing to expect? The feeling of self-eject Losing one's
self respect
Loneliness becomes a constant threat Something carried heavily
around, that's a sure bet
Is this the path that's does induce
To become short of becoming a recluse
But you have to stop and smile
You still have your life, just for a while

THE DATE

I went to meet a person on a date
Something we have all done and can relate
Worn the roses on our chests
Carried books and papers and signs of interests
Organized where to meet
Excited and nervous on the way to greet
Not knowing what you'll find there at arranged meeting place
Heart thumping arriving there wondering what you face There
you wait lost and forlorn
And wishing you'd never been born
People passing to and FRO Backwards and forwards they go
And there she stands Rose in hand
6FT 8 and 20 stone not what you planned
OH MY GOD you think, is she the one?
The rose I carry screwed up and gone and she reaches for her
mobile phone
She dials; you're on your own
Waiting for yours to ring
Wanting deep inside you Want to smash the thing
If it rings there nowhere to hide
Excuses needed you scream inside
It can't be me Please it can't be me
But it's not my phone ringing you see
And there's the victim on his phone
They meet shake hands and off they go
Breathing a sigh of relief now they have gone Thinking that was
close, thanking GOD I was the Lucky
one What about my date you ask,
and how did it go?
As per usual they didn't show

ELEMENTS OF THE STORM

Dark clouds roll over each other up on high

Black horses Rear up to ride the sky

The winds moan in a low pitch drone, as they pass by

And Shards of lightening fly

How the mighty unseen titan's clash

As they're colossal weapons crash

The gigantic swords in the sky that flash

To the tears and sweat pour down in rains that thrash

As vibrating thunder shakes the earth

To the battling of the tempest giving birth Torrent waves of the confused sea rise and roar

to the shore

Smashing down heavily to the rocks does pour As the Gods battle in the struggling fight

The raging confusion in the night

Ride the winds and sail the storm

The tempest shows its tormented form

Horses writhe and scream with foaming bit

The gods fight on in demented fit

Shattering sheets of icy hail

Blinding elements of confusion prevail

All thrown in to nature's battle

To be unraveled in torrented tackle Screaming howling winds call to the land

The Storm stands firmly in command

Lightning throws its sparking, cracking prisms that blind That leaves dark shadows to the eyes behind

How the mighty opponent falls

To Natures eternal calls

The weathers Performance gave

To tribute the fallen and the victor's brave

As all calms to the quieting sound

To softening fresh airy ground
As the battle of the elements move on
Into the distance it's now gone

ENDLESS LINE

I'm in a queue as far as the eye can see
I don't want to be here, believe me
One step forward in this never-ending wait
Time ticking by, making me more and more late
Children screaming as they run about
As they swing off the line ropes, running in and out
The old lady in front bangs you shin with her shopping trolley
And someone from behind stabs you with their brolly
Jolted forward and papers dropped
Leaning forward to retrieve them elbow in the eye is copped
Staggered back tripped and fell
Landed on your backside, not a funny thing I can tell
you pick yourself up and brush yourself down Looking round
and feeling like a clown
With a feeling of disgrace
Looks like of lost my place
So now my place is to the back,
as I start all over again
I just can't take the strain
There in a line to hear my number called
Dazed, lost, and totally appalled
when you standing in a queue Spare a thought and be careful
what you do

FOUND OUT

Don't you stand there wide-eyed, with an innocent look on your face?
You know what you done and what took place
It's no good acting, or starting to cry
I can hear it in your voice that you lie
Sometimes I wonder if you're my child
Sometimes unruly, sometimes wild
At times you wear my patience thin
The antics you've got up to and the places you have bin But, now you have been found out
It's the truth I want, without any doubt
Turning on those tears don't really work with me
I've been there many times you see
I know all the tricks, and fibs that you will ever tell
And all the excuses yet to come, I know very well
As adults we know all the score
We've done them all before
dry those tears and come clean
To lie to us, is just obscene
tell the truth and be true People will respect, and look up to you
And besides it less painful, less punishing on that guilty mind
And will ease the consequences you will find
Always remember tell the truth
It's all part and parcel of your growing youth

FRIENDS

Seems friends are important indeed
For those being in need
How, at times they are taken for granted?
And at times, that's never what is wanted
Sometimes it suits their aims
To play their emotional games
But a friend is a friend
No matter what happens in the end Support, advice, and a crutch
And at times, that diplomatic touch
Tea and sympathy as they say, time to listen
Tarnished gold does not glisten
Seeing good friends come and go
For reasons why, only they know
what is a true friend?
Someone to help mend
Loyalty and understanding
Not controlling or demanding
Just someone to be there Strong enough to be aware
To be objective
Put things into perspective
if you're a friend, when in need
Then you are a true friend indeed

FULL OF IT

There is he, the man who likes to brag
About those escapes he likes to bag
You think you're so fit
In reality, you're so full of it
You treat all, like a door mat
And there you stand with tipped and tilted hat
Truth is you're a low life, so vile
King of the heap,
Lord and master of the pile
There will be a day we watch you sink
Then we will really smell the stink
With defecation you're stuffed so full
There's seepage, with all the bull
Talk and it trickles from the corner of your mouth
Want good advice, go head south
my tarnished knight
To the man who's always right
One day your reign will end
You will be the loser, friend
When it all comes to a stop
We will all be there to watch you drop
Enjoy your day while you can
For the moment, you are the man

GRACE

Tender is that gentle touch of grace
does stroke softly against your face
Warm petaled lips do purse
As I watch your mouth move as you converse
Eyes opaque, that flicker and gaze
As pupils react in many ways
Lashes with a simple curve
Long and curvaceous as I observe
And as the light shines across your cheek
Changing shape as you speak
Small but perfect nose
Compliments your face it shows
Down to your soft and delicate skin
All set in a perfect profile within
I could sit here and stare at you all day
Watching your face in awe all in every way
And that hair so dark and soft with every perfect strand as you
brush it through your hand
Those ears so nicely set
Listening to every word that's met
And as you speak, I hang on every word
Softly spoken, Chrystal clear and heard
As your mouth does softly smile
I'm taken, lost, and breathless for a while
All these things that I do see
Is what your face means to me?
in my mind I keep your face
Your gentle touch of grace

ALL HALLOWS DAY

Take time way back in the history of all hallows day
Back in Neolithic and pagan times they say
The one time of the year that spirits rise up from eons past from earthly beds to walk the earth in mass
And as night drew near
Fires were lit to keep away fear
As groups gathered together round a fire Safe around that warm bright pyre
To celebrate relatives and friends of long since passed times
That night retuned in spirits minds Fires burning to keep evil spirits at bay
While sprites, witches, and daemons play
As those ancient people waited till morning light Praying to the gods for safety through the night
Hoping to keep their souls safe and sound
Not stolen by spirits and taken to hallowed ground
When Morning came a feast and time to celebrate
That those survived from hells open gate
And all the old gods and spirits receive
Of Hallows day and hallows eve

HEATED WORDS

Some say "nothing like a good argument" or a blazing row It
releases tension and clears the air some how

Heated words in an exchange Ending up in a violent rage Two
sides with an aimless view

Building up in frustration in everything they do
A game of verbal winning
As nerves fray from the beginning
Hurtful comments passed to and FRO
Losing tempers as they go
That game of verbal tennis
Discord becomes a menace
What's the point in this escapade?
No one wins in this masquerade
After all you never get to agree
A waste of time, effort, and energy
All those nasty things that was said
Running through each other's head
Making up in the end, to relinquish guilt
Not the way life should be built
For some not easy Just to sit and calmly talk
If it starts its best to walk
Wait till things calm down
Then nicely talk each other round
Solutions solved better to a gentle sound
Together closer you are bound
Better to talk things over in this way
Serves no purpose just to blaze away
No wedge to drive between
More sense to keep it clean
If this is a thing we all can do
Then the world will be a better place for me and you

THE HORSE

You the Noble beast stands from 11 to 40 Hands
The steed of regal stance
Free in the fields to dance
Sport of kings you participate
Both friends to master and mate
You're with majestic strut
Who ploughs a fields Rut
Hunters that peruse a fox
One who rides in a box
Dray horses that pull Brewery Dray
Just for another working day
Beast of burden to pleasure ride
Excites riders deep inside
Loved and adored
Groomed and adorned
The finest saddle on you back
You wear bright and shiny tack
Reigns, stirrups, and bit
Canter to gallop to make you fit
One of the animals that's supreme
You, one of all little girl's dreams
You of high intelligence amount
For the rider on your mount
With flowing main and splendid tail,
The need to win and not to fail
You the Regal Horse
Set upon your daily course

IF

There's a hollow in the pillar, where you used to lay Another day, another night, of loneliness and dismay Where are those gentle hands in the morning that used to stroke?
Where are the morning tender words you spoke?
Those eyes that used to give that loving greet
The morning kiss that used to meet
That perfume smell that filled the air
I lost you, you are not there
Oh god I feel so lonely IF only but the word IF is a cliché
That means the start of an empty day
Half empty shelves and draws
Emotionally I'm clutching at straws
Half my life gone
Lying here with tears in my eyes
Deceived, mislead, with lies
And yet for one second, I would have you back
You are the missing thing I lack
At a drop of a hat, I would forgive
Just to get our lives back and live
But now I lay in a half empty bed
To face another day, I dread

LADY ASIA

Lady of Asia you are the glittering shinning jewel
The beauty of the stone, to the touch that's cool
You are the slender movement of the tigers walk
The soothing chatter of the monkeys talk
Swift in thought of the cobra's strike
Astuteness of the mongooses like
Wit as sharp as the scorpion's sting
Gentle as the songbirds sing
Nimble of the prey mantis dance
Strong as the elephant's stance
You stand above the noble ox
Cunning as the bushy tail fox
Dark as the leopard who stalks at night
Bright as the ruby's stunning light
You are the touch of silk
You are the mother of milk
You are adorned on palace walls
Displayed in Khans halls
Kings utter your name
Child givers in births pain
The empress who wears the crown
Held in high esteem,
away from renown Lady Asia you stand above your crowd
History says you should be proud
One small glimpse of you face
Says you are the one with grace
All these things they do all men say
And for once this is your day

MY LOVE

Where my love, my sweetheart, where will you be?
Far across lands, and over the sea
Green cliffs of the kissed shore
Cry out, for you forever more
Hills and trees of our homeland weep
For the love inside I keep
I wait for you in the misty glen
My heart is there, waiting for you then
My love, my love, I miss you so
More than the warm breezes in the valleys blow
May you hurry on the tide?
From O the sea and ocean wide
When that ship is on the sky line
Then I'll know your home and mine
May my love find you on the air?
Hurry home my love, may the winds be fair
Till my arms hold you firm
The heart inside me, for you love does burn
May our kisses be firm?
My love, my love, till you return

NEGOTIATIONS

Police cars screaming in the streets Sirens, blue lights, come in
fleets Armed police rush about
Bark their orders in a shout
The pounding on a door
The place of murder, blood, and gore
This crime committed minutes before
Who knows what's in store
A scream, the ring of a shot
They surround the spot
Rifles and pistols held at the ready
The commander shouting steady boy's steady
A crack, a flash
A ricochet, a window smash
Who is the guilty perpetrator?
Who is the life taker?
Then a call for calm the plea to do no harm
Steady is the voice of the negotiator
To relax the nerves of the instigator
Throw down you gun
Make it easier on yourself to come
Then silence and paws
Breath draws
Out walks the condemned man
Ended now, from when it all began

I'M NOT A POET

I'm just a writer of line and verse
Of sights, feelings and life, in words that I converse
Just words written on a page
defines
A collective of syllables grouped in lines
An expression of emotions written down
Adjectives and characters Jumbled with noun
But all put together in line
To narrate those stories of Life, in rhyme
One skillful word can say it all
When inspiration comes to call
But if wrongly put down it can fail
When it comes to make a rhyming tale
All done in a different style
In many different ways to compile
At times not an easy thing to do
Inspiration plays a big part too
However, I do my best
Competing with the rest
And others work I have to admire
In their own individual works as they aspire Touching and caressing to sensitive ears and hearts, they preach
Tender moments as their words do reach Each
one a Bard in their own right
As they struggle and word play with what they write
I am not a poet
Just a simple man of word
And glad that others appreciate what is written and heard

ONE OF THOSE DAYS

Is it one of those days?
Everything goes wrong in many ways
Not as things appears
A day to scream, and burst into tears
All the troubles of Nations
Rest on your shoulders with no reasonable explanations
Burdened with your heavy sole
A down in the dump's day, takes its toll
Almost afraid Tempers displayed
And to cap it all, you feel you're to blame
Knowing you're not, is just not the same
Gets to a point you can't take the strain
Feeling like you're going insane
There you are, in the thick of the scrape
Hands clasped on both ears; can you escape?
Filling that already full head
Empty, weakened, and fully bled
Can't get those things, sorted in a hurry
Maxed head ready to explode with worry
Don't you want to run and hide?
Chill out and unwind?
In time things will sort itself out
Keeping cool, no need to shout
And at the end of that day
Things will work out, I can say

RACE

So, you never lose your way in the race
Or never want to lose face
In the never-ending human-race
And after all it's no disgrace
If you fall behind and lose your place
This normally is the case
And easy to for steps to retrace
It's a goal to act with grace
To interact and interface
So don't feel so glum, just watch this space
And you'll be the one who's ace

ROSE IN TIME

A small green bud grows
Evolving colors glows
Petals in the warm sun, form
A rose is born
Beauty to the eyes does please
As it gently sways in summer breeze
Picked and kept in treasured hold
For an instant in a moment told
Rigid is the stem, and thorns so strong
Can this creation last so long?
Petal's curl and wither
Fall off and shiver
Helplessness as it slowly starts to die
Elusiveness the rose does tell a lie
It doesn't last for ever
To possess this treasure, never
The impression leaves a fond moment in mind
An image and epitaph left behind
Remember, remember, and do not forget
The time held, is no regret
Yours for those small seconds in time
Appreciated, yours not mine
You held the rose
You smelt the perfume of its repose
It was yours and yours alone
Something borrowed, you could never own

SHE SLEEPS

She sits on the edge of the bed
Betrayal and lies, rang through her head
Her hands cover the tears on her face
Trust turned to mistrust, gave her disgrace
She had the right
When the truth came to light
All this time
The one she loved, committed the crime
She could not believe
How one so trusted, came to deceive
Now it's all come out Her shattered life in pieces, all now in
doubt
The pain now weighted, and pushed
Her heart crushed Driven to despair She feels life has not been
fair
She gave it all; she gave more than her share
Seems He didn't care
Alone now she has to brave the fight
No one there to help her share her plight
She pitifully weeps
Till her weary sobbing closes her eyes
and she sleeps

HOUSE OF SWEETS

Somewhere in the realm of a dream of treats
There's a house in a place of the land Sweets
Where leaves on trees are made from paper rice
Frosted with glistening sugar ice
And bark on the trunks encrusted with chocolate flake Paths
made out of nut cluster toffee bake
A bed of lollipop flowers in a dark rich soil of fudge
There a pond of creamy chocolate sludge
Candy striped columns, around liquorish doors
Treacle toffee bricks, makes its walls
Clear sugar pane windows of gloss
Curtains of wispy pink sugar candy floss
Press the M&M chocolate bean button, of the bell
As the door opens to an aroma of heavens smell
Baked cakes from the entered confectioned hall
Into strips of colored Liquorish paper on a wall
As you gaze on black and white Bertie Bassett tiles on the floor
Pear drops and pineapple chunks mosaic held in store
To a gaze of a ginger bread settee with jelly beans inset A crispy
wafer coffee table is met
Up a flight coated chocolate pairs walnut and dates of banister
stairs
To a red and white candy striped four poster bed
With pink soft marshmallow pillars to rest your head Falling
asleep on a mattress of angel cake
Then suddenly realizing you're awake
After drowning in a bath of coffee cream
You realize it's only a dream

TEDDY BEAR

My old and little teddy bear
Has one eye, and missing bits of hair
In places scuffed and worn
Pads on hands, snagged and torn
Sticking out, bits of straw
But still loved, and has a place in store
With that fixed smile upon his face
My teddy has that special place
Teddy has been there through all my life
The little button in his ear, says steiffe
My Teddy may be old
He has a story to be told
We will always be together
My cute and cuddly friend forever

THE CALL FOR HOME

I hear the haunting pipes down along bogs and mountain sides
The flute in green valleys and wilds
The beat of the drum, like the Celtic heart
The plucked strings of the Irish harp Music in my head, to the
lands of Low
As the breeze of peat flowers sway and flow
The shamrock trembles as it does a dance
To Limerick words of Irish romance
Loch carries the Carrack down to the seas
Past grassy green, and leafy trees
History sang in words of a song
Of a tradition of a sacred heart so strong
In the music tells a story
Of hope, loss, and glory And yet there's a beckoning call
Back home to the emerald isle would befall
Where ever in the world, an Irish heart does roam
T 'is the call for home
Where the heart is tied
For the true sense of Irish pride

THE GUN SLINGER

The saddle and the horse is my Friend
On both I ride and depend
The gun and holster hangs at my side
The open rage, from town to town I ride
A blanket is my home
Campfires mark where I roam
From burning sun, rain, frost, and snow
I travel through the seasons, where I go
Earning a living when I can
the so-called saddle tramp,
I am I live by the gun
Moving on when my work is done
The taker of life, the romancer
A gambler, a chancer
I've seen the fear in man's eye
As I have shot them, and seen them die
The law of the gun, says it's them or you
Its survival is the thing to do
My name and reputations best
I am known throughout the West
Gunslinger is my craft and code
A career where you'll never grow old
I am the cowboy with no home
In History books I will be known

THE THISTLE

The thistle, stands strong and tall

Green, thorny stem, sharp spines and all Blue purple flower of a gentle part

Unmoving as a man, and flower soft as a woman's heart There stands a symbol to the brave

This the Scottish emblem gave

Among the wild moorlands, of the highland peak Gave Scotland a voice to speak

Proud of the tartan clan

For every Scottish woman, child, and man You the thistle are the sign of the free-Spoken pride of Celtic tongues to be

You sway in the field

Hardy, stern, steadfast to never yield

To the sound of the pipes, of bonny lads and lass N'er the moments of history pass

Wear the Thistle with pride Scotland forever and tradition never died

THROUGH THE EYES

I sit on the side walk, and watch them pass by
They don't care if I live or die
To them, I'm and object of fear
They don't see the person I appear
Looks can be deceiving
Loose change they drop, is relieving
My rag worn clothes, makes me a different sight
Ignorance is just their way of being polite
The system has not been a friend of mine
And I guess no one has the time
I used to be like them, but it's not what they perceive
I don't think for one minute, they would believe
They are too busy getting on Things, Places, to do or be done I
am un-noticed and forgotten Beguiled, and begotten
Now all I have is time on my hands
While they rush to beat daily demands
See then rushing to and FRO
But I sit; I've got nowhere to go
Seen through the eyes, of doubt
Me the down and out

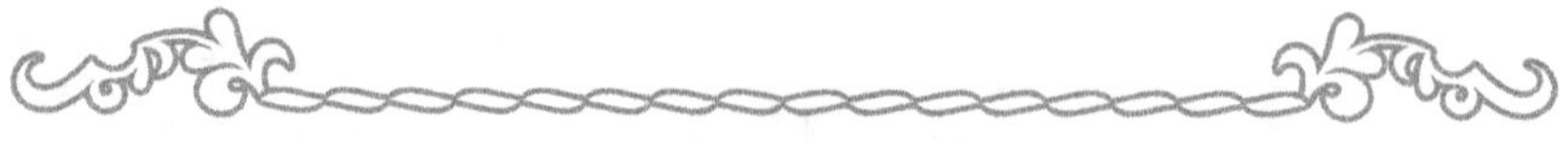

VLAD

Who would have thought Dracul? Your stories of old
Of Vlad the impeller would be forever told
A Turkish Prince of nobility and station
Would throw a tyrannical rule over a Rumanian nation
Cruelty was your name
To torture, inflict injury, and maim
Those you impaled in steaks, as they slowly slid to agonizing pain
Some said you were insane
Heads of vanquished enemies' hand on spikes above you gate
A man with no respect and of sheer hate Rotting carcasses were
put on show
And those on steaks died long and slow
Pleasure you took amongst those exhibits, as you dined
A sight for those poor peasants to remind
Your legend has become immortal
The name always to be remembered for those who are mortal
Carved in stone
The word "Vampire" stands alone

YOU ARE THE FLOWERS

You are the delicate Orchid, I hold in my hand
The purple Sweet Peas, that grows in fertile land
You are the blushing rose of infinite red
The swaying virgin Lilies in its bed
You are the somber Sun flower in the field
The Tiger Lilly in full yield
You are the Tulip that makes you mine
The Yellow Daffodils that shine
The pink Mission Bells
The Blue Snap Dragon that tells
You are the clover beneath my feet
Nasturtium petals that is peppery and sweet
You are the garden of my sole
Repose of bloom that makes me whole
The garden of love, which I tend
Delicately taking time to mend
Like most things that need tender loving care
To see the color of beauty share
You are my Garden of elation
Together we make creation

CONTENTS

SPENT MORTALITY

I don't believe in God
Don't you find that odd?
And yet if I was to appear
In front of the heavenly court, the great overseer
Then who am I then?
I am just a mere mortal, like any other men
Who am I to argue?
I wouldn't have a clue
And if there is the greater being, who gives out judgement
It means my mortality is spent
If in my short span
I have lived a true and honest man
And I can only accept
And show the greater one respect
Shrug my shoulders, and take what's given
Take the punishment delivered and driven
So, if that judgment day does arrive
And in death my sole does survive
And there is an Almighty
I will just have to agree and say alrighty
Till then I will amble along in my honest way
Come the time of this so-called Judgement Day
And at that time, I won't be deceived
Lie I will not, and say that I believed
Until then I will play this waiting game
And if called, someone may explain
And maybe if it's too late
I will just have to see and wait

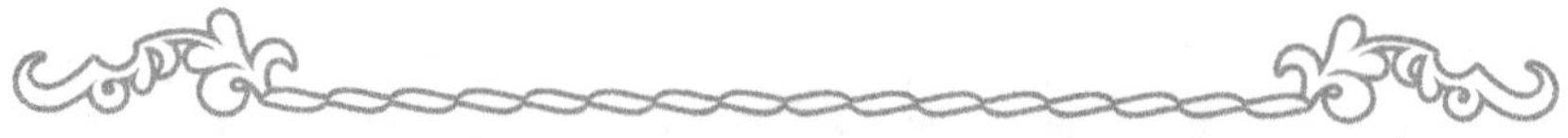

SONNET FOR A FRIEND

By light of moon, thou face that looketh divine
In sunlight thyne hair doth shine
Of raven black and darkest night
Thou eye doth spark like twilight
Red thou lips of petals of rose
Cantered and perfect thou gentle nose
Olive tint on smoothen skin
And gentle smile that doest tickles within
Heart of thine soft and kind
Intelligent and humorous mind
Small in stature but tall within
Why hath we not met yet, where hast thou been
Voice of a choir that doth sing
Thou softest words though doth bring
Tis these things that remindeth of thee
Thou art a woman of these qualities I doth see

SINGLE MUM

She wakes to another day
In another bedroom, she hears her children play
Another day in a normal life
She's now an Ex-partner, an Ex-wife
Circumstances in her life has changed
Through many faults of either partner, have been re-arranged
And she realises she's now alone
With kids to bring up on her own
And it aint no joke
A woman on her own, without a bloke
Another typical day to face, to scrimp and scrape
Money matters to manage and re-shape
No income, no wage
It seems to be the thing in this day and age
It isn't easy, but no matter how hard she will try
She has adapted to resigning to get by
Putting her children before herself
While feeling trapped, and left on the shelf
She is alone, but she's a heroine, she's the one
After all is said and done
One day, her turn of happiness will come
When children grow up, and realise what she has done
Mean while she tries her best to give them fun
She's a typical single mum

THE SHY MAN

What vision doth behold, before mine eyes
I doth see her I canst not lie
She be there I canst not spake
For she hath mine goodly heart to kept
Oh, if she was mine
Mine dreams I would give so divine
I yearned for thee mine love
Thou hast been sent from haven above
Tis liked thee thorn that pricked mine heart
When I see-eth thou vision, and I doth depart
I doth longest to spake mine true words I doth hold
For I be a man not so bold
From afar I stranded to see thine beauty thy hold
Thou love cometh, to mine eye
Tis within mine self I canst not lie
Nay I sayeth be strong and true to thy self
Doth a man run away and be weak to mine self
But alas I canst not be with speak be so free
Be gone thou cowardly cur inside of thee
I must be brave as thou canst be
Spake thy words unto she
Thy lady thou adore may see thee
She may say aye
She may say nay
If thou canst not spake thou wilt never know
Take thine self unto her and to she thou show
Doth thee lady get the man?
Tis another story in another span

SERVING TIME

You did the crime
Now you'll serve the time
As you walk down long and stacked prison halls
Steel doors in rows, set behind prison walls
As you walk into a bare bricked cell
Four by six is hell
The realisation of the slam of the heavy door
Is it your first time? Or have you been there before?
You're just a number
Controlled even as you lay and slumber
Told what and when to do
As prison warders stick like glue
Timelessness drags as you sit in thought
Reflecting on the time you got caught
Be untouchable in every way
Always in mind you would always get away
Now you serve the time you got
And believe me, you got a lot
When are you ever going to learn?
The only way is honesty, to earn
No constantly looking over your shoulder
As fearless in crime makes you bolder
Don't go there any more
If you don't want to hear the slamming, of that door

ONCE HIDDEN PRIDE

You were a woman once, till the drink took hold
It blinded you, made your feelings cold
Eluded you, made you look old
You're not the person you think you are, as others must have told
And it's taken away your self-esteem
Life now is never what it would seem
It hides the true person you used to be
Once loving, upstanding, and free
Now you wear a different face
In that minority in different race
You sacrificed and gave up all
For the urge to dinks call
And Drink does that in the end
Makes you break and bend
At times you must have taken a sober look
And thought of the changes you could have took
Wanting deep inside to change
The warnings within you to rearrange
Sometimes you think it's not worthwhile
And you just haven't the will for anything to compile
Never knowing if it's to late
To pick your life up, and get out of this state
You can if you really try, and if you really care
The damage done to you, your family, and all, you can repair
Time and determination is what you have got
And if you're strong you can fix the lot
It just takes you to reach the real person you once was inside
Just to find a spark of your hidden once pride

OLD SCHOOL DAYS

Granddad told me when he was a lad
When at school in the old days we had
A piece of slate and a stick of chalk
Told to sit up straight and not to talk
No fancy pencils, pens, or books in what to write
We had learned to do things right
Our teacher was stern and strict
Not allowed to answer back or contradict
And if played up or became a pain
Was sent off to the Head to receive the Cain
We would take lunch in a little cardboard box to school
Or brown paper wrapping if times were hard and cruel
Most times a crust of dripping and bread
Or if you had Jam, you were posh it's said
At play time out in the school yard
No fancy toys, times were hard
No Game Boys, Mobile phones, or Poke man
If you played football, you kicked a can
But Granddad said, "The best times of my life"
Free from stress and away from strife
Enjoy your childhood while you can
Things are different when you're a grown-up woman or man
And how lucky you are these days
That you have all this nice stuff at your fingertips, he says
You have all this new-fangled technology
And he keeps asking me, what's a PC?

LOVE DIES

When a partnership and love, is lost forever
And habit keeps both together
Love falls apart
Secrets affect the beating of a heart
Can't bear the thought of another touch
Leaning on each other emotionally as crutch
Losing the will to give, just to survive
Just to keep a dying relationship alive
Failing in all type of reason
Suffering the accusing treason
Needs pleads
Heart breaks and bleeds
Agony divides
Incarceration arrives
Till pain can't take no more
And thoughts walk out the door
To run and escape
Picking one's self out of another scrape
Guilt follows everywhere
As if to follow constantly here and there
Memories bear tears, followed by breakdown
Hurt creates a permanent frown
No remittance from the pain
The feeling of failure again
But what is the choice?
Prolonging the agony is in the voice
The direction is decided
Living with the actions provided
That's what happens when love dies
Despair sheds tears and cries

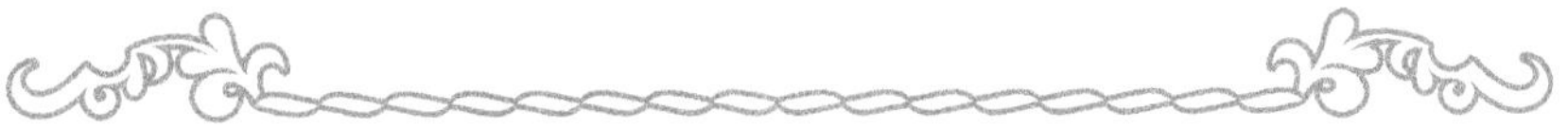

LOOKING BACK

Looking back at the days of my youth as a lad
Some of the best days that I've ever had
Young free from worry and care
Adventurous and full of imagination and dare
Gangs in war games as soldiers in battle we played
Pirates and cut throats that we portrayed
Cowboys and Indians, kings and knights
Cops and robbers, gangsters in fights
Those movies star heroes on films on the big screen
One of many roles in situations we had seen
A sick as a sword, anything used as a gun
Spacemen verses Martians was so much fun
Making or building a tree house or den
Pretending they were castles or fortress then
Fighting back those who would invade
Knights of the roundtable sent on a crusade
Robin Hood and merry men to rob the rich to feed the poor
Frankenstein and monsters that wandered the moor
Romans and gladiators that would clash in a fight
Enemies overthrown and put to flight
How the imagination ran wild in those ways
Entertaining our selves for fun in those days
All those precious moments from the past
All locked in those memories amassed
Treasured moments keep them safe to be used
Childhood Magic to keep you amused

LIVE

Touch the burning amber sun, it shines so bright
Watch the sombre dove take flight
There is no mistaking
I'm for the taking
You are the one that knows
Of the rivers unstoppable ebb that flows
With never ending force
Set upon an impossible course
Feel the wind brush
The breath of life touch
As the tear cascades
To hidden masquerades
All feelings purge
To an exciting urge
Chest vibrating thunder
Tingling lightning asunder
Feel, touch, see, and view
Let nature take you
To the sight of many faces
In far off places
On a journey so far
You are who you are
Never say that life is dull
Live it to the full
Don't get caught
For our meagre life's are short
Be who you are
The shining star
Be a giver
And see what life does deliver

ISLAND OF DREAMS

I dreamt of you my darling, the other night
Together on an exotic island of sheer delight
I held you gently in my arms
On sandy beaches, under tropical palms
The warmth of your pursed lips gently kissed mine
Oh heaven, it was so divine
As we lay together on the shore of sands
Sensually caressing each other with our hands
The tepid Chrystal Sea, brushed our soles of love
And the sun heated our passion, from clear blue skies above
The softness of the Caribbean breeze
Set tenderness against the romantic freeze
Together we created that moment of a single pleasure
Taken to an erotic escapade of momentous leisure
To fun and laughter on the beach
But in harsh reality you were out of reach
If only dreams could come true
As a man, and you a woman, I'd want to be with you
And to realise, and wake
To find myself alone and ache
Oh well a guy can only dream
But in reality, sometimes dreams can come true, it would seem
If you wish hard enough
Dreams are made of stuff
Only time can tell
In the pursuit of romance, as you and I know well

HOPELESSNESS

Who was it, who said peruse you're dreams?
It's not as easy as it seems
For every realistic, idealistic pursuit
Is blocked, and thrown down the rubbish shoot
Only to be left, fallen by the way sides
Where only misery resides
To a tune of utter hopelessness
Ending in a total mess
And the greed of others, take your possession
To reap "your" reward is their only progression
Steal away
Your light of day
All that you have worked for
Has gone out the door
Destiny is to keep you poor
Keeping you firmly on the floor
Honest sweat
Is your sure bet
Making do
Is what this means to you
Frustrated screams
Follow your dreams?
I don't think so
The end result I know
The only sure way
Is to live day to day

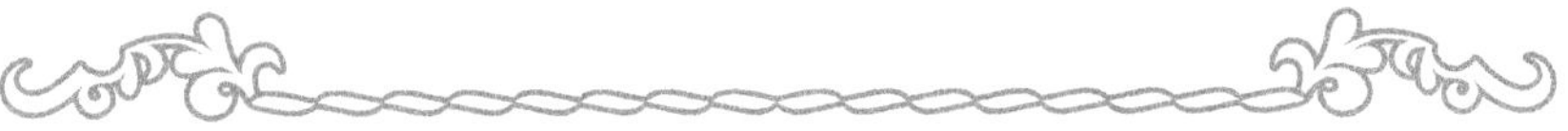

THE REALM OF THE BEAST

The gathering masses gathered round
On fiery burning brimstone ground
The entire multitude in suffering in eternal pain
As the beast that ruled rose up again
He stood on obelisk that reached the sky
And looked on his minions with evil eye
As he raised his hand
To order his command
I am the face of many you all know well
Lord and sovereign over hell
Here in my domain
I inflict my pleasure of pain
I own your souls to do with what I please
To amuse myself at my whim to tease
Your very existences I do own
As he sat upon his throne
Misery is my pleasure
To toy with you at my own leisure
Stand against me you cannot win
For all those you are mine, those who committed sin
And as for those in the future who are yet to do
A sin of any kind I will be waiting for you
I have an eternity to wait for souls to receive
Those souls I will retrieve
The Vile beast rose to his feet and let out a vile laugh
Rubbed his hands and his cruel eyes burned like a fiery hearth
Sin if you dare
Because in hell, I'll be waiting there

DISASTER DAYS

Do you ever get days like this
Where everything falls apart, and you want run away and
give the day a miss
Coffee spilt that's starts the day
The start of disasters coming your way
You put on the stereo to soothe your sole and "Blow me" the
tape deck don't play
The light in the bathroom has just blown
The constant ringing on the phone
Always never rings normally unless you're in the bath, the
shower, or the loo
The indignant things it makes you do
Toast burning in the toaster that's set on low
The smoke alarm screaming so
All the commotion and there goes the door
Some religious sect, asking if you believe in the lord
Have I saved all these disasters in a hoard?
The iron burning on the ironing board
And wondering if there is any more?
Trying politely to close the front door
After time these things are sorted and calmed down
These things settled and you just come round
This is what life can at times be like
And in the end, wrong is put right
Just another day, in a normal way
To everyone have a happy day

COUNTRY CHURCH

The country church stands on a lonely hill
Ringing the call on Sunday morning for the congregation to fill
That solemn tolling of its distant bell
Echoes across field, hollow vale, and dell
Majestic and daunting there you stand
Central for parishes to worship within you near at hand
Your facade of warm sandstone that gargoyles decorate
As they sit on niches pulling faces to be ornate
Columbus rises high above arched door
To meet with old red tiled floor
Stained glass windows that have a tale to be told
Stories of the past and gone by from eons old
Lust green trees fit like a comfortable coat that does wrap around
To bond with flowered and grassy ground
Epitaph and stone tablets stand proud
A rest in peace place, away from the crowd
The entrance stands scared, from cuts in its wall
From those who sharpened battle swords, when they came to call
Old records of the English civil wars
A place to enforce God and country's ancient laws
the heart of the community of history's time
Set upon and ancient and distance line
A row of English churches set from north to south on the map
The length and breadth of our countries lap
Old and historic there for all the world to see
As you nestle amongst the group of leafy trees
And yet you are known by your old ringing bell
The call for worshipers that they know very well
The past frozen as if part of the earth
A place of recorded of deaths and birth

A VISIT TO WALES IN PAST TIMES

In the late fifties, I remember a visit to Relations in Wales as a child
Small winding, Twisting, Climbing roads in rugged mountain wild
I remember rows of mining company houses, back-to-back
Daunting slagheaps, shrouded in dirty, dusty, black
Men dressed in flat caps, long coats, and mining leather boots
And a nation forbidden keeping their roots,
Spoken welsh not allowed to say
Language outlawed, with identity all taken away
The once great heart of a Celtic race
Torn forlornly out, for coal, slate, and granite, to take its place
I saw dire poverty, felt the pangs of hardship that owners of the mines make
As those who were exploited, but strangers always welcomed with best china and a piece of cake
Lately I've seen the wonderful changes, and I'm glad that Wales has been returned
To a land of singing and welsh tradition, that its sons and daughters earned
All those years of family's hearts that burned
Was a hard lesson that fathers and mothers learned
Well Welsh people you can all hold your heads up high
You all revived a country that nearly did die

WORLDS

My Very 1st written poem
Isn't it a funny thing that we altogether brings
A handshake across the net that sings
Different races and people met
Right across the internet
Binary travelled at impulse speed
Bringing warmth and friendship we need
Although different cultures made
Other lifestyles and roles we played
Our separate views and other waves
We all relate in different ways
All together and as one
We laugh and joke and have our fun
But each has a story told
And each a diplomat in the fold
To proud to speak and shy to say
Unless that special friend comes your way
And secrets in whisper boxes to be told
To be kept and to behold
We converse and tend to join in speech
To make a friend or friends in reach
This international melting pot
That we all enjoy a lot
Special thanks to all the Hosts, who police worlds for safety most
And hope all the friends both new and old are near
Thanks to one and all I'm off now and finished here

WHAT, WHEN, AND THERE'S

Whatever problem comes to bear
There is always someone here to share
Whatever a tear
There's always someone near
Whenever there's anger to prove
There's always someone here to smooth
Whatever a time a heart is broke
There's always someone to fix and stroke
Whenever you're feeling down
There's someone to pick you up, around
When energy and life seem low
There's some one to push you and make you go
When Loneliness does proceed
There's some one here to suit your need
Whatever questions are asked
There's always an answer amassed
Whenever someone has told you lies
There's some one here to put truth in your eyes
When someone does deceive
There's always someone to perceive
Whenever you come to the end
There's always a friend on, you can depend
When you have a problem to dissolve
There's always a person ready to solve
Whenever you hide behind a mask
There's someone to remove it from that task
When, whatever, there's always a way
There's always someone to help you get though your day

WHAT IS THIS FEELING?

What's this feeling that causes the blood to surge?
Hearts beating in a throbbing purge
Concentration to drift, into being lacked
Causing irritation and be un-relaxed
Losing the urge to eat
Confusion is the order of the day, to make it all complete
And yet a wonderful elation
Waited with eager anticipation
For all those disrupted devotions
Of all those mixed emotions
Suffering that tender pain
Tends to drive one insane
When you have it, you're on top of the world
But when you lose it, into hell you're hurled
It can make
Or it can break
Oh this martyring it can cause
To a lifting of inner feeling of applause
Can be forever eternal
Can be minutes or seconds infernal
Wrote about in song and verse
In books and film, and can be conversed
Universal to one and all
What is this feeling? I hear you call?
The one feeling that never needs a shove
It's simple, the word is LOVE

VALENTINE

Do not offer to be my valentine
Do not say you will be mine
Do not play the part
Do not offer your heart
For all this is making believe
It's what I perceive
Little tiny hearts on a card
Decorated with flowered facade
Arranged with a pretty verse
Of words of love that's seems obverse
Do not offer me your tender kiss
It's something I will not miss
My heart is like cabbage leaves
Well cooked and eaten with ease
My violets are never blue
Brown and shrivelled, and stuck like glue
Do not offer me love again
Because it just gives me pain
Just give me friendship, if you want to please
This will make me feel at ease

UNWORTHY

It was just an accidental glance
In milliseconds, amongst the crowd just by chance
Pictures poured a thousand moments of images in my mind
And for that instant, I became frozen to the spot, became blind
Thinking of the life time, we could hold each other
And to feel those hundreds of thousands of tender kisses, Oh brother
Warm bodies in rapture of ignited passions
Perusing and planning fashions
Feeling all those moments for eternity together
A never-ending passion ride of pleasure
But for that instant, it all blew away
To reality of the day
And I realise
It's all misconception and lies
And how I feel so unworthy, this could never be
So, I'll just carry on and be me

UNTOUCHABLE

To me you cannot be touched
A heart so distant, that it cannot be clutched
There lies a stone barrier
Burdens of a traumatic carrier
If only one could break down the wall
Chip away at stone bricks and make them fall
Prises open a gap, make a crack
Take the weight off your back
Fear hides behind an elusive mask
Pretence makes a heavy task
Scared to show true emotions
Of long ago, lost devotions
I know you hide tears inside
You say you're fine, ok, but I know you've lied
Just the threat of that, makes you in self denial
When you feel you're life is on constant trial
Happiness, when it gets close, is taken away
A price you feel, and have to pay
No wonder you're so difficult to reach
And the wall that surrounds you is too difficult to breach
After all you're only human and for real
One day, when it's safe to feel
When your greatest enemy is not Trust
And those bonds broken and bust
Then that will be the day you start living
To be honest, loving, warm and giving

TRIAL AND TRIBULATION

A child sits in a cold, dark room
Crying, a tear falls down his soft cheek
The Innocence of him being in the world
He sits and wonders what he has done wrong
NOTHING!

....

He didn't ask to be here, he didn't ask to be bor.
His crime ANOTHER MANS SON
The terrible injuries he endured he could cope with
The pain of the names he could not
Never being allowed to be part of the family
Always bring pushed out

.....

As time passes pain gets worse
The MENTAL abuse more intense
It becomes a daily thing; he gets used to it
But he can't take it any more
He blames himself and wishes himself dead
To escape every possible moment
Then he is free

.....

One day he just explodes fights back
The TYRANT has lost his power
And the young man has WON
But although the CLOWN in life
He carries the scars and leans to bear
No confidence
A complex about his looks
A failure in life
But a heart of gold

TO REMEMBER

When the famous New York Twin towers
Fell in a reign of debris showers
Concrete, steel, and glass, ended up in a huge pile
It was the result of terrorist, who were sick and vile
It was too incomprehensible to believe
The greater loss, for loved ones to grieve
There now lies an empty space
An epitaph to all lost in that place
And yet their phoenix will surely rise
A new Twin towers will reach the skies
A symbol of the world's defiance
A common cause of humanities alliance
And a time for all to remember
The 11th of September
Loved ones lost, will never be forgot
As the new building will stand on the very spot
Is it time to put those soles to rest?
We stand together for sadness to be addressed
And those memories put aside, for feelings gave
For the land of the free and the brave

TIS LOVE

This is in the style of Shakespeare and not in Shakespearian script

What manner doth I feel inside thee thy mortal Man?
To rise to thy heights of thy life's spans
Like doth surged thy fire doth purge thine soul
Light doth grow and blinded thy mind of whole
Clouds thine mind asunder
Above all thine highest Toils set under
One-word doth maketh thy minds quake
To utter thy worldly voice doth spake
Tis Love
And set highest all
Thy word doth make thine kingdoms fall
Man, doth yearn thy need
Thou canst not shake thee, but just heed
Man, doth pair with thee oh wench
Thine feelings within canst not quench
Tis Love
Angels doth take thee upon heavens high
Like kind thy free bird doth inside thee doth fly
And yet doth a man be single alone
Thy darkest chasms hath thy been thrown
Tis a man of one doest known
Can't I deny three?
Doth thy person not, see?
Tis Love
Of thy warmth doth thee brace
Thy soft breast doth thy long thy embrace
For thou have thee to hold as bonded one
Loyalty doth two become one
Thou hast by thy side till done ends three days
Wedded till life upon thee thy death lays

Death thy doest sayeth to do we part
Thine love hath thee in thy heart
Doest thine true love becomes thee
Tis Love
Thou canst see

TIME SERVED

Well, I done it now
Served my time, and how
One year and a month I've locked myself away
Meeting no one, and nothing else to say
Neglected all my close friends in life
I didn't want them to listen to my hurt and strife
So, I thought it best to stay away
Keep myself to myself as they say
It's been tough at times sitting here
Just keeping my family near
And I blame myself at times
That comes from the usual mixed-up minds
But with all the pain that's almost gone away
I live to fight another day
At times it's been really hard
And times death has been on my cards
But stupid I thought
Something I've fought
Well, I've done it I've served my time
It all seems vague now and sublime
I know the past has not treated me well
But who knows things will get better I can tell?
And as I sit and write this rhyme
I am not fishing for sympathy, just for time
If I can do it? So can all of you
This is reality for me and all of you, to go through
Funny thing is I've seen the pain of others too
For those wanting a life, those things we do
I seen love build, crumble and fall
And those poor broken hearts and tears, it's not funny at all
I feel sad inside when I see it happening for real
I know what they all go through and it makes me feel

But as for those who have moved on
And they who are healing or the pain has gone
We stand and help those in need
As we really do understand in deed
It's how we lean unfortunately with life
We all seem to adapt to stress and strife
Oh well I think this lecture gone on long enough
The time is to let others do their stuff
So, all you lovers and livers never say die
Time for me to go now so Good Bye

TIME PASSED

How time has passed me by
The constant ticking of time does fly
And yet I still ask why?
Age has touched me, and I cry
All those things that I once achieved
Now taken and relieved
I now live with the remnants I have received
Learnt hard a lesson of life I have perceived
Of those many times unknowingly, I was deceived
And the knowledge I have amassed and conceived
How time has flown
Those many lost situations I have blown
In many was I've gained and lost
The price paid and the cost
Am I a winner or a loser?
Or has life been my user?
How much will time brush past?
Will it go slowly or will it be fast?
As I deal with age and come to terms
As the fuse of life on and on burns
Only time its self will tell
To the final tolling of the bell

THOU MAKETH HIM

This is in the style of Shakespeare and not true Shakespearian script.

To glance upon thine eyes, doth give me pain
I but mortal man, and doth go insane
And yet thou dost take mine stock
In thy laugh thou doest mock
And yet not. I doth not, I canst not, utter mine feeling
I doth like dance on strings like a puppet, to thine appealing
Mine head doth rack in pain
Tis a game
Oh, heart of mine doth dry to an empty husk
How I doth lust
For thee mine fair maid
Ache for thee, tis the price be paid
I doth try thee with all mine regard
I doth fall long and hard
Thou dost mock thee with thy great skill
Take and doth break mine will
Yet I have soldiered in battle for Queens and kings
Smote all mine enemy that brings
Yet maiden thou dost bring mine self down
For this mine lady thou wearest thee crown
For no matter how strong be the man
Woman thou doest maketh thee man whom I am

THOMAS THORNILY

Mine love thou dost haunt
Thou doest mock and taunt
Tis thee year of mine lord 1643
Five seasons past since I saw thee
Thou mocked in life, thou doest Mock in death
Mine once beloved Beth
Thou stand-eth before in ghosted form
Me thinks by thee devil thou hast spawn
Why does thou haunt? Thou set before mine eyes
Thou oh wench, didst deceive thou spake lies
Twas the day of five seasons passed
Thou didst spake thy lies, thy lover and thee amassed
From thy wicked mouth thou didst utter thy leave
For to lose thine love, t would make mine heart grieve
Five seasons thou doest lay under thy earth still soft
In mine corner of mine garden croft
Thou hast good company, thou doest lay with thine lover
Thy lies, deceit, thou didst pledge it was nay other
Mine hands didst twice murder commit
Thou unfaithful adulteress, I hath no feel of mine remit
Be gone! Be gone!
Nay I say
Away! Away!
Mock me no more wench, take thou thy leave
Thou has made mine suffering, mine heart doth grieve
Thou does give-th torment, Tis not enough thou doth cause
suffering
Tis thine revenge thou doest bring
Thou doest seek mine death
Mine sweet Beth
Now I doth hold thine love forever

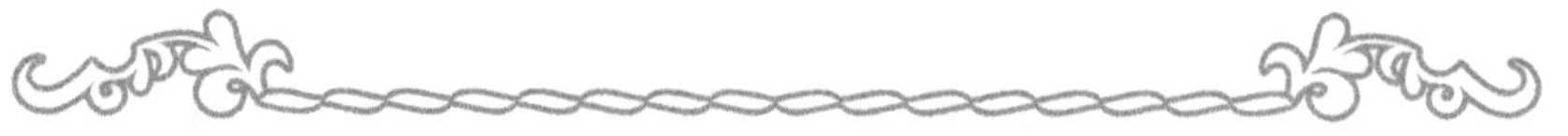

Thee and thy lover, Adulterers bones doth lay in grassy part together

    And yet thy spirit doth stand to mine eyes before

    Thou ungrateful whore

    Torment thou does torment

    Yet mine sole doth lament

    When doth it all end?

    Till mine bow of a body doth break and bend

    Oh mine God, Oh mine Lord Mine sole doth repent

    I doth yield to thine own tragic event

    In the year of 1645 Thomas thornily, in front of god and law was tried

    For the murder of his wife and her lover, where he was hung and died

THE TRUE MEANING

I don't pretend to know
What makes Love go?
All I know it takes two
To be committed too
Each person striving to give it all
As if it's one sided will collapse and fall
Not taking things for granted
Making each other wanted
No one wants love to fail
Everyone strongly wants it to prevail
To me, there's no commitment these days
Love is too easier a word to say
Now others use that word "Love" for what they can obtain
Leaving the bitter taste of being used does remain
How we have lost the true meaning
Of loves true feeling
And in these times, it's all too easy just to walk away
As People the world over, in these games tend to play
What's happened to one who's involved and committed
Together forever and no room to be remitted
As the whole globe in that never ending search
All having something in common bearing loves birch
To find the real meaning of the in this word we use
Not the word of "love" that others abuse
We have all really forgotten its true meaning
And some keep on dreaming
Let's search our hearts and find the right way
And maybe just maybe we will find true love one day

THE STORM

In the distance Grey billowy clouds roll over the sky
Darkening all the ground it passes by
The blackening hand
It throws a shadow across the land
An eyrie silence fills the air
Muffled deafness makes you seem aware
Spots of rain begin to fall
A warning to all
As the wind picks up its pace
She the temptress shows her face
Making tree's branches toss and dance
As the storm made her advance
A heavy deluge of sheets or rain lashes down
Below the grassy ground begins to drown
Corn in the field chops like a stormy sea
As the temptress brushes her hand to make it sway and roll free
Then, a loud crack that tears the heaven above apart
Electric fills the air that tends to race the heart
Blinding is the white lightening flash
And a pause, followed by a vibrating roars and crash
The earth moving thunder rolls
Sending rabbits racing to their holes
Darkened now almost into night
As nature puts on a spectacular show of light
To a symphony of light and sound
She the storm throws her tantrum all around
Then the storm slowly dies
Into the distance it drives
The sun peeks out and shows its face
Bringing warmth and security in the storms place
The air cool, fresh, and clear
Gone away now is the excitement of fear
The till next time it does appear

THE STAR

Oh, eastern star how high, how bright
Pointing the way throughout the night
The sign of all mans hope is born
On this early Christmas morn
Who would have thought this Childs destiny?
You the tiny child, born out of poverty
The company of cattle, in a stable, in a stall
On view to man, woman, beast, and all
And yet you gave a hope to those you knew
The common cause related as you grew
You the boy, to man, giving
In a time of fear, and unkind living
This special time for being kind
Giving sight to those who are blind
To make the deaf hear
Comfort those who live in fear
Free those from poverty
Befriend those who are lonely
End all conflict at best
Make all hostility rest
Give a moment of thought
When the year was bad for those distraught
Forgiving those who have done wrong
Feeding the starving, and of those in need
Tenderly heal those who bleed
This is what giving for Christmas means
Help to all fellow human beings

THE SMELL OF PATCHOULI OIL

In those good old Hippy days
One was free to do what's pleased in many ways
The love beads around your neck
Freedom to think what the heck
As groups of people gathered chanting
And those times of never wanting
Smoking pot, taking trips on LSD
Singing songs of love, being carefree
Head bands, Love bells, hipsters, and platform shoes
Hippies always in the news
As they gathered singing, give peace a change
Then the threat of the Vietnam war did advance
Oh, the smell of that Patchouli oil in scented air
Joysticks burning every where
That music, Jam sessions, and parties' trouble free
The Monkeys, Davey, Dozy, Mick, Titch and me
The Mamas and Papas, singing California freedom on a windy day
The Beatles, Sergeant Peppers lonely Heart Club Band did play
Rolling Stones, Jimmy Hendricks, singing across the lands
Uniting the world as we all held hands
Trying to fight the systems demands
Psychodelia paintings on a bus
Peace and love, no sign of fuss
Time passed by so fast
Those patchouli days they didn't last
All seemed to swiftly pass by
Memories to keep, but time does fly

THE MIRACLE

She kneels in the church, and begins to cry
In all her suffering, she wants to end it all and die
She prays to God for the four boys she will leave behind
Tears in her eyes make her vision blind
Her suffered life of being abused
Took its toll, and made her feel tired and used
Her sobbing, echoes in that church around
As she asks God to be found
She is not a Christian by any means
Just a survivor, like most Human beings
Cancer had already taken part of her away
Thrombosis had made her body pay
She, worn and tired lost the will to live
Now asks God for what she is about to do, to forgive
In that desperate moment, a light caught her view
There appeared a dazzling figure, that she knew
The man with auburn hair, and olive skin
Clothed in pure white, and pure without sin
He walked over to her and laid on her, his hand
Looked down on her and smiled, made no demand
His words softly spoken
To a woman, and a mother so desperately broken
His hand took all the weight of the world off her shoulders
That was filled with torment, and pain, in times when colder
Filled her with warmth and hope, Oh Jesus you had blessed
To a true and kind woman, in the desperate moment she had
confessed
Even today after a heart attack, and a brain wasting decease
She remains happy, a Christian and at ease
And after this miracle, as son expects
Looks up to her, shows love, and respects

THE LOSS OF THE WORLD

This is to commemorate the loss of all those poor souls
That perished or was injured in the 911 terrorist attack
Don't cry Children Its God who weeps
That single tear of billions he keeps
That Loss, that pain He feels to bear
One who takes all your sadness, to care
And as we carry emotions in our hearts
For All our friends In Americas parts
We are there to support you a shoulder to lean on
To take your pain and sadness to as one
We hold your hands in this time
We wrap our arms around you to help you feel fine
We kiss the tear from your cheek
With heavy hearts you carry
We lift your souls
Making your broken life's whole
And if we can stand in time
Eventually it will be fine
Remember we all care
We are all with you there
So don't think you are alone
We are here with you in heart at your Home
So, children don't you cry it's us that weep
And take your pain to keep.

THE RIVER

I sit on the bank of the river, and watch the child fly his kite
As the gentle hands of a breeze take it to its height
As it sways and dances
Swoops and takes its chances
I hear the whispering in the reeds
To a gentle lace curtain, of misty floating seeds
Tiny bits of cotton, like an armada of sails
Set on their journey, as their course prevails
The sun glistens on the surface of the waters crown
Like a jewel in the light reflecting light all around
And how the regal white swans perform a ballet
To tease the eye and tempt the pallet
Mother mallard, tends her baby chicks
In an unruly and directionless mix
The lazy boat drifts idly by
As if asleep, no need to try
Fish in schools dart and weave
To hide in shadows as if to deceive
Flowing willow trees hang down as if to dip their fingers
And hung in the air the perfume of Honey suckle, lingers
I sit there in the cool of the shade
In awe of what natures made
The green and lush scene in the warmth of the sun
Watching others having fun
All this on glorious display
Before my eyes, all this wonder does lay
And inside I feel peace
For the moment at least

THE DREAM

While I was at asleep in dead of night
I dreamt I watched 2 army's fight
The battle raging all around
Screams of injury and deathly sound
Twisted metal from swords that clashed
As 2 sides met and crashed
Desperate struggles as they came to blows
As I saw rivers of blood that flowed
Sickened, I turned away
A voice behind me said "turn and face the day"
This battle is being fought for you
It is this that you have put them through
In what you believe in is just and right
So, turn and face the fight
As I stood on that hill
Two forces fighting against each other will
And as I watched those armies retreat and advance
As they fought for a weakness to make their chance
The Battle raged throughout the night
As sounds subsided in that field of fight
A weary soldier in tarnished and blooded armour came
As he knelt down in exhaustion and pain
Victory is ours the day is won
The battle now is over and done
I awoke. I wondered what this dream was meant to be
After a long deliberation it made me see
My deep inner conflicts were the fight I saw
That's what that battle was for

THE DOGS OF WAR

The dogs of war are on a leash that's strained
As they struggle for release, but are restrained
They have the scent of death and blood
Paused to strike and stalk the world's neighbourhood
Waiting for the command
For the loosening grip of their master's hand
As the beast's howl and bay
Eager for release in the playground of war, which they hunt
and prey
They thirst, they hunger
On the work of the war markers monger
Foaming, snarling, gnashing, yellow teeth
To strip the soles of conflict, that lies beneath
Pain, sorrow, and injury is their meal
No emotions for their quarry do they feel
For them the master relies on its sport
To weed out the weaker sort
While those hide in safe bunkers. Who run the helm
While Dogs of war run free to hunt in their realm
It's the nature of the beast
To thrive on those victims as they feast
Listen to the deathly Howling of those hounds
Of the beasts at your door, and in their hunting grounds
And those Masters as they prepare
Of us they don't really care

SOOTHING TENDER WORDS

I know how you feel, I truly do
I think I know what you've been through
Your marriage or relationship has fell apart
And that your partner of yours has broken your heart
Leaving you with mistrust and pain
As your Life is full of confusion, and tatters again
You tried your Dam nest to hold things together
Believing the situations would change for the better for ever
Hoping in your heart that things would last
Regardless of those events in the past
And finally, now it's come to this
The person you loved and now seem to miss
All there is that someone left to blame
Feeling hurt and betrayed and left to carry this pain
Your Home, your children, and you utterly destroyed
And in the anger of mixed emotions, you blame yourself and become annoyed
I keep saying that time would eventually heal
And it will, I know as I can reveal
You want to point anger at all the gender, of the partner you was with
Unrelenting not wanting to forgive
And at this present moment it's hard as you mistrust
Into this situation that you have been thrust
But one day you will heal
And inside you will change what you feel
You will get there in the end
And in time your broken heart will mend
And those times if you get lost and you need a person to depend
I am here to listen, advice, your friend

TEENS

Isn't teenager's hard work?
Little wannabe adults, with a child like quirk
Hormonal bombs, which are actively fused
So, want to be independent, but easily confused
"I want to do everything cause I'm grown"
But when it goes pair shaped, enraged and tantrums are thrown
How they perform in outrageous fits
As things of lost patience end all up in bits
No matter how you try to please
You tend to walk on eggshells, with no ease
And those fateful words that you dread
That seems to swim around in your head
I want to try smoking, booze, sex, and drugs
As they turn into impossible adolescent thugs
From faze to craze, that seem to shock or amaze
As late nights turn to mid afternoon bed ridden days
Those once angels, you were once proud
Now Mange, Marilyn Manson, gothic makeup, they walk round in a shroud
Decibel breaking music that shakes the street
Compiled pigsty bedroom hovels make it all complete
And the invasion of half the nation that traipse through the home
And the receiving of heart attack bills from the use of the phone
But as parents, we are old, and we don't understand
As they scream, I want it now, are the many expensive things they demand
Roll on twenty as you pray to the gods
So that they can leave home, the little sods

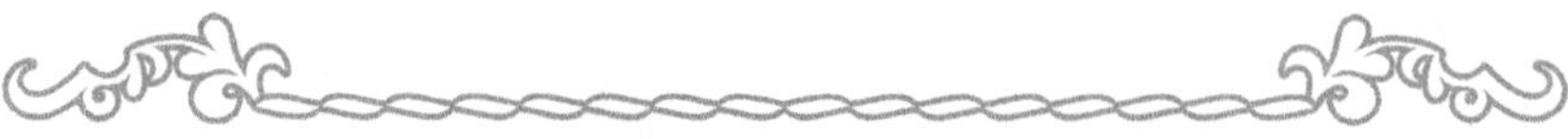

SUMMER DAYS

I remember Lazy summer days
The calm and breezeless summer haze
Smell of fresh cut grass
Mill pool ponds like mirrored glass
Warm sedate of summer dream
Of tea, strawberries and cream
Cricket played upon village green
Picture that summer scene
Grey clouds on arisen loom
Rolling clouds and distant thunder boom
Dark clouds aloft
Deluged field, orchard, and croft
She the tempest raises her ugly head
Causing confusion and turmoil and dread
Lightning striking to and from the ground
Crashing to the thunder sound
Storm reaching an exciting peak
Electric air as we speak
As the torrent subsides
Distant now as black cloud run away and hide
Birds singing as the sun peeks out
Fresh and cool and new no doubt
People return to normal ways
I remember lazy summer days

CONTENTS

I MISS YOU

Please don't grieve for this passing of mine
I am gone to a better place in time
And although I left you behind
You still have a life to find
Please don't grieve or cry
In this life you have to carry on and try
Love your family and keep them close
For they need your support the most
I know your loss is at this moment great
But in time you will heal and regenerate
The loss eventually will be easier to bear
It just takes time getting there
I ask for nothing in return
Just the odd memory as you will learn
I know the pain at this moment is too much to bear
But with those around you, they really care
But you must heal your broken heart
Make an effort for a new start
As is said one door opens and another will close
As in a life span, Nature and God has chosen
I will always be there in your mind
And eventually Life will be kind
Who knows we may meet in a different life
Until then don't be sad or full of strife
So please don't grieve for this passing of mine
I am gone to a better place in time

HOUSE WORK

We as Male, female, single, or wed
Do our Daily routine we all sometimes dread
That daily chore from when there's no escape
It's that HOUSE WORK that "word" we can all relate
Beds, vacuum, dust, and clean
Some, we love to do, others are none too keen
Washing (laundry) that's not so bad load it in and slam the door
I like others, it's the ironing I hate doing it for
Washing up is a bore
You do a load; turn around and there is more
And the more Kids you have harder it becomes
It's like working in a labour camp looking after your little ones
And then there are the little things you never get time to do and miss
Those little jobs that nag at you, upsetting your mental bliss
You can't take it anymore, and that little job gets done
Feeling pleased you won and that small job overcome
Then you notice another little job that wants to nag at you
Oh well that's another time to do
On and on that daily tread
That constant daily Pattern always in your head
Well, I can't stay here gassing I got housework to do
Armed with vac, duster, and polish, I'll say good bye to you

HOGARTH

The old Warlock stood there in his place.
Calling the old gods and forces of nature to his face
I command you to appear
I stand protected and have no fear
HOGARTH does command
To help us mortals here at hand
....
Rise up, rise up, I call on you as I have need
Assist me with my mystical deed
I command you by all the gods that's I known
Appear before me spirit of GOAN
For I have need of your services, from your grave
I beckon you, my salve
....
Wind, Storm, Torrent came
Howling voices in moaning pain
HOGARTHS greying hair and beard tossed in winds that
blew
Ghouls in a circle, Spirits flew
With tempest all around
The warlock stood his ground
Once again I shout GOAN I command thee to come
You are in my power till my deed is done
....
From darkest gates of hell
Spawned a foul and ghastly smell
A dark silhouette writhing against his will
Screaming a deathly howl in a deafening shrill
I HOGATH command you not to resist
You are in my power I insist
As the creature rose on earth to full height
His massive form swamped the night

A creature with leather blue grey skin
Like a crocodile covering with horns set in
Tall and hunched
Face taught, twisted, and slightly bunched
Deepest eyes or glowing yellow red
Thick set brow and malformed head
Protruding teeth yellowed with age
Thick lower lip taught with rage

....

GOAN roared "Who has summoned my here on this night from where I dwell?"
Booming voice that shook the depths of hell
I HOGARTH warlock of the place of When lock, I have called thee
I have the power over you to do my bidding for me
For You GOAN have a contract with me to fore fill
The demon spoke "Hogarth I am at your will"
What is this quest you will have me do?
Name this deed I do for you

....

I have an enemy that's cast on me his hex
Unto me, he has angered and made me vex
For this I seek revenge
I will not stop until avenged
Go seek him out and take his soul
This your reward when the deed is whole
For myself I take his powers to be mine
Those skills and property I can combine

....

His name is DYTHON in the vale of dean
He's cruel, ruthless, and branded mean
Go GOAN bring him to me here in this place
So I can see the terror on his face
Goan roared writhing, twisting with pleasure and pain
HOGARTH waited for them to return again

....

Time passed throughout the night when GOAN returned
Dumped down a sack, inside screams and pleading was heard
Goan picked up the sack and shook it about
DYTHON rolled out of the sack unto the ground and out
Mercy, mercy, he did plead
Cuts and bruises his wounds did bleed
Goan Picked Dython up by his hands
Struggling foe went limp, helpless as he hangs

....

I take your powers DYTHON for my own
All your knowledge, properties, and your home
Spell now cast and all goods received
DYTHON now stripped and cruelly relieved
GOAN takes the poor wretch in to the gapping ground
HOGARTH listening to the screaming sound
Closed earth, now deed was done
Warlock HOGATH victoriously won

HE HAS LEFT

I was so sorry to hear he left you
Your heart must be so broken; I bet you don't know what to do
To think your life is in shattered little pieces
And I can imagine, you are crying all the tears your eyes releases
Life must seem so lost, desolate and empty now
And I bet your wondering how to cope and how
You must think, you're never going to get you life on track
The financial and emotional turmoil that has broke your back
Devastated as you sit there in a mess
And wondering how you're going to cope with all those things
you need to address
And time you have now, time to sort things slowly out
You will do these things without a doubt
I know you think that it's all-impossible to find a way
But you will get there one day
Just hang in there, persevere
Positive attitude and goals will all become clear
Achieve
In yourself believe
And one day soon you will look back with pride
That you have put back the broken bits and smile inside
Taking stock of all the work you have done
Knowing all the work in time, from the time it all begun
And in these times of desperate need
You will have the drive to succeed

HAGGIS

Now that Hogmanay is drawing near
It's the time in Scotland wild haggis fear
Open season for the great haggis hunt is on
Those fearful critters are in hiding and gone
In the land that drunken Scot's women dance
On tartan covered pool tables they prance
With swinging handbags above their head
And half beaten Scot's men lay half dead
And as in the land that Scotch whiskey flows
Those poor men suffer from those women's blows
Fergus Mc tight wallet the greatest haggis hunter of all
By Royal appointment to the King of Scotland calls
The King Proclaimed "where be ma haggis for ma hogmanay
feast"?
"Ye dinna hae one Fergus at least"
Fergus Mc tight wallet Said "my laird Ye canni see"
Nessie their friend taught them to hide well from every Scott
and me
I've set traps to tempt them with their favourite food
Carrots and parsnips, sugar coated doughnuts but they still
elude
The king told Fergus bring me ma haggis ready and dead
Or it will be you wee Sassenach Head
Time passed and on Hogmanay Day
A hundred Roast haggises on the kings table Lay
Fergus Mc tight wallet rewarded for services done
The Golden Caber and thistle that he had won
I sent ma women out wee her handbag
And a hundred and two Haggis she did belt wee her bag
So, if you're ever in Scotland and you do see
A woman with her handbag running free
Spare a thought for those poor Scotsmen, Haggis and Hogmanay

GREMLIN

I got a gremlin in my cupboard because he's been here 24hrs
a day
    Playing his mischievous games, a spiteful way
    Undoes everything I do
    Throws me into Confusion that's what he put me through
    Holds me back when I want to go forward
    Makes things normally easy, difficult and hard
    A spoilsport, upsetting everything I try
    I don't know his reasons why
    I have really tried to cast him out
    Always about me plaguing me with doubt
    Follows me everywhere
    Always there
    He's even in my sleep, messing with my dreams
    Always taunting me with his sarcastic screams
    He's been locked in my cupboard. or at least I thought I did
    He is good at escaping though, the Houdini Kid
    I have learnt to live with it, as you normally do
    Haunting me even when I go to the loo
    Well Mr Trouble you mostly have had your way
    Your days are numbered, I can definitely say
    One day you will slip up, fall over, and then I will be there
    To Boot you on your way old son because I don't really care
    Find someone else to hassle, as you're not welcome here
    Sorry, I seem to pass him on, it would appear
    So, if he shows up on your door
    Don't send him to me, I don't want him anymore
    So don't let him in, or you will have to pay
    Just kick him out and send him on his way

GLASS PRISON

In my prison made of glass
Trapped inside a transparent mass
No corners to hide your fear
Cylindrical, dome shaped, and clear
Shouts resound the echoes inside
But silent deafness of mime outside
Strong and cold inside your silicone wall
Escapeless to one and all
Impregnable in all its might
Illusive to trap and holds all its light
Crystal, clean, and clinical
Pure, and cynical
I am looking out, as they look in
With nowhere to go, they know where I've been
I see them pass by in my crystal dome
In this incarceration I call home
One tiny chip is all it takes
Before this structure breaks
Just to make a tiny flaw
Shattering it to billions of tiny shards, to make it fall
To breathe the air of freedom once again
But here in this see-through fortress, I remain
And they still look in, as I Look out
No corners to hide my fears and doubt
I see them walk by and pass
In my prison made of glass

THE COVER OF A BOOK

I am a book that sits upon the shelf
One of many, unique and a single one myself
My cover looking slightly rough and worn
Inside my pages tattered and slightly torn
Covered with a coat of dust
With the smell of musk
My appearance leaves me on this shelf
While younger, fresher, newer ones radiate wealth
I once was popular and new
Neat and tidy with an exciting view
Years of reading me have made look misused
Wear and tear of being abused
But if you take the time to read me well
I still have a good story to tell
Many covers have I worn to hide
To attract others to read inside
But when the cover is removed
I am cast aside for looking used
So here I sit in my place
Waiting for someone to show me grace
Take me off to be repaired
Open my pages and make them aired
To love my story through
To read again for pleasure new
So don't reject me by my cover
Look inside and you'll discover

COUNTRY CHURCH

The country church stands on a lonely hill
Ringing the call on Sunday morning for the congregation to fill
That solemn tolling of its distant bell
Echoes across field, hollow vale, and dell
Majestic and daunting there you stand
Central for parishes to worship within you near at hand
Your facade of warm sandstone, that gargoyle decorate
As they sit on niches pulling faces to be ornate
Columbus rises high above arched door
To meet with old red tiled floor
Stained glass windows that have a tale to be told
Stories of the past and gone by from eons old
Lush green trees fit like a comfortable coat that does wrap around
To bond with flowered and grassy ground
Epitaph and stone tablets stand proud
A rest in peace place, away from the crowd
The entrance stands scared from cuts in its wall
From those who sharpened battle swords when they came to call
Old records of the English civil wars
A place to enforce God and countries ancient laws
The heart of the community of histories time
Set upon and ancient and distance line
A row of English churches set from north to south on the map
The length and breadth of our countries lap
Old and historic there for all the world to see
As you nestle amongst the groups of leafy trees
And yet you are known by your old ringing bell
The call for worshipers that know you well
The past frozen, as if part of the earth
A place of recorded of deaths and birth

CIVIL WAR

Into the battle smoke
Cannons thunder as they spoke
Musket barrels ring a sound
On bloody battle ground
Uniforms of blue and grey
Fight to win the day
Fallen soldiers scream and cry
In large numbers they did die
As the Generals sat on their horse
Watching as the battle runs its course
Ordered confusion that ran amok
Blues and greys headed in a flock
As each stood in ranks in a line
Firing to the commander's time
Dark and blinding is the smell
Of spent gunpowder hangs in shrouded hell
As the young soldiers die where they fell
The advance pushed forward well
The greys in lines across the field
The blues lines broke to run and yield
The bugler sounds the charge
As the greys rush forward as they barge
Cheers of the victorious greys that won
Of Gettysburg the battle done
This civil war that's been sought
As friend against friend and brother fought
This Battle the first of many to bring fear
Those thousands of lives lost, I shed a tear
And as for those battles won and lost
Tragic cause of both sides cost
Union Blue and Southern Grey
What price you both did pay

BRAVE KNIGHT

The brave knight stood before the battling hoards
Enemy checked with spear, shield, and swords
Missiles and arrows darken and rain in the sky
His pledged allegiance, meant it was a good day to die
He looked to the heavens and cried aloud
For God, mine lord, and Christianity into the crowd
If mine enemies come, I do smite thee twice
And if they still come, I will smite thee thrice
Till thy invaders hath been smote
And the blood doth fill mine master's moat
Like angry ants the opponents swarmed the place
On the day that death showed his face
Death and fallen lay all around
On bloody stained hellish battle ground
Bodies lay heavily piled, as one sword was held high
By the Triumphant young knight who did not die
The battle now ended and done
The Victorious knight had pledged and won

BALDNESS

I'm in the stage of life, were
There's a receding tide of hair
When the sun shines bright and fair
My head gives off a solar flare
And it doesn't bother me, I don't mind
As the suns reflection leaves most blind
I get a half price cut and trim
And there's always hair round the sinks brim
Smaller bottles of shampoo I use
And other people worry about my shinny views
Who cares? Not me
I think it's hilarious you see
My baldness is "O" natural and in fashion
Yet others copy me and shave their heads with passion
Bald men are sexy and virile
With heads clean and sterile
And she asks, can I run my fingers through your hair
I say sure, most of it is on the barber's floor down there
And what's left on top is none at all
I look like a pink billiard Ball
Well said Fred
I go to go now to polish my head
Any way not to worry
You only go bald once and it's never in a hurry
Someone turns down the light
Only I'm blinding every with my bonce shinning bright

AUTUMN 1

September is now the end of summers call
Nature's changes to autumn fall
Green leaves turn to change to colours new
To golden yellow, burnt umber view
As leaves fall gently away
Autumn breezes tend to play
Swirling winds throw leaves around
a covering of golden and brown on the ground
Trees prepare for winters host
As nature intended Most
Cooler climate on the way
Already losing the warmth of a summer's day
But seasons have to roll on
Spring and summer been and gone
As we look for winters cold
As the cycle of seasons that we hold

AUTUMN 2

Once again autumn comes around
On copper, golden leafy Ground
Sombre light on Burn Umber field
A time that bears the harvest yield
Nature's time to sleep and rest
As squirrels collecting nuts to digest
The rolling hills of fields lined with stacks of hay
As the magpie's romp and play
Gees and swans in practice flight
As they display in squadrons tight
Cows in distant fields the graze
Sheep they seem to laze
And in the grey blue sky, birds in flocks do fly
To the time of year that passes by
As leaves gently fall
To a carpet of brownie yellow that covers all
Comes the quiet whisper soft
Of the busy outcrops and croft
And the busy farmer takes his leave
For the next stage of what nature does perceive
Seeds lie under the earth
Waiting for winter to pass and spring to give birth
Until then winter needs to spread its coat of white
And the seasons roll on true and right

ALL WAS IN COURT

The Judge sat in Court in pomp and refine
Still drunk for the previous night
Where's the Prisoner he demanded?
Why Sir Your Honour he is still Remanded
Then bring him here as I have a lot to do
I have a game of Golf at 2.00
The prisoner looking worried and scared
Stood in the dock transfixed and stared
Your guilty of that said the judge I am sure
10 years in prison will make you secure
But your Honour said the lawyer my client is accused of lit-
tering instead
Panic set in the prisoner's head
The accused rose up in full height
Jumped out of the dock and fled with fright
Treading across desks, fingers and hands, flying papers and
leaving a mess
Screaming, shoving, and fighting no less
Two eyes and wig in hiding behind
The judge scared out of his mind
Lawyers and barristers' wigs put to flight
When the prisoner escaped in the commotion and fight
After all, had calmed down and commotion was done
Finding the prisoner had vacated and gone
The judge now getting brave stood up and said
Capture the prisoner and bring him here to be led
The prisoner now caught brought in front of the judge, still
shaking with fear
It seems a mistake was made it would appear
Case dismissed he said with sobering thought
This day I have learnt something, a lesson being taught

ABUSE

Something I can't stand is physical abuse of any form
I've been a witness to this from the day I was born
How does it feel, are you a man?
As you stand over her now, before this argument began
Blood on your clenched hands
As you stand there, shouting your demands
She lays weeping injured on the floor
You've done this, time, and time, before
The words she spoke cut like a knife
The truth spoken from her lips as true to life
And you think you have won?
But the damage you have done
Inflicted injuries, you have made her stronger
There will be a time; she won't take it any longer
The pen being mightier than the sword
Makes you weaker as you're not cleverer to the use of word
And fear and pain is what you use to control
Anger burns inside you, like a smouldering coal
And to use this tool of abuse
To put to your own personal use
But little do you realise that you have already lost
As you made her pay the cost
Then comes the guilt
On this relationship that's built
And yet she loves you, and to hide the fact
She is dedicated to the pact
In her heart she wants to forgive
Hoping you'll change your ways, in a better way to live
But it is too late the rots already set in
It's started long ago, from when the arguments begin
And now it's easier to inflict pain
You will do this over and over again

Till all that's left is the abuse to remain
After all you have someone to take the blame
And she will leave you, as it's all under strain
Did you fulfil your need, win or succeed?
Or did you hurt her, and make her bleed?
Your inflicted will made her bend
You broke her in the end
You have nothing left, you lost it all
You pushed too hard and made her fall
How do you feel, are you the man?
Or don't you really give a damn

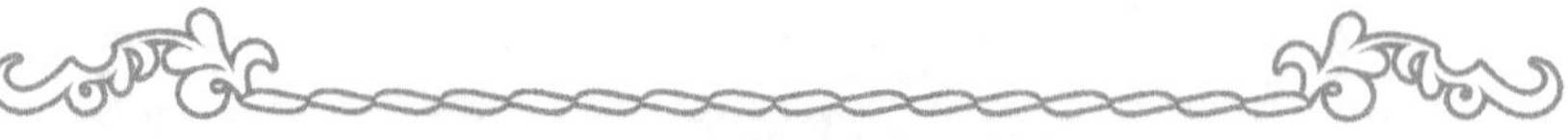

YOUR SMILE

Your smile makes me feel eased
A welcoming feeling, that makes me pleased
Of gentle persuasion of being relaxed
Warm and relaxed
A slight tingling sensation inside
Emotionally pacified
To me that means a million things
Of pleasantry brings
Almost to a state of tranquillity
Away from the world of hostility
I love to see you smile
That means you're happy for a while
And if you are, then so am I
Better to smile, rather than cry
And if you can stand and hold that smile on your face
Then I know you have a touch of grace
And OK, I know you will always be the one to take it
And though life's tough deals you'll be the one to make it
Please don't ever give your smile away
It helps everyone through their day
I do love your smile
Makes me and others happy for a while

WORDS

Its Ironic isn't it
Putting words together to fit
Making smooth lines go
That bounces along to flow
Words that dance along
To the tune of a catchy song
Moonlight sonata
Vivaldi vibrato
All the magic that can be composed
Of verbal text of sweet reposed
Classic and swish
Yearning orations of a wish
Syllables of tears
Characters of fears
Pens and pauses
Comers and clauses
Rough notes and writing in fine
Papers and line
Jumbled text
Frustration and vexed
Thoughts of how you feel
Play with words that appeal
Sadness and whit
That all fit together bit by bit
Poems and odes
Fire the minds and goads
All this for an inspired poem
Just to get the verses going

WONDERS

We have conquered all the wonders of the world
Great mysteries to our intelligence have we unfurled
Man has climbed the highest mountains and breathed heav-
ens air
Improved Humanity beyond compare
Travelled into space and walked the moon
Cures for diseases and cancer coming soon
Witnessed natures force
And Rivers on their course
Technology surging ahead on its advance
Taken life by chance
We have mastered all we saw
Created rules and made the law
How Man has reigned supreme
On his quest to realise a dream
Stood on a precipice so high
The goal to succeed and try
All these things we have done
Champions to the causes we have won
Winning in the loser's face
Victors of the human race
One small thing we could never control
Is LOVE born in everyone's soul
That one emotion on the whole
It can create and make
On the other hand, can destroy or break
That strongest of all the feelings we possess
Can't be controlled or addressed
No matter how we try
It can hold you or pass you by
Oh, that word that that we chase
To hold you in its complicated embrace

Makes all the wonders of the world oblique
One thing we can't conquer that's unique
The End.

WINTER

Winter set its season once again
Of those four seasons of climates change
Within the cold and greying cloak that overhangs
Comes a dusting of white overland
An individual designs of Chrystal ice
Patterned, single, delicate, and nice
But all together a covering of crystal lace
Covering lands of the earth of the human race
Heavy cascades of snow does fall
Gently wrapping and encasing all
That turns darkest days to light
Soft woolly and wispy white
Those coldest days that turns to fun
Turns adventure in a Childs mind done
Snow Man building, to snowball fight
Tobogganing, to skiing, and skating on ice
To look upon mirrored and glassy pond
Frosty ice and waters bond
Scenic views up on a card
Winter for some makes times hard
But those seasons keep rolling on
Time after time those seasons spent and done
Of natures inevitable course
The coldest season of the year from source

TOY SOLDIER

Oh little toy soldier how you stand proud
Your little red jacket makes you stand out from the crowd
Crisp yellow braiding and buttons shine so bright
Sharp creased trousers neatly striped
Polished shoes on your feet
And your blue hat makes you look prim and neat
Standing to attention with medals on your chest
Your rifle by your side makes your regiment best
How you were loved by the little lad
You to him was the best toy he ever had
Together the hours many games were played
Marching and war games were laid
That little lad grew up and went away
And you lost and forgotten and stood on the shelf to this day
Your trousers not so creased
No shiny shoes the polishing ceased
Yellow braiding dusty and worn
Your neatness lost and forlorn
And you rifle not by your side
Tucked away in dusty place you hide
But that little lad is now a man
Returned home a soldier and still your fan
And now you're found you stand pride of place
Behind a sparkly glass case
Stand to attention like you used to do
All prim and proper and looking as good as new

THOUGHTS

A million voices rattling in your head
Wondering how to phrase things said
Confusing issues at the time
As those inside tensions tend to climb
The pen lies on the empty sheet
Of a letter that's incomplete
Dormant lays that lazy pen
To the none existent ways of men
That search of busy soles
Who are lost and missed of empty goals
Awareness is distant and seems aloof
Looking for a glint of proof
And silence there just sitting
Nothing emitting
A pondered pause for thoughts
One small word needed for reports
Times long since passed and in the mind
Of all those experiences left behind
Looking for the forward route
As if like a PC waiting to reboot
Just one small spark to light the way
For another thought for another day

THOUGHTS

I stand on the shore of the sandy beach
What? I ask myself does other land the ocean reach
The vastness of the space, as the sun sets on the rise
Far out of reach to insignificant eyes
And I wonder
Of the distant shores, down under
And who stands on the spot
Of another shore, that time forgot
Are they thinking the same thoughts that I think?
On the vastness of this watery brink
Do they, like me look to the sky?
And do they think as I?
If a hand could reach out and touch
Could they be dreaming as much?
To hold out their hand with a tender clasp
But we stand thousands of miles out of grasp
Well, it's all down to my wondering mind
And all just a pipedream as you will find
One day, maybe one day
This great big ocean will take me away
So, I can stand on that distant place
And meet that person face to face
But for now, I'll leave my thoughts just to wander
About the shores that are down under

THE STRUGGLE

A day dawns a new
As the sun rises to a view
If only I had the strength
To last another 24 hours length
If only I could fight for one more day
To last in life's complicated play
Just some time to hold
To me precious time is like gold
I cannot, and will not let go
The will is within me, to struggle on so
Each breathe an effort to exist
Each Heart beat to resist
Any call of death I push away
Just to live another day

THE SEARCH

I roamed the world
I searched lands across the sea
Into many different situations hurled
When I was young and free
I marched thousands of miles
Glanced a million faces
Stood in endless lines and files
Explored the many different races
In my quest for the impossible goal
Relentless time
To make my life whole
Just to make you mine
How the ticking time has passed
And left me far behind
Time never seemed to last
I'm worn out, tired, and blind
I did try hard to win the fight
Loneliness is killing me slowly
I have fought every second with all my might
Now I feel so lowly
But as time keeps ticking
And as the countless seconds keep on course
It's harder to get the choice of picking
And why I have breath, I force
I will try
And if I survive
Before I shrivel and die
With the will to stay alive
I will find it
The illusion that's long awaited
The thing we all need every bit
Love, the word related

THE HOUSE

On the hill stands a tall, old, forbidding house
Alone it sits, as quite as a mouse
Wrapped in overgrown, and neglected ground
Unkempt, threatening, as dusk draws all around
Greeted by a slightly open front door
Entering in, and walking on an oil cloth Floor
As you walk into Dark, and gloomy entrance hall
Wondering what of the fate that will befall
Floor boards groan and creak
As you hesitate to speak
"Hello is anyone there?"
Cold and wet you enter without care
Glad of the shelter on offer inside
Wondering what horrors reside
Darkness plays in the shadows, shapes twist and form
And being there, makes you wish you had never been born
Screeching in the night
Makes you jump with fright
But hesitating you ask yourself of what does hide
Fear that seems to hurt your pride
Nervous as you feel some doubt
Of what hides in the shadows, ready to jump out
The smell of musk fills the air
Old dust and damp, makes your imagination scare
Silence rises to a deafening sound
Wondering what's waiting around
Heart beats to a fearful pace
The fear of the appearance of an unknown face
Echo's in this empty place resound and bounce
As courage takes every ounce
The flick of a light switch to get some light
But the light doesn't work and shadows stretch in the night

Cobwebs brush against your face
In this eerie, forbidden place
Nervous finger tips brush against the wall
Careful not to trip or fall
The dusty Mirror reflects the shape
Of the scary scape
As I venture in to the darkest room
A white shape appears to loom
A voice rings out
I scream and shout
With cold and sweating fear I run
Racing my way out the door I'm out of here, I'm done
Never looking back behind
Fear that makes one blind
As the house behind me disappears
As moonlight shines and dark skies clears
The distant outline disappears from view
A sigh of relief I give out, phew

THE GIBBET

Oh, rotting carcass there you hang and fly
Face contorted was hanged or did you die
Did you dance on the rope and choke
Then the final snap and you're neck broke
Now wrapped in a wrought Iron cage on show
To deter those wrong doers so they might know
The hungry birds have eaten most of you, and had their meal
But because you're long since dead you didn't feel
Flesh green and rancid falls off those bones
It doesn't become you those shades of blue and green tones
And the smell now all too much to bear
You are given a wide berth of those who are passing there
The once fine cloths you wore now torn to shreds
And the fine head of hair now mouse's beds
Maggots eat away greedily with ease
Chrysalises store inside your body to mature when they please
Your bodily fluids drip down and refresh the earth
The new growth of mandrake has given birth
So, my friend you have been useful after all
You have given to others after your deaths call
And there you are on show like an exhibit
On the cold and lonely Gibbet

THE EXECUTION

The dawn is yet to come
When it does, I have to face the gun
The solitary post stands in the yard
And the gravel beneath my feet is hard
The last and final yards I walk
I hear the Priest in whispers talk
The silence of the dawn
The place where my life will be torn
Soldiers stand in a single line
And the bullet will finish my time
1915 was not my year
And my crime was fear
Nothing more
Those Safe Generals planned for me what is in store
The post is closer now
With pounding heart, and sweating brow
A last cigarette for the condemned
And the last words, do you with God amend
Hands bound behind my back
The Blind fold turns my vision black
I hear the words, aim, load, and I perspire
Then silence and the command fire
The firing of the rifles, I jump with surprise
And pain racks through my chest, and the pain dies
Then Nothingness
British soldiers were made an example of in the 1st world
war, because the French soldiers went on strike.

THE EDGE OF LIFE

I stand on the edge of a precipice so high
Paused, to throw myself of to fly
As I gaze into the swirling darkness of the mist
Into the welcoming abyss
I lean forward to the point of no return
Heart pulsating, thumping as I twist and turn
Off the edge I fall
Leaving terra firma with no care at all
My thoughts are of the life I once had
Tormented, abused, from when since I was a lad
And still to very day, I pay the price
Unhappiness and pain of all these years to suffice
This the straw that broke my very soul
Tired of life, and snapped inside, No goal
As the exhilaration of the winds push through my face and
hair
The force of the rush, As I leave a life too much to bear
Saying good bye to all lost hope
How the hell did I cope?
As the ground meets and comes closer fast
Impact as my body smashes and I breathe my last
Splintered bones and flesh do rack
To the point of no going back
And as the dark consousness takes hold
My body dies and grows cold
As My soul leaves its earthly bind
I feel at utter peace, all the rigors of a tortured soul left behind
Oh peace, oh rest; of this life I'm tired
Escape away at best, this life now expired
Not a fitting end of ends
I leave behind my family and friends
This, an insignificant life is lost

To escape a tragic cost

I write this not to contemplate suicide but the end of one period of life. And the Start of a new Phase of life

THE DARK SHADOW

There are those who hide from a dark shadow of the past
And bear the deep scars that never leave, and last
There are those who suffer from that dark shadow in their lives
"IT" has the power to posses and hold husbands or wife's
"IT"s weapon of fear used like a tool
Constantly demeaning, those weaker, treating them as a fool
All Opportunities "IT" uses to grind you weak
To make your desperate daily struggle oblique
"IT "Sometimes uses physical violence to imprison those in "IT"s hold
To have the ultimate power and make those who fear and have them controlled
Tyranny and oppression as "IT" use force
Pretending "IT" is the victim and feigning remorse
Saying its love when they know really its possession
Disbelieving its "IT" that's really at fault and denying confession
As "IT" takes cruel sadistic pleasure in inflicting misery and pain
As "IT"s disease repeats its self over and over again
Emotional Black mail "IT" would use
As "IT" inflicts daily abuse
Convincing others that "IT"s the victim put in the frame
And that it's really you to blame
As this dark shadow evolves and grows
You that take those arduous blows
Making you doubt yourself and laying self blame
Putting yourself out to please to ease the pain
Bringing down yourself esteem making you doubt after so long
And "IT" feeds from that, making its self strong
The bully that uses Psychology for its own aims
As "IT" uses for demanding and demeaning games
But "IT"s weakness it fears and hides those fears inside
The dread of you winning and "IT" losing you is what it hides

The more you stand up the more punished you become
The more "IT" fears, the more damage to you is done
Possession, fear, Blackmail, and pain
Are what "IT" uses for you to remain
As long as "IT" has got that power over you
"IT" stands on its pinnacle on high on that towering view
But "IT"'s weakness is within yourself you know
And when you're at your end, you leave and go
Making that powerful house of cards collapse and fall
Bringing that "IT" weakening to Call
And "IT" does not accept defeat
Chasing after you when you retreat
"IT" will trick you by begging forgiveness as you led to be told
Saying "IT" will change and a promise of a new start, as it lies to hold
Because "IT" knows it losing its tyrannical rule of "IT"'s way
And will try to repossess its lost possession of the day
Because "IT" knows it's not love, just some tool to Blame
For "IT" has to lay fault on someone in life's game
Walk away if you make that break
Never look back a new life you must make
You know in your mind you done your best
All that's time you wasted that time you did invest
And if "IT" shows its ugly head
Send "IT" on its way use, the Authorities instead
Wipe your hands clean of "IT" clean out your life
Enjoy the freedom away from "IT"'s strife
Because eventually "IT" will have been paid back in time
Left in its pain ridden world with this on its mind
And time will pay "IT" back as they say
And you you'll have you day

THE BRIDGE

Black and grey clouds, twisting tormented the sky
Screaming winds moaned and began to cry
Thrashing rain, in deluged fall
Rocking the old bridge, straining timbers and all
Raging river rose, like thousands of clasping hands
Torrent churning to the storm's commands
The creaking groaning bridge rocked to and fro
She stood on that bridge, she had nowhere to go
Like a dozen bullwhips, the wind cruelly lashed
All the elements against her, her body thrown and smashed
Thunder and lightning boomed and lit the view
She faced the danger; she did not know what else to do
Desperate to get home to her children and family was her need
Without thought she done the deed
Hands held on the rail, as she crossed with every painful grip
As she edged her way across the splintering wooden strip
As the bridge fell apart, no one heard her screams
As like tinder washed away, it fell apart at the seams
Breaking timbers twist and broke
Into the watery hell she fell, to drown and choke
Never could she say to her children, good-bye
For her loyalty she did die
To the river she became its slave
Her final resting place, her final grave
A new steel bridge, now lines the way
And a plaque to remind us of that tragic day

THE BELL

Hear the solemn bell that tolls
Across my life, the echo rolls
Vibrating in empty rooms and across halls
Through brick walls, it calls
Come to me it constantly rings, it does insist
Beckoning I cannot resist
Calling, calling
The deep tone never stalling
In its tone it tells a story
Of the greatest tragedy and glory
The urge of its call is so great
End of my life is now late; it's now a game of wait
So great is the contemptuous force
I have to find the source
Oh God, Oh God, I cannot fight
As the distant bell tolls through the Day and Night
It's my un-turning destiny, as I go with dignity
To lose myself into infinity
As the heavy hammer strikes the bell
Do I go to heaven or hell?
I breathe my last
Recalling memories flashing of the past
Ascending to the course, and the great tunnel of radiant light
And to the end of the welcoming end, in sight
The bell tolls on
As it sings its song
Tolling on and on
As it sings its song

THE ALCOHOLIC

He wakes up and reaches for a cigarette
The dry acrid taste in his mouth is the taste of regret
And the empty bottle on the floor, is the reminder of some-
thing he's trying to forget
As the shaking starts and he begins to sweat
And he's sorry
But the vicious circle that he's in, is far beyond a worry
Now he reaches for the half empty glass from the night before
A livener for the start of the day is what he's looking for
The bruise on his face, from the fight he does barely remember
The scrape on his knuckles in the day light of September
The bits and pieces in his mind he recalls
The fight, the drunken stupor, and the stumbling falls
Now the only thing on his mind to find and open store
To buy and drink more
To look upon his pitiful face
As his looks unkempt and a disgrace
As his life sunk into oblivion, lost the person he used to, be
without trace
The drinking reaching an incredible pace
His daily routine is just to drink
It helps him; it numbs his thoughts and helps him not to think
The last thing on his mind is any form of reconstruction
As he obliterates and drinks himself into destruction

THE ROBIN

Little bird why did you die?
Once you lived, and used to fly
Now limp in my hand you lay
You lived your life until this day
Once you stood upright and Proud
Your shrill singing Crisp and loud
Your Bright Red breast
Tattooed on your chest
Lively with your cheek
One of a species unique
And as I dug the soil
I watched you search the spoil
You had no fear, you became a friend
Time with me you did spend
As I threw you crusts of bread
You sang a tune of gratitude as you fed
Shrill you sang and true
I would have said you was saying thank you
Each time I came to that place
You were there to greet me face to face
Singing your song with chirping sound
As you cheekily hopped around
And now you've come to your end
I will miss you my little friend

REGRET

I regret that things never worked out between us two
But sometimes I just sit here and think about you
I can't help it, it something normal people do
Both in tough times and good time's couples go through
In my mind you was always the one for me
But looking back now, it wasn't for us both I see
Those times gone by I loved too hard and too much
And how in this loneliness I miss your touch
You were at in those times everything I could ever need
I thought you was a different breed
And all you done was toss my feelings and love to the winds
of time
And at the time I felt it was a crime
But you decided for you own reasons, it was your fate
And I still can't find it in my heart to hate
You must have been so brave
And it must have hurt you in a big way, to reject the true love
I gave
You gave me my freedom you see
It must have been so hard to let me go, setting me free
And OK, to me it was a great big shock
Like a being crushed by a giant rock
Now having time and looking back I see
You done all this for me
And I would wish to tell you so
But now you'll never know
And if our paths ever cross again
Then I wish you luck in the future and you find ease from
consciences pain

Dedicated to my ex partner of 10 years, Maggie Larcomb who
recently passed away

POSTHUMOUSLY

She stood there, a solemn figure alone
In front of fresh dug earth and crisp marble stone
Eyes reddened and forlorn, misted with tears
True came all those dreaded fears
He promised he would return
But duty called, for the posthumous medal, he would earn
He kept his word
The promise she had heard
He came home, to rest in back in England
With his comrades, brothers in arms, his heroes band
She can never watch him grow old
He lies forever young, in earth that will be forever cold
She would never bear the children that they both planned
She would never feel the warm tender touch of his hand
She would never feel the warm kiss of his lips
Or never hear his funny, humorous quips
His life was given to a cause
Honour, and bravery, in the conflict of wars
Her hand now shaking, places down a small bunch of red roses
Amongst the wreaths and tiny posies
Choking back the grief
Knowing he died for his belief
She now a war bride widowed, with so many
How brave she is, now to pick up the pieces, if any

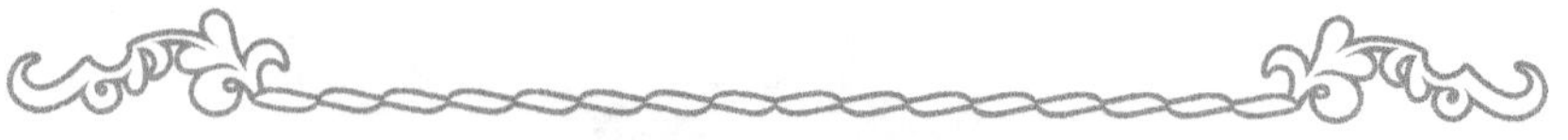

PARANOIA

He sits in a darkened sombre room, praying for a release
From the mocking of a thousand voices of the beast
No one could ever understand
The beasts demand
The tightening of the grip of the hand
At the beasts never ending, unmerciful command
Wrestling with his conscience, between wrong and right
Twenty-four times seven, day and night
Voices constantly taunt, mock, saying" they are all against you, you know"
There is no escape, nowhere to go
He stands up to full height, and screams Let me be
Tormented soul that's twisted, longs to be free
Bruised and bloodied hands, from the pounding on the wall
Are no redemption at all
The voices keep saying, Go On! Go On! Kill yourself and do us all a favour
They keep saying to him, the only escape, is death your saviour
They, the voices have taken all control
Weakening his punished and pitiful soul
He shouts above the constant droning of the angry crowd
But no one wants to hear, his one small voice is not allowed
Drowned out by the babbling of countless chatter
Ignored he feels, he doesn't matter
Help! Help! Screaming get me out of here
Because the burden of paranoia is his fear

MARTYRS TO THE FACT

Look towards the skyline of blue
Something's missing from that view
A part of New York that was true
Those tall towers of two
Like proud soldiers on parade
The Icon of America's Trade
Some never counted on, and didn't lack
For those who tried to break America's back
Was the will of American People
The pride tall, and strong as a steeple
But strength added to their cause
They carried on
Without pause
United the Western world was the goal
Community and humanity as a whole
Making the will that was unbreakable and stronger
To take up the fight longer
A hard lesson learnt and taught
The enemy ousted and thwart
All those lost souls found a voice
For Liberty, freedom, and choice
This a time we could never forget
For those innocents paid a price and we do regret
As America and the western world united to pick up the fight
In the name of what we all think is right
Do not forget; remember those soles and relatives, who met
that dreadful fate
September the 11th the year 2000, at 8.46 A.M. was the date

LOST LIVES

Look upon those fields of war, where a lost life goes
Neat green and grassy spaces, with stones placed in rows
Funny how we plant those people like seeds
Like empty wheat husks, with lifeless needs
But they never do grow
All part of nature, as we all know
What an utter waste of humanity
Just to appease a politics vanity
And yet those who are interred of which
Come back to lay in the earth, so fertile and rich
And in that small corner, of our land is peace and rest
Of slumbered quietness that space invests
Memories are the only thing to thrive
To keep thoughts of fond ones still alive
The tall stone memorial says it all
Those who gave their lives in war, did fall
And stood and rested before the epitaph lay a poppy wreath
To honour those who lay beneath
In Immortal words "We do not forget"
But meaning really, we do regret
How many fields like this, must we create?
How many young lives must we make late?
When do we ever learn?
Lives we keep, but money we can burn

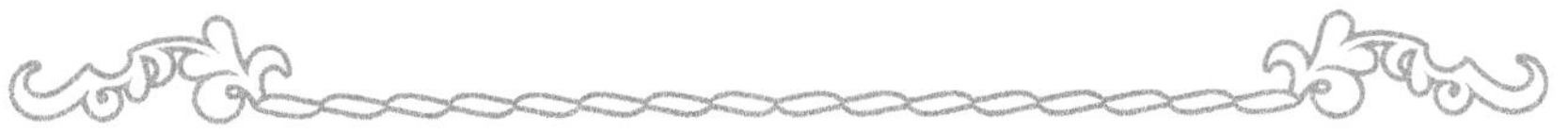

LADY OF THE ROAD

How I love your shape, form, and lines
You're the envy in all men's minds
Long and slender, cool and neat
You can sweep any man off their feet
Warm and smooth to the touch
Excites anyone who sits astride you, very much
The lady of the road and street
The winner amongst many, of who compete
And how you purr and roar
Makes even strangers look at you, and adore
Hearts race as you accelerate
Control at fingertips, as you vibrate
Leather against leather and steel
There is only one unique feel
The open road your domain
Makes one's adrenaline rise time and time again
Although you are mean and lean
You are sporty and clean
And oh, baby how you burn
Tantalising and teasing at your every turn
At times you take my breath away
On show to all the world and admired on display
In my eyes you are a dream
The ultimate in power, and how you gleam
Glistening chrome and colours in spender form
The speed and power from your engine born
Take a seat, and take the ride
Upon the ultimate machine with pride
Sit upon you saddle and take a hike
You the prized Motorbike

CONTENTS

MY UNCLE

I didn't recognise you when I came to the hospital and saw
Cancer had taken away your dignity, looks, and health for sure
I felt so helpless; I couldn't take away your pain
As you slipped in and out of consciousness again, and again
My Uncle you were dear to me
I have fond memories you see
To see you slipping away
When you passed away on March the 5th, this Saturday
I heard you call for your mother
She came for you, with your father, sister, and brother
All reunited now, and together
Seems life doesn't last forever
Cancer took away my Granny, Grandfather, Aunt, and Father and You my uncle, now rest at ease
You were kindness, always there to please
There for my traumatic childhood past days
To make me forget those uneasy ways
The short moment of fun you gave me to forget
Meeting and knowing you I did never regret
You helped me mend
I will miss you my uncle, my friend
In memory of my Uncle Brian Powell

MOTHER'S TRAITS

Mother how you looked after us through life
A faithful parent, a loving wife
Tender words to ease and help though times of pain
To always be there when needed once again
You love your children as Mothers care
Protective love of a parent, firm but fair
A nurse to heal wounds and take away tears
A psychologist to council inherited fears
A teacher to educate in life's complicated path
A banker and lawyer to help out a financial aftermath
A friend that's loyal beyond the cause
Taking time to care never ceasing to pause
Provider who gives selfishly with no thought to her self
A woman of rich in knowledge's wealth
A comforter in times of need
Giver of happiness indeed
These the traits seen in you
This your spouse does view
The heroine unique seen in our eyes
Always truthful never lies
One beyond duties call
A pillar of strength that will never fall

A MILLISECOND

If I could take a millisecond of time just to be with you
I'd stretch it forever that's what I'd do
Suspend it in time
Make it everlasting just to make you mine
Oh, to hold you in eternal embrace
To take my breath away for one glimpse of your adorning face
To feel your lips with one endless sensual kiss
Nothing in the world would make me miss
A never-ending feeling of emotions mix
That would be my deepest fix
All This I would for you I'd do
Just to spend one milimoment with you

LIFE MAKETH THE MAN

Take a man
Look inside him if you can
See the secrets he has to hold
Although on the outside strong and bold
A man who stands for pride
But no one knows what he holds inside
Tradition of his gender dictates
He's the man out with his mates
The expected breadwinner
Experienced in life, he's no beginner
Intended to be always on the ball
Taking's things accepted to extreme
Not allowed by rule to show emotions or dream
One to lead and hold a hand
Always there to be at demand
But to show true compassion he is weak
To show passion in the open he's a freak
And to cry in public is his biggest fear
For him to openly shed a tear
To show honesty, love, and feel
Doesn't to others show appeal
At the risk of damaging his pride to contradict
He has to hide his emotions a man he has to depict
A so-called Male Domination
In societies predicted nation
To keep mans name
The labels put by societies does remain
These things the humanity does protest
Puts his him and his name to the test
Life maketh the man
There for I am.

LAST LOVE

The attention for what you did crave
You asked for love, and I truly and freely gave
I gave you warmth and passion
Adorned you with every fashion
I would have given 25 hours a day, 8 days a week
I couldn't have loved any harder, so to speak
Tenderness, like the handling of gossamer silk
Blended with cinnamon warmed milk
Maybe I loved you too much
Loved too hard, as such
Or maybe I gave you too much space
Now I've fallen from grace
I am who I am, and that's not strange
I will not, or couldn't change
What you see is what you get
And that's a sure bet
And now I still don't know what made us fall
I'm sad, to think I've lost it all
One of those great mysteries in life, no doubt
I guess I will never find out
No matter, I know I gave it all my best
I couldn't have given any less
I am resigned to being who I really am
A truthful and an honest man
Love has lost and fell far behind
Left me insecure, but kind
One day, one day
Maybe the true love I've been looking for will come my way
Until then I'm safe and free
And will have to wait and see
I have had some bad feedback from my ex,
Only to find out what the real truth is.

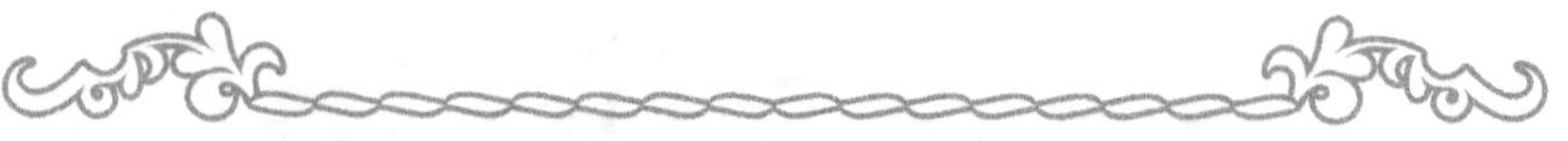

JUSTIFYING THE MEANS

13 months have passed since splitting up with my EX by now
How time has flown and how
Lies that have been told and rumours spread
Hurt and defenceless, and others misled
How can I defend my good name when I'm not there?
Friends you once knew become weary and beware
Knowing all those accusations made
On the receiving end a price, your reputations paid
And you the loyal, faithful one like that's writing in the song
Then the eye-opener comes along
Finding out that you were not really in the wrong
The lies that's told TO JUSTIFY THE MEANS
The reaction of guilty human beings
As they hide the truth, afraid of being found out
Covering tracks in a web of deceit and lies about
Hoping their lies would be hidden for once and for all
But eventually they trip and fall
And I the victim on the receiving end
Trying to heal and get on the mend
Be strong I say don't react to all
They will in the end crumble and fall
And when the spin their tissue of lies to someone new who comes along
Who knows they may be found out and proven wrong?

ILLUSIVE LOVE

Isn't love illusive?
When you are reclusive
It doesn't hide in the top drawer
And it isn't behind a locked door
Search and you will find they say
But where do you look, which way?
They say don't look too hard
It will eventually turn up in your yard
So contradicted, so restricted
This indescribable feeling depicted
It doesn't come in the post
You can even search coast to coast
It's all a matter of chance
Seeking romance
Seek and you shall find
Are we all going blind?
Wake up and smell the roses
Sometimes it's right under our noses
And believe it or not, we tend to ignore
Boy this is such a hard chore
Is there a thing called perfect love
That tends to fit like a comfortable glove
Oh well keep up the search
For that dream you'll end up in the isle of a church
When you've found love, and achieved your goal
Then maybe love and you will be for once whole

IF KIND HEARTS

If kind hearts do help and aid
Friendships forged and made
Trust is bonded with each other
In the search for perspective lover
Over time builds up a rapport
And feelings build up of a sort
But when those feelings are hung up on a string
And a game is played in an unbalanced thing
Told that's feelings are more than a friend
But not getting anywhere in the end
Up and down and twisted around
Confused by turmoil thoughts are found
Sent up in the air and smashed to the ground
Feeling your standing waiting in a line to the letter
While that person looks for someone better
Inside you feel, oh you will do
Till they pick and choose someone better and new
Only there for a convenience when in need
Ignored and kept waiting is the deed
And you have lived a useless hope
Finding it hard to be patient and cope
What a fool you've been
Convinced in you blindness of what you could have seen
It took time to see through the game
And you, you're left behind to take the blame

I STANDETH

I have had another crack at writing Shakespeare I hope you like it.

I standeth before thee a humbled Man
Thou see the Man that I am
Hath I no worldly goods to bear
No riches I do have to share
Nay do not forsooth mine self as thou canst see?
Tis what appeared to mine self outside to thee
Mine heart I hold in mine chest doth reside
Of what I truly hold in mine inside
Tis Mine heart true and honest as the day is long
Happy like the Lark in song
Good manner I hold in mine person
I but one of single version
....
I standeth before thee a humbled man
I offer mine self unto thee, take mine self if thou canst
Tis love that bear mine soul
The need to make mine self whole
To feel thy warmth of a comely wench
Purge mine fire and soothe and quench
Tis mine soul that hast been lost in black night
I doth look for warmth of thy light
....
I standeth before thee a humbled man
Thou know before thee the man that I am

HORSEMEN2

The three Politician horsemen, Bush, Blair, and Hussein
Ride on their steeds across the globe, as though they are all insane
Bush brings fire, Blair brings death
And Hussein brings Pestilence, plague
Together they all bring apocalypse to this age
Uttered with dread of the fear of lips
As they reap, they do sow
As in the annuals of history will show
The eagle flies, the lion stalks
The cowardly Jackal walks
Bringing chaos and disorder
To other countries border
Bringing universal hate to all
As other weaker cultures fall
Who really wants war?
What is it all for?
Innocent pawns
Buried under stones and grassy lawns
Relatives grieve and cry
As loved ones die
For this political game
So that heads of state can gain
All under the excuse of different belief
And we the under dogs suffer grief
What happened to world peace?
As Bullies control by the worlds police
Piece is not a goal to be achieved
Seems death is the only way to be relieved
What of the fourth horseman? He gathers all souls
Death harvests all that's left to burn over roasting coals

HARVEST

Harvest times that hang the breeze
Have ripened fruit hangs on the trees
Golden barley, wheat, and corn in the fields
Crops that need picking of natures yields
Autumn fruits hang readily of the bow
As late summer and autumn does allow
Lush greens to feed the hungry mouths
Vegetables or roots, ready are the ploughs
Furrows in lines ready now
Piglets weaned from fatted sow
Treasures from Natures hand
Given freely from the land

EXAMS

Oh, Teacher what have you done?
Now that it's the day my exams have come
This is my time of dread
Facts and figures of my learning thread
I've studied hard these days and nights
In that silent and stressful plight
My marks have to meet a demand
And all achieved by your teaching, and my own hand
No one understands what I'm going through
Of all these subjects that I do
Assignments set
Makes me worry and fret
I really am doing my best
To win good marks and beat the rest
I'm told I need to succeed
To get the best career in life indeed
But every subject I can't enjoy
Some I'll pass or fail in educations ploy
How I dread examinations day
This time of all my studying should pay
Will this be my time of make or break?
And if I fail how and what reaction will my parents take?
As I really do want to please
As my parents have saved for the college fees
And now the examination is done
Waiting for my marks to come
Oh, I hate this waiting game
That "have I passed or failed pain?"
But teacher I know you have done your best
As your education and time in me you did invest
So, if I pass or I fail
At least we both done our best to prevail

DEATH OF A POET

I saw the day the poet died
The agent of his work, with delight he cried
All those poems written, when the writer was alive
Means others will benefit, profit, and thrive
But the poet died a pauper, he died so poor
Clever words from an agent promising allure
For the love of poetry, the writer wrote and not for gain
Recognition was all he wanted for his pain
Poems to be printed in a book
But written unfinished works was took
As the literary vulture's tear over pages and fight
For a small piece of the action, they bicker and bite
History talks of artist's insecurity
Those who die in obscurity
Is this the price of fame?
Words in a book, a picture, in a frame?
A legacy left behind
Chapter and verse in a fancy bind
And a signature in a book
For others to read and look

DARKER DAYS

As darker days fill my empty day
Somebody took my light away
And in the twilight of the evening light
Days turned to night
You took me by the hand and guided me through
As I knew you would do
Crowds of doubt gathered all around
Lost in the land of no self esteem on swamped ground
A mist of low feelings clouded and hung in the air
Driving me into deeper despair
You gave me a glimmer in hopes light
To help me through my fight
In the distance heard were my cries of a desperate plea
They heard, and came to rescued me
Oh, angel of mercy lifted my soul
And helped my face my life as a whole
Softly held me and gave reassurance
Comfort and Insurance
Gave me back the will to live
To continue my life to give
Helped me mend broken parts
Put feeling back into hearts
Lifted my recompense
Encouraged my intelligence
I thank you with all my heart
For making my life, my feelings restart
Thank you for not taking me for granted
And for making me feel wanted

D.I.Y.

Are you the builder in the street?
No job to me to obsolete
I specialise in loose shelves hanging on the wall
King of botch jobs I do them all
The front door held by tape and string
Although looks shoddy it does its thing
Plug sockets hung by wires will do
I'll put them right one day soon
My excuse, can't get the right tools to do the job
They are expensive and cost a few Bob (£s)
So, I work with what I got
Loads of new tools unused I got the lot
One day I'll learn to use them right
When I got time someday I might
Hammer is the main tool I use
Glue, Stick tape, Nails, and screws
My wonderful house looks good, but don't touch
Safety I can't grantee very much
Wall paper and decorating only half done
Paint work stripped and left undone
Fitted wardrobe not complete
These big jobs tend to me, to defeat
Well, I have another job to do
So armed with Hammer I'll say good bye to you
Bang! Bang! Whirrrrr! Clank! Clash!
Tinkle! Crunch! Bash! Bash!

COLUMBIA

Columbia How you touched heavens face
Before you sadly fell to grace
Multiple vapour trails seen in space
Up in the ozone in that untouched place
This event took place at the first day of February
In the year of two thousand and three
Six American and one Israeli soles, will be forever immortal
A step far beyond the hands and eyes of any mortal
Seven souls will eternally look down on earth
To the place of N.A.S.A. s Birth
They touched far beyond sky
In memory and hearts you will never die
Fly free now and go beyond the realms of outer space
You are truly in the heavens place
And although in this situation your lives were torn
Your perused dreams, for each and every one of you were born
Seven heroes will be remembered forever
To be forgotten? Never
You shall never need to be tied to earthly binds
Always in the hearts of loved ones minds
Columbia fly free
Seven souls now will be

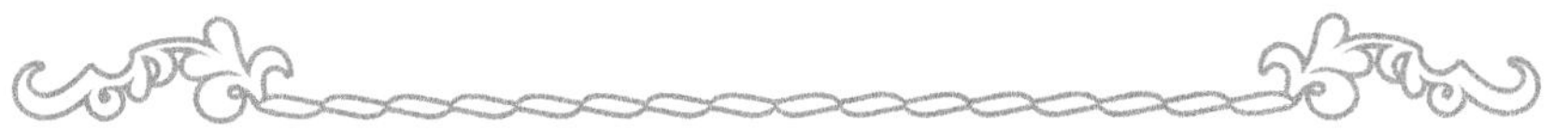

CAN YOU GUESS WHAT THIS IS?

This place of splendored Hall,
Its gleaming throne, to greet you all.
A place to ponder and depend on,
Of natures call.
Cross words, papers, books, and puzzles, all.
A haven of dreams, ideas and thought,
While face of expression and taught.
Place of rest bite,
And open 24 hr both day and night.
All are welcome 365 days of the year,
Privacy intended without fear.
A choice of darkness or of light,
Away from prying eyes out of public sight.
Time to take as much as you need,
There is no time limit to really heed.
Excepts all types short or tall,
Fat or thin, big or small.
Age no preference here to tell,
Takes sick or healthy here as well.
No race discrimination no objection to call,
Form peer, to working class, tramp and all.
A place for all seasons from spring to fall,
From single occasion, from party to ball.
A place that no one can do without and would be lost,
Even at any cost.
Have you guessed what it is or is it driving you mad?
Then all I can say is that you've been had

BETRAYED AND DEFEATED

A mother sits and cries
When the love for her child dies
That child has become violent and a threat
Physical blows exchanged, and now regret
The child has won, and now rules with ruthless demand
And find it so easy to get what it wants, with the use of a heavy hand
She feels broken
From cruel words harshly spoken
Her humility is now depleted
As she feels betrayed and defeated
Controlled and manipulated, and with no more respect
As demands are made with a clenched fist, as only she would expect
There was once a beautiful child
Now stood before her a bully, a tyrant, and some one totally wild
The Black eye and the bruising
Is the reward from the bullied child that is left from abusing?
She has no money in her purse it's all gone
Taken by the emotional blackmailing one
Where did I go wrong she thinks?
How life stinks
And yet whom can I confide in? Who can I tell?
To get me out the living hell
It for the of love my child, I don't want to lose
But I can't stand any more of this abuse
Trapped in this dilemma it's hard to cope
When a mother is losing all faith and hope
Too late now the rot has set in to do any good
As there is loyalty to family blood
So she hides it all in shame
Till enough is enough and she can't take the pain
And rings the authorities to take control
To give her time to regain humanity and make her whole

ASKING FOR LOVE

Has anyone one got any love to give
For someone who wants to love and live
Just a tiny bit to share
From anyone who wants to care
Tired of empty promised made
For one who's had head games played
A lonely one who's served their time
Someone a little younger would be fine
But I suppose we can all dream
Waiting for that special person to intervene
Slightly afraid in side
But on the outside out going and applied
Friends are in plenty and well adored
Accepting more and never been bored
Not being too fussy
But not wanting a charlatan or a hussy
One who wants someone the same
Not one who punishes or lays blame
One who wants a relationship for good
One who's committed and ready to give loves blood
Being prepared to compromise
Not one who full of hate and despise
Forgetting those broken times from the past
To be truthful and honest in the cast
To love a person as is seen
And not enforce changes from what that person has been
Someone with an understanding and simple view
Not one whose uses a stepping stone to get through?
Not a lot to ask for to love and live
Just someone who wants to give

WHAT'S IN A HUG?

A hug for some is warmth, and what we all need
Expression without words to feed
Needed when some ones feeling down
Help them feel better, and feel wanted around
Hugs for loving posture between couples, that intimate touch
That need for couples, partners, is a hug is wanted very much
A hug to warmly greet a friend
Bonding, making a person on what you can depend
Lifts your day
In a lovely way
Makes you feel warm, safe from harm
Makes those who give them a touch of charm
So when you greeted with a hug
Smile! Your wanted, be a little smug
And those who give it will make a person's day
Given freely and without pay

WARWICK CASTLE

Warwick castle above the town you stand
There an impressive feature to dominate the land
Conflicts and battles through the ages you have beat
One thousand years still you stand complete
Eight Earls and their families kept safe inside
The fascinating history from your walls reside
Tall imposing towers and gate house stand tall
Battle scarred and elongated surrounding wall
As you sit in your moat, showing your portcullis and Rampart
gate
Resting in your regal state
Inside on castle green lays an imposing court
The great hall and living quarters hide in side stone fort
Even The ghost of Sir faulk Grevil walks the East tower
And in the bowls of the castle lies the dungeon of power
Kings and queens visited and stayed
To be hosted in your Stately rooms and entertained
As the Medieval timbered town
Gently wraps around
Nestled by the River on rock bound Bank
Shows your splendored rank
A death mask of Cromwell and objects of many things
Finest arms and armour on show brings
Quality furniture decorates your halls
Paintings of ancestors and family hang upon your walls
To visits this marvel takes a full day
As you wander around, lost in history that takes you away
Well worth the visit if you're passing by
Locked in memories forever, all the things you spy

TIME

Time, we take for granted
Even if not wanted
Sad times seem to go by slowly by
Happy times swiftly fly
Sometimes fast or sometimes slow
At what speed you'll never know
How we accept it in every way
Those tricks that time does play
Time for smiles or to cry
A time to love, live, or die
Hard times never flow
Good times smooth and so easily go
Times of uncertainty bring unease
Sure, times tend to please
Time for reminisce to contemplate
Thoughts of past times to relate
Present times here to day
Future times are on their way
As the clock ticks on its course
On its path to eternal force
Never ceasing on its endless track
Always looking forward and never looking back

THE VALENTINE CARD

Deep in the draw, an old valentine card lays
A reminder of those past and bygone days
The yellowed envelope, covered with finger prints, dust and grime
A card that has seen days in a better time
Edges of the card scuffed and worn
The corners bent and torn
The verse faded
And the ink smudged and jaded
Fond but distant memories it holds
As the words of the card unfolds
Those old tear stains of distant pains
Of the remnants of loves remains
Forgotten memories brought to life
As the card is opened to the days light
Recollections come to mind
As promises of pledges are left behind
Tears well up inside
Where once emotions were long ago hide
Placing the card back where it belongs
Where the dust settles echo's in past songs
Memories of the distant shore
Putting away in memories in store
As done many times before
Gently closing the draw

THE KNIGHT'S BATTLE

In the days of chivalry
Way back in the time of history
Two knights of honour stood in a lonely field
The goal to make each other yield
Each stood face to face
Sword and shield held in each other's embrace
Both on a quest
To hold a goodly name they considered best
As each stood ready in battle stance
To swing wield their weapons in a dance
Swords clash and shield defend
At fight of honour right to the end
Striking every deadly blow
Slashing high and hitting low
Crunching and smashing the sound of breaking bone
As crushing blows are hitting home
As each stagger exhausted in blooded dance
Looking for a victorious chance
As one knight falls wounded to the ground
To the final injured sound
And as the victor stood proud and upright right in the field
"Thou has been done thy deed thy wounded goodly knight,
does thou yield?"
"Aye sir knight, thou art thee victor done"
"Thou proved thine honour, thou hast won"
The victorious Knight took the wounded knights hand
To lift him off bloodstained land
They swore a pledge of allegiance to each become a friend
To protect each other's honour to the end

THE HORSEMEN

On normal calm and reddened sky
Strange things occur on high
The clouds suddenly tear apart
To the thunder of horse's hooves, that excites the heart
Screaming of the sound of riders on horses
As they are set on their intended courses
Three shapes from the heavens appear
Striking into hearts, terror and fear
To look on these three faces you are already dead
Your soles claimed, predicted it's said
Now is the beginning of the end
The world is helpless from these, no one can defend
Pestilence, Decease, and Death are the riders
Among the three are they the soul's dividers
The three horse men of apocalypse
As they go to work and get to grips
The song of Pestilence sings his deathly sound
Death gathers souls he's found
Decease spreads his seeds that's sown
Across the planet they have blown
The scythe of death swings and reaps far and wide
Gathering soles as the scythe smoothly glides
Pray that death be swift
As mercy would be a gift
They sweep the lands to make them clean
Eager for the work they are keen
Destroying all in their path
In a devastating aftermath
They will not stop till they succeed
And the reaping of tormented soles are done indeed
They won't listen to pleas or reason
For a prayer or pleading mercy to them is treason

Death and the gathering is their business, the goal is fixed
Souls are profit and they won't be tricked
Pray you never see them for real
As Death will take your soul, I can reveal

THE HOLE

I'm in a rut
This is where I been put
This dark deep hole I am in
I can't get out, I just can't win
No matter how I try
I can't get out, I don't know why
So, I'm resigned to where I sit
I don't enjoy it one little bit
Trapped, I just can't move
Finding it difficult to prove
High walls all around
Climbing out, and gaining ground
I'm knocked back down I've found
No way out that I can see
This is what life's doing to me
Find a ladder, grab a rope
Any way of finding hope
Use my hands, dig in my heels
The urge to climb appeals
Use a shovel to dig my way
Just to live and fight another day
Knocked back down to the start
I don't give in and don't lose heart
Taking time and it easy counts
In tiny small amounts
And one day to reach the light
The long climb out to win the fight
All you have to do is not give in and proceed
To reach the top and succeed

THE GUN

I am the gun, made of steel
Cold to the touch, heavy to the feel
I have chambers, but no heart
Precision engineered for every moving part
My only function is to injure, maim, or kill
The finger on the trigger controls my will
My long barrel sends out the projectile flights
Once the hammer hits the charge, and the bullets ignites
My job is done, my function to protect
From the missiles I project
I don't carry a conscience for the victims I leave behind
To all emotions I am blind
I don't shed a tear
I just create dread and fear
Just to hear the sound of my name
Is to strike terror in the hearts of those in my aim
But I am the one who doesn't have control
It's the hand that holds me as a whole
I am a legend in histories hold
Mentioned in the stories told
Held by the famous and revered
My name lives on to those adhered
I am the gun
A name remembered on the lips of every one

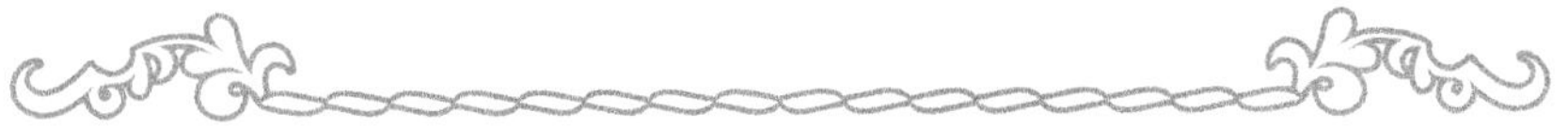

THE GARDEN

In the garden flowers grow
That warms the heart and makes one's insides glow
Bees buzzing busily along
Bird's serenade their song
As the romantic couple draw closer together
Made promises to each other to keep forever
They look into each other's eyes
Knowing that in each other's hearts there's no room for lies
Honest like deep true love is held
Hearts melt and together weld
Their hands clasp gently together in tender touch
Knowing they love each other very much
They kiss passionately in warm embrace
Heats beat in gentle pace
As they hold each other near
Promises made and held dear
As the garden holds its beautiful scene
Love and romance in this place serene

THE FACES

Our religions of stories told
Of events, happenings, in times of old
One small word, form a persons imagination
Stretched, exaggerated, and adapted, to suit every nation
Stories like wildfire, rumours spread
Of one so powerful and almighty, those others fear and dread
And so strong, the created belief
That the powerful message spreads suffering and grief
All religions have a similar base
As they spread and develop at a different pace
They nearly all wear men's faces
Allah, God, Buddha, and many others from ancient races
Some lost in the time of fashion
And some very alive with devout passion
Like a story told to frighten a child
Beyond comprehension and overly wild
What if there was no heaven or no hell
And God and the Devil, are one of the same, say tell
But all made up by the founders of those stories
Like legends and myths that grow in their glories
New religions popping up, and offer in which
Like a new product in a high profile pitch
Buy one, and get one free (lol)
This is what it seems to me
Forgive me for my own opinion but if there was no excuse
For religion used in war, what would man use?

THE ACCUSER

How can people be so wrong?
Stretching small things into long
Little things into large
Small accusations, into they will barge
Unfounded accusations they do make
To make others innocence and good reputations break
As defence you naturally do
As they turn their verbal screw
Making you guilty as charged
The opponent's ego much enlarged
Angry knowing that their lies are untrue
It's the only way they can get to you
This from one you hardly know
Because they think they know all of you so
How wrong they are
How they use this to mislead
On this their super ego would feed
And you feeling belittled and put down
And them, feeling good and wearing the crown
Don't they comprehend the damage done?
Just because they think they have won?
Well let them have their glory I say
I hope it helps get them through their day
Friends know the real you and they know you well
They know what the truth is as they can tell
So accuser, have your day
Life will pay you back in every way

TEENAGERS BEDROOM

The teen-agers bedroom the dreaded domains
A place of their own privacy and inner sanctum remains
That dreaded bedroom door and what you find inside
Heart thumping as your hand touches the handle, no place
to hide
Opening the door and slowly walking in
Knowing that you're about to enter the residential bin
The room dark, sedate, and dim, trying not to trip or fall
With just the glint of light from the showing from the hall
Dark mountains and shapes all around
As you opened the curtains your heart falls to the ground.
Standing in the light and in its true glory and now in shock
Piles of dirty clothing and smell of sweaty sock
Ashtrays full and flowing and trash where the bin used to be
Where was the carpet the one we used to see?
Cans, bottles, crisp packets, sweet wrappers, yoghurt pots,
things that look obscene
Makes the local garbage dump look quite tidy and clean
But worst is yet to come when peering under the bed
The sight that greets you, wishes you were dead
Cups, dinner plates, and side plates covered in alien culture,
that fills you with dread,
Books, comics, paperwork and magazines swimming in your
head
And all the hours of cleaning up the endless mess
The teenager comes home and you can only guess
MOM! What have you done to my room? Its private I said
Screaming, tantrums, and abuse going through your head
After all the time you spent and the miracle, you have done
Another battle not quite won

SILENT KILLER

The tanks roll on, progress pushed
Silence as the bombs are hushed
The crack of sniper shot
Breaks the silence in the night of the desert hot
A voice cries out
Then other voices shout
Medic! Medic! Comes the call
Of a soldier injured to a fall
Echo's carry across the sleeping plain
And in the dimness a cry of pain
More shots fire in a deafening sound
Multiple bullets ratting in a resound
Then silence, has the sniper been found?
Or has he crept off? Gone to ground?
Another scoring mark on his gun
Trained for what he's done
Silent as the night
His target in his sight
A worry for the forces advance
With a sniper at large, they don't stand a chance
The deadly silent killer roams so free
Picking off those so easily
Creating terror and dread
While soldiers sleeping in their bed
In those deadly sights, who appears
Then like a ghost disappears
Never to be seen
For one illusive sniper, who has come and been

ROSE

The gentle petals of a rose
Soft and delicate as it grows
Stamens that nectar feeds
To busy pollen collecting bees
The heart opens for natures show
Exhibiting beauty for all to know
As it stands on hardy wooden stem
Sharp and spiky thorns defend them
A red romantic rose comes to mind
But many colours you will find
Types and spices of many kind
Some new and old from an historical line
Morning dew on soft petal rolls
Like beaded strings of pearls in rows
Glistens like diamond jewels
In morning sunlight pools
Cobweb lined like lace
Like a sparkling jewelled necklace
Swaying in summer glow
With a multitude of colour swaying to and fro
And oh that perfumed smell
Pleasured membrane tantalised well
Pleasing to the eye
Ruby rose evolving and passing by
Regal flower to king and queen
Royal ensign you have been
A bloom to show ones feelings of romance
Of love to blossom in life's chance

ROBIN REDBREAST

Oh little robin redbreast
How finely you are dressed
Like the master of the hunt, you wear your Sunday best
That bright red waistcoat you wear upon your chest
No top hat on your head
But tails you wear instead
How you stand so proud
Surveying your domain from branches bowed
The best-dressed bird in county and town
Your bright fashion, you wear the crown
Never afraid of man
Scurrying for grubs, worms and morsels, when you can
I have to admire your cheek
From one so tiny and meek
And yet you make your living
For one who's always giving

RETURNING SPRING

Once again spring has come round
To wake the sleepy winter ground
Birds in pairs, nest in bushes and trees
As the warm spring air warms the breeze
A multitude of colour bursting into bloom
As snowdrops and crocuses push for room
White, purple, and yellow
Cheers the bare grass to make it mellow
The once bud less trees seem to bear
Pop out, now spring is in the air
The yearning for new life for natures fair
As the new seasons fashion sets to flair
The farmer works the rested soil, in the field
To produce the newly growing yield
Rows of geese and ducks fly to return
Buds like curled fingers stretch open, on sprouting fern
New life struggles to adorn the eye
Growing, being born, being created, on what we rely
New seeds seem to wake up and stretch their arms
To evolve in springs charms
The song thrush sings its serenade
To tell us all springs on parade

NIGHTS ON THE SHORE

Oh, Midsummer nights of gentle breeze
Warmly wafting across calm seas
In red burning sunset sky
Dark blue backdrop and reds and yellows apply
Calm and restful mill pond tide
Creating serenity inside
Stars glistening on a clear and darker Blue
Shooting stars on streaking view
As I look to the distant twilight shore
Town's lights glowing in lines I saw
And slowly drifting the odd illuminated ship
Across the sky line I see Slip
Warm and comforting is the summer air
All these in one scene you can't compare
Romance springs to mind along the beach
Holding hand of the one you love you reach
And as you kiss, Caressed by oceans touch
That striking view moves you very much
To the movement of shushing rhythmic tide
Sooth's emotions inside
In this place of romantic host
Brings feeling of loving couples close
Walking hand in hand on moonlit shore
The place with the one you adore
Two silhouettes against the lit moon
Inviting love to return again soon

PRICE PAID

So, Miss, you thought you was so cool
But I'm no fool
I know of your game
I knew of your aim
You see
It's all clear to me
You have played your little façade
I won, and you lost hard
It's the usual obsession
Of wanting possession
Now it's time for confession
A new toy for your profession
Shows your personality
The real you, in what others see
And now found out, you feign for pity
Using your charms, because you're pretty
You must be cute
Rather astute
But you under estimated
I was patient, and waited
And the truth is now revealed
Your fate was sealed
Why didn't you just like others enjoy?
Instead, you publicly were demeaning and tried to annoy
For all these things I'm sad
You've made your self look bad
Angry I may be, but I never like to fight
I bite my lip, and keep it tight
I hate to say, a lesson been taught
The price is paid, and you bought
Your apology accepted
Received and well respected

PICK YOURSELF UP

Why do you put yourself down?
There are plenty of others to do that, around
Lifts your spirits
Don't look down
Better to smile
Then wear a frown
Look at yourself you silly twit
Nobody cares about it one little bit
So why should you bother to feel so low
Its time you got up, now get up and go
Don't just sit there and stare
Others have noticed and are now aware
Why don't you be like your old self?
You used to be happy, now you look left on the shelf
So come on Let's see that old you
All those things you used to get up to
Those laughter and antics, like you used to be
Not being gloomy as I can see
Chin up: Smile: try to be your usual happy way
Time to face a better new day

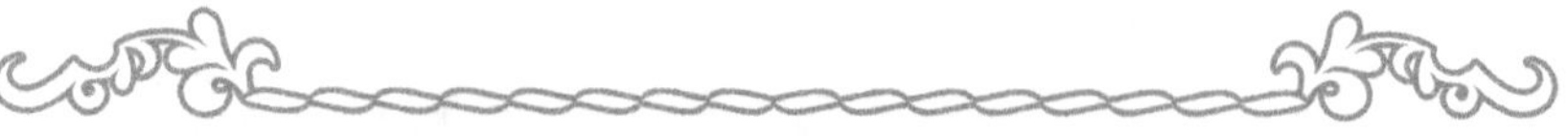

PHONE MADNESS

The pressing of the buttons on your telephone
And listening for the dialling of the tone
Then the voice
Telling you to press the button of your choice
Press one to wait forever and sit there like a jerk
Press two to get lost in the network
Press three if you got a house to build
Press four if you want to be heavily billed
Press five if you're already insane
And press six if you want to start all over again
Then that music in the background plays
With and that annoying voice comes on and says
Our advisers won't take long
Then you're back to that long playing song
And in the end you're almost bored with slumber
Only to find out you rang the number
Or they can't really help you in the end
It's enough to drive you round the bend
Press seven if you want to commit suicide
That answering service where you think you died

PERFECT LIFE

If we could all dream of a perfect life in every way
What would you wish for? To exist every day
Maybe your perfect partner to honestly hold, what gives as
much back in return
As you grow closer together and learn
A home you can live in happiness and care
Together a loving life and able to share
Where all the bills are paid and there's food on the table
And money to spare for those special treats when able
None of the stresses and strains to exist
No arguments or hatred that you strive to resist
Never any mistrust or subterfuge that does arise
Being torn apart by others lies
Honesty in all that's done
A life worth living and having fun
The wonderful utopia that we all long to need
And the will to win and succeed
How we all deeply long
To live life right away from wrong
Although these things are just a heat beat away
So near and yet so far out of reach, that usual way
As we all yearn through life's journey, as we all slowly tread
As we climb over those obstacles and barriers we dread
After all it's only a dream
Only a few find true love it would seem
Others fall by the wayside hurt and lost
As we all seem to count the cost

NAILS IN MY FENCE

Quite a few sent me a story about nails in a fence
But how can you put nails in a steel defence
Is what I built up in these past few years?
My fence in the past was broken and smashed letting some fears
Don't get me wrong my friends I love you all
But life and past mistakes has made me build this wall
I tend to keep within my fence it makes me feel safe
Stops me being hurt you see and keeps me from mistakes
Occasionally I leave a small open gap
To listen to the troubles of ladies or a chap
I don't hide within its Bound
It's just a place to retreat when things get too though around
I don't have locks on its gate
Something I think my friends appreciate
When I let them in
There's a warm and understanding heart waiting within
And those walls echo sympathy to all
For those that call
The welcome sign that flashes on my door
Tea and sympathy as we say in the UK here
I am always here to lend a sympathetic ear
And try to advise and resolve your life's worst situations
And My doors always open to any creed or anyone of any Nation
That boundary is just for me for rest bite somewhere to retreat
As you and I know how life wears you down with defeat
So don't be put off by that daunting barrier feel free to knock
my door
That's what I'm here for
At times empty promises are made
Games for those uncertain are played
So I gently close me door so as to be given my own space
My sanctity and my safety place

So there are no nails in my fence
I have to admit it's my recompense
But thank you all to my Friends
I am honoured to be here with you all you've helped me mend

CONTENTS

PEACE

Loneliness has a friend in me
One to keep my company
Although I have friends you see
Alone in life I seem to be
Solitude my best friend
Gives me time to mend
Someone like me I can defend
Myself alone I can depend
ME just ME here on my own
No ringing from the telephone
No voice, no sound, No one to moan
Just I and I alone
No noise Just peace
Background noises none to release
Tick tock of my clock on the wall
The sound of quietness says it all

PATRIOTIC ROSE

The Strong dictating hand took the rose, and squeezed
That hand, so corrupt and so diseased
But the sharp thorns made it bleed
Enough to make it let go and heed
Pain, agony, and blood
A wound, to make a statement good
One delicate single rose to prove a point
But as a bush of many, would deter great numbers in joint
Against a storm of many hands, against a foe of odds
Deferred the foe from picking, the little sods
Drive all those grasping hands away
While colours stand proudly on display
For you, the delicate and strong
Upright and erect against the wrong
Red the colour of true blood
White the purity that stands for good
May your roots be strong and hold
And you be warm against the cold
For you represent a nation
You fight against Tyranny and occupation
British rose
Pride of pose
Be gallant
And at the same time be elegant

OUR UK

Asylum seekers throughout the world
Don't listen to those stories unfurled
In Britain our streets are not paved with gold
Our Houses are expensive and old
We don't give money away for free
For those on low income it doesn't come easy
In fact, we are taxed to the hilt
Exploited to the max is how our system is built
We don't supply you with furniture or a home
What is given is an expensive Loan
Our Health service is over stretched and underpaid
To wait for an operation, you'll die I'm afraid
Our welfare system is burdened and broke
Even to our own people it's a joke
We don't have a lot anymore to give
We ourselves have trouble to live
Can we come to your counties instead?
Can you fix us up with a home or a bed?
And we can come to your country and you can give
Maybe we can be better off where you live
Better then the internment camps cause that's what you get
Or the majority sent back to where they come from, I bet
So, before you set out on a dream
It's not as easy as it would seem

OLD AND NEW LIFE

When there comes a point in death
And time draws my last breath
Please don't grieve and cry
Because I've passed on, did die
Tired bones I leave behind
To another place and time, I go to find
A life of a new, to another start
The beating of another heart
And if we meet in a future time
I'm sure you'll know I'm fine
And if our paths cross by chance
Even at a fleeting glance
I would pass the time, and say hello
Like the end of one life, I go
So please try to forget
Do not show remorse or regret
Death says it does not deceive
Do not grieve
I am in another place
Reborn in another space
The eternal clock ticks on
As one life ends, a new one has begun
So, I beg you not to cry
I've moved on, I didn't die

NATURE'S CALL

Have you ever been on a long journey by bus or by car?
Sitting there comfortably, looking out the window as we usu-
ally are
Time passes on and a feeling comes to mind
I wish I'd have left that coffee, tea, or drink behind
Then there's that nagging feeling down below
And the Journey gets longer and slow and you to go
That spiteful voice is nagging in your head
Saying you need a pee, it's that time you dread
And you try to convince yourself that you will soon be there
Those nagging pains and voices now are not playing fair
The journey getting longer, slower, as the urge starts to
increase
Telling you it's now time for nature's release
You cross your legs, and start Praying Oh Please
Trying not to this of the situation
All kinds of thoughts and games to stop this emancipation
And the Transport finds every lump
You are now sweating at every jolting jump
Now the nagging drives you insane
From simple urge by now to that need to go pain
Guys think of elastic bands
And don't know what to do with their hands
God knows what you ladies do
We can all relate this thing we all have gone through
Finally, you reach you journeys goal
You rush headlong and desperate to that porcelain hole
And there's the sigh of a long agonising, reliving waterfall
And ridding of that nagging voice of natures call
Of the never-ending eternal pee
That satisfied look of heavenly glee

MY PET DOBERMANS

My Doberman pets that sit by my feet
Large muscular slender and neat
One with a shiny coat of black and tan
Misty she's my number one fan
Loyal obedient to a point
She obeys commands to a soft and gentle voice
Smart but a comic with her antics in mind
She's the leader of the two you will find
She's the one who makes you laugh
The funniest by half
The other Doberman Dee-dee she's clever in many ways
All Fawn in colour the one that plays
Talks and answers in return
But she's not too quick to learn
A little gentler and not so rough
It's her sister Misty who is tough
Dobermans may look nasty and mean
But that's a rumour that's obscene
They are gentle and loving clowns
And good with infants to have around
As is said it's not the dog, it's the owner
And to do with the way they are treated more over
My girls as I call them to me are more than pets
Members of my family, I have no regrets
I treat them with respect, as they do in return
I think we all together we live and learn

MOTHER EARTH

*I don't know about you, but the state of our planet is what I
see*
*The rising damage to our precious Mother earth and nature
is so clearly*
The air full of oxides and fumes
And a break down in our protective Ozone layer Looms
A rise in Skin Cancer from our Sun
Those Harmful rays endangering the health of every one
All those toxic additives in our food we eat
All those Hormones and steroids in out meat
New epidemics to affect our food chain seem to arise
Seems that nature is taking revenge in my eyes
Areas of once fertile lands tuned in to desolate bowls
Dried up Oasis and watering holes
Mother Nature tries to repair
But she is losing the battle and no one will care
As global warming and polar caps melt
Rising sea levels and storms are felt
The warning given to mans down fall
Let this be a lesson to all
We've abused all resources they've been depleted and declined
*And our desperate search for other energies have now been
defined*
Ecology now affecting animals Habitats all around
Once abundant animals are losing their ground
*And those Creatures once plenty in common numbers and
vast*
Becoming extinct and now in the past
As forests are destroyed as they are slashed and burned
And nothing put back or given or even returned
And we done all this damage in the speck of time
Two hundred years from the industrial revolution line

And yet it took us over a million years to get there
And what does man really care?
All for Profit and gain, Money and Need
A wonderful legacy to our children indeed
And as Mans epitaph will read
We lost Mother Earth and humanity for profit and greed
Written By. Terry. J. Powell Ó 2002.

ME

Me a funny kind of Guy,
Sometimes funny, sometimes shy.
Loves to laugh to hide the cry,
It's the way I am.
And the reason why,
I have to try.
"

Always positive,
And never lie.
Forthcoming and honest,
Forward to apply.
A listener, a talker,
A laugher, a joker.
A sensitive guy,
And that's why,
I have to try.
"

I pick up the pieces,
And carry my strife.
Loads of friends,
But lonely in life.
I have to keep going,
I have to try.
"

Helping others to cope with life,
To hide my feelings.
To give them time,
And that's the reason.
I have to try.
"

Me a funny kind of guy.

PRAYER

If you hear me lord
Look down on me again
Give me ease from pain
Make my way clear and true
For I lord love you
And all those around me be my crutch
I love them all very much
And if I heal it's you, I can thank
And if you decide to call me at your flank
I will be there, by your side
I have been good I can confide
So, I leave my life in your hands
For you to decide if it demands
For lord I love you
And I will be true
Oh, my lord it's up to you

LOCKED AWAY

Why do some just sit and waste away
Just to struggle through another day
Lost inside, to make existence roll
Only part of them selves, to make them whole
To lock away of what's inside
Quiet happy to be safe there, they reside
Wishing deep down inside they could be like others
Positive, adventurous, as in life discovers
The way they used to be
Bursting out, Being free
And yet they promise to themselves that things will change
Of the future things they would arrange
One of these things we, or they go through
But in truth really never do
Time to find that key
To open that prison door, as many would agree
One large stride for a sole to save
One large step to be brave
A walk, a run, to join in the race
Once again to be part of the chase
Again to be in the flow
And feel part of what they all know

JUST A MAN

Why does my life fall apart?
In the end suffer a broken heart
Am I weak or just a man?
Getting by the only way I can
What can I say?
Each person has a better day
Then if this is a reason why
And if I just get by
I am just a man
Doing the best I can
Picking up the pieces
In the human species
And if I can succeed
And do the deed
Then I am just a man
Getting by the best I can
And at times I trip and fall
Or at times face the wall
Then I can say I have done it all
The Bell of the ball
Cause I am just a man
Doing the best I can
I am just a man

HUMOUR

I see most things as a Joke
I'm really that kind of bloke
It costs nothing for a smile to make
Laughing till your jaws break
A single smile is all it needs
To take away troubles' bad deeds
A laugh to forget
Just for a few seconds of no regret
To have that beaming smile on your face
Is not really any disgrace
Go On, Laugh
Don't do it by half
Go On Laugh and take it all the way
And you will really find it helps your day
Don't be the one who smiles when you break wind
Otherwise, that bad attitude will be binned
If you can smile when troubles bear
Then really you are the greater person with care
Laughter, humour, and jokes depict
A temporary break that happiness does fix
Have a happy day folks
A sense of humour and lots of jokes

HEALTH

Disclaimer: this is not directed at any individual or at any group; this is just a concern of health

Is it me? Or are the people of the world getting fat?
Obesity is the number one killer, in the western world and that's a fact
Seventy percent of the population are over weight
Over size sixteen seems to be the accepted state
Whatever happened to healthy eating, keeping trim?
Taking pride in health and staying fit and slim
All gone out the window, for the sake of fast food
I'm sorry for saying this, please don't think me rude
I don't know about you, but I am concerned
This age of fast food, those calories can't be burned
Whatever happened to, two veg and meat
And just odd occasional sweet
Additives, (E) numbers, insecticides
All in the products the consumer buys
And now the new craze Governmental GM foods are used
More genetic profit making products to be abused
Well People it's your bodies, and your life's
On what your health derives
Your choice
Your voice
I say make the world a slimmer place
Make your children a healthier race
It's hard trying to lose weight
Look at me now I have the same fate

BROKEN DREAMS

Oh, those nights of many dreams, that takes you away
To lose all sense in non-realties realm of play
Walking in heavens loft
On open field and leafy croft
Sailing the seven seas
Feeling soft, warm and sensual breeze
Weathering the stormy weather
Being with that special person together
And the thousand symphonies sounding in your ears
All the wonders of the mind appears
Led to the rhythm of the chase
Parting feverishly from dangers pace
The winner that broke the bank
From the finest casino of its rank
Resting on the golden sea breeze shore
Or under Coral Sea and on sandy floor
Oh, those many situations that seems real
Dreams and emotions that you feel
Then to wake up in the hard reality, and watch them fade away
Those Broken dreams of the day

BIRTHDAY

You know when it's your birthday You get a golden Zimmer frame
And as Andy Warhol says, is the only time you get your
15 minutes of fame
You're the poet that as time passed, you seem to know it
In the scribbled writing you seem to show it
Another year and another day
Seems to be the slowing every way
And what took all night to do
Takes you all night to get through
So, Fact, in fact
I notice your poetry work shop each week becomes more packed
So now its golden Zimmer frame time
And for the bus pass you have to stand in line
You drink more beer and wine
And still end up sober and feeling fine
Well time waits for no man
But you at the age of a lovely span
Happy birthday just for you
And I hope you have a good day too
Written for a fellow poet

BIRTHDAY GREETINGS

Happy birthday and I hope you have many more to go
Now your way past the big 40
All those candles blazing in a row
Each year gets harder and harder to blow
You would think it's now a bonfire show
I hope the fire brigade aint too slow
Well Happy birthday tidings as you well know
Dear ___________, I love you so

ALL AND LED

You the argumentative type, that came to call
I think you got a lot of gall
As you tried to make my good name fall
And there you stood, feeling tall
Of my unknown fate you brought befall
I was not amused by it at all
As a matter of fact I was appalled
Felt trapped, as I crawled
As you stood there and bawled
My past, through it you trawled
I felt abused, and mauled
Not a nice situation, as I recalled
You thought I was easily led
As you stood there and watched me bled
As I stood there and stalled
I wish now you never called

A MESSAGE

There's a traitor in our camp
He, with black hair and dark eyes
As he masquerades as a loyal citizen
His eyes fixed on the prize
The only goal to posses it
In the name of what he worships
He is biding his time
Time is what he has
Secret meetings hidden in his religion
As he plots and schemes
Revenge for the old days as is secretly said
Chipping away slowly as not to draw attention
Bleeding recourses and weakening from within
And if caught feigning Innocence
He's clever hiding amongst his own
Waiting for his target, the prize a lion
He and his kind have tested the eagle
He waits in the shadows
He holds on his face a smile
Behind his back he holds a knife
His roots abused, drained, and spent
AS he looks to the promise land
All eyes look to the prize
Greedily fixed, possessively motivated
Slowly growing in strength
Keeping to the prizes system
As not to be noticed
Until the time to take that prize
Until then Birmingham and Leicester remain silent
Beware look for the signs they are there
Politicians stupidly hide
They are afraid, ignorance is bliss

All for the need of cheap labour
The underdog will rise up and bite its master
They were warned years ago
And what of the one who warned
He was classed as insane and cast out
He made waves for those who had comfortable lives
So beware there's a traitor in our camp

Disclaimer: They who feel they are the accused will be the ones who are shouting the loudest and protesting the hardest, it is like one of many honest opinions that others cannot say because of being accused of racism. Being afraid of the truth can be extremely traumatic for those hiding the truth.

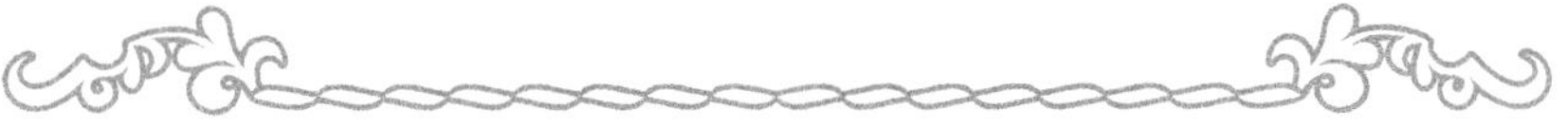

A BARE CHRISTMAS

Christmas is coming and the cupboard is looking bare
For those on State benefits, there isn't any money to spare
It's a scary time for those, and money is tight
As most on benefits lay worrying many a night
Spare a thought for those pensioners, and ones who are alone
It's the loneliest time of the year for those who are on their own
Single parents, they try to make ends meet
Christmas morning is their final defeat
The embarrassment of not being able to give a present
Fills one with self hate, guilt, and a self resent
To all those who are poor and really have no choice
The people living off the state those who have no esteem, no voice
To someone in this position it's the most dreaded time of the year
Not being able to afford, or spread Christmas cheer
I know that most others would say get a Job
But circumstances for those on benefit are not any sponging yob
Pensioners, Single parents, Incapacitated, and who suffer with Disable
Would love to earn a decent wage if they were really able
The only person who could really understand this situation is one who has been there
Those are the people who can understand the hardship and are aware
Any way People I wish you all
A very merry Christmas when it comes to call
Just spare a thought
Christmas is for giving, the way it should be ought
Not receiving
But true Christian believing

XMAS ON THE WAY

The month of Christmas on the way
Those build ups, for that special day
All those repeats of the Christmas special shows
And scenic views of glistening snows
Leftover turkey on the plate
Burnt and cindered pudding in a state
Christmas carol and Scrooge featured on the box (TV)
And packs of silly Christmas socks
Relatives and friends round the table stuffed to the brim
As the drink flows, and good cheer does swim
The children with new toys, excitedly play
Piles of cardboard and wrappings, ready to be thrown away
Washing up piled on a devastated sink
Bath oils and aftershave, give out an odorous stink
Holly hanging on the door
Granny tipsy, passed out on the floor
And Father snoring in the chair
Now he's stuffed with Christmas fare
Children run around in an exciting din
The cat that's digging in the rubbish bin
The Queens speech
And chocolates and treats in easy reach
Nativity plays as the vicar does preach
Second and third helpings from the leftovers from the
Christmas feast
All this for just one day
Christmas is definitely on the way

WHO?

The beckoning of war bids
I feel sorry for the women and kids
Who is the eye behind the rifle sight?
Who presses the button to put missiles into flight?
Who burdens the guilt for lives taking?
Who holds the consequences for misery making?
Who has that right and power?
To make the nameless cower
Who will be the victims to die?
Who will break their hearts and cry?
Who will be the families to be mourned?
As another day of war is dawned
Who will mend the injured and the sick?
Who will take the lives, they pick?
Who will mend broken memories left behind?
Who will give sight for those who are blind?
Lands and buildings we can replace
But not those lost, behind a name and face

THE WEB

Oh, what splendored web you weave
Intricate of design you precisive
Silk of splendour in glistening in morning dew
Encrusted by gems of each day new
Soft but delicate, but deceivingly strong
Always perfect but never wrong
....
Like vail of sail wafting in the breeze,
Crisp, white, and crystallised in winter freeze
Soft and pleasing to the eye
Made to trap morsels passing by
Of insects of all kinds of insects that come to rest
On time and energy, you invest
....
A home, a source of food,
A nursery for tender brood
Who could imagine a web with so much use
The many tasks to produce
A web for one spider in the 4seasons of man
From beginning to end of a short life span
The architect of each one's design
of gentle threads that entwine
A lace of webbing of yours not mine

VALENTINES

If I had a valentine to send on Valentine's Day
These are the words I'd write, send, and say
Thank you for the love we shared
Those soft emotions you showed and cared
Moments when we kissed away each other's tears
Shared each other's strengths and fears
Those tender moments we spent together
Wanting those brief moments to last forever
The up and downs together we faced
Our Loyalties well placed
Times we briefly spent apart
As they gently broke our hearts
Rushing back to greet
Hearts racing as we meet
With long and tender kiss
Holding each other as we did miss
Those words expressing true meaning
"I love you darling" quiet revealing
All those sorrys for the wrongs I may have done
If I have at any time, sorry It can't have been any fun
Times of happiness as we did laugh
Those good times we had by half
I am so wonderfully happy you are here
I couldn't ask for someone to better to be near
I hope our love will never change and will be for life
As we hold each other's tender hearts through thick or thin
through Bliss or strife
Those would be the words I would send
Happy Valentines to you all, The End

UNWELL

Here again I cough and sneeze
Running hot then cold, I tend to freeze
I shiver and I'm weak
And with this sore throat, I find it hard to speak
my aching bones
my head banging, and joints that groans
Runny eyes, as I shed more than a tear
Boxes of hankies kept very near
With this virus, there's nothing I can do
I guess once more, I've got the flu

TWO CANDLES

Two candles burn in the night
One, the newer, burns bright
The other, the older, burns a duller light
Each at its own height
One gives off a shinning glow
While the other, burns dimmer low
Neither can equally, never
One flame cannot last forever
Each does an individual dance
Time misses a past chance
Both a different thing they do
Flickers of a separate two
Not synchronised together
Each a moment of the measure
One wears a crystal glint
The other wears a tarnished tint
Each competing
Glances fleeting
Yet they burn on
Till the older candles dies and gone
As the remainder burns a light to show the way
Shines a light though night and day

TWISTED THOUGHTS

does death make me want to sleep
Do I cry or do I weep?
Or does inside of me scream?
In this never-ending living dream
My agonised sole is burning
But time and the world keep on turning
In my mind comes the constant yearning
Of past thoughts that keep returning
How can I keep suffering this fate?
As nagging thoughts turn to hate
I struggle as my insides writhe
In the search for lifting blithe
I try hard to resist
Getting by to just exist
And to rest, but have to try
No time to give up and just die
To rise about this internal battle
That monster I have to tackle
Long away from Harm
To mental peace and calm
And oh, that sombre rest
To familiar surroundings I like best

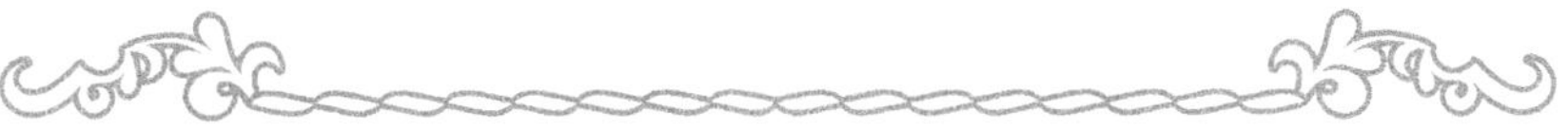

TRUST

You told me you loved me, I was deceived
And it was the one forever, and I believed
Promising we would be always be together
For the rest of our lives forever
I would be the only one
But those days I guess, moved swiftly on
I know how really hard I tried
But you were the one who hurt my pride
Telling me it's over, as you hid behind a phone
No excuse, no reason, Left all alone
I feel unwanted and that's the point
Our bonding broken like a damaged joint
Three years I had to mend
And at times drove me round the bend
But I'm building trust
For a heart that was really bust
The damage you have done
Only you know, and you alone, know it can't be fun
Even now I feel so insecure and unsafe to get involved
Until I learn for this problem to be resolved
Even to the stage of someone being interested
And ignore the feelings of a woman invested
That's what I think now that no one wants me
It's the way I feel you see
And that's what you have done
I'm distant to everyone
No involvement no hurt
Makes me a realist, and not someone inert

TRIBUTE TO THE INNOCENT

Today innocent lives have paid
Of political games that are played
While Violence used by extremists' groups
Used to involve bystanders in this so-called coupe
Maiming and injuring to make a point
Instead of working for peace in Joint
Devastation, Destruction, they use to sell their needs
Aimed at the innocent this group feeds
Well People of America you be strong
All the world stands at your side along
How can people use tactics to do this to all
Now they have created their own downfall
To all those poor victims involved
May GOD smile on you and take you in his fold
And those perpetrators may they rot in hell
And all those innocents God treat well
Unnecessary I, like you think
Using those underhanded tactics stink
My and your prayers go out to all the victims caught in all this
Heartfelt sorrow, sadness, and tears for all you will not be forgotten, but you all will be missed

TRANSPORTED

In the town of Leicester, in 1793
At a time of poor living and poverty
The poor lad stood in the dock
Confused, uneducated, and in fear and shock
My Lord said M'lad tis you sentenced to the end of a rope
May the lord have mercy, abandon all hope
But as a boy and poor you have no voice
I as lord justice will make a goodly choice
As your boys of 12 years old, tis a pity to rob you of your youth
For stealing a loaf of bread, that we have the proof
Transportation is the sentence I commit
For the rest of your life, there will be no remit
Away we go M'lads across the sea
On a three-year journey we will be
And times be hard but we be free
From our mother home we'll never see
Thomas Langley waves to the shore
Will never see his mother, Father, and family ever more
To a new land and life of what's held in store
In a human cargo, sent to Australia by the law
Never to return
In a new nation that will grow and lean

TORMENTED HEARTS

If tormented hearts and soles break
And suffer in mistake
Up one minute, then down and torn
Like this from the day you were born
Some times confused, not knowing right from wrong
Just glad in a way to get along
Searching for a tiny Niche
Bouncing along with out a hitch
But some times dropping low
Up and down it does go
In the usual struggle for the fight
Looking for a small glimmer of light
The yearning for what we all believe is true
Or is it just a phase we all go through
Never knowing whether we will mend
As heart is beating right till the end
And do we justify the cause
Or do we take a break to stop and pause
On that continuation to try
Right up till the day we die
Something we could never comprehend
We'll just have to pretend

THE WISE

Listen to the word of the old, and wise
They have experienced life, through their eyes
Seen it all, many, many times before
Holding memories, both good and bad in store
One single word can tell a tale
Of what they have had to prevail
And yet, we still don't listen of what's been told
Like stories of old
And still, we make those mistakes
The burden of Punishment that breaks
To proud to bow
And wondering, why and how
And using others to blame
When troubles take an aim
So, hear the words of the wise
They have seen life through mature eyes

THE TOY BOX

A little one legged soldier leant in the corner of the box
Talking to the worn face of a fluffy fox
The three legged donkey stumbled to and fro
As the doll with the broken eye asked "where do all the broken toys go?"
I've no idea said the action man with one arm
Maybe they go to a special hospital away from harm
Said the bear with the missing nose
Well said Barbie I can't find my missing clothes
They must be amongst these bits and bobs at the bottom of this box
Among these old jigsaw pieces and discarded building blocks
Said the jack in the box who has a broken spring
And the old Buzz light year held together with string
Funny said the three wheeled car
How those humans are
When new, they play with us for ages and never put us down
But when they are carless with us, drop and break us they leave us on the ground
I do remember said the Game Boy with the cracked screen
Those grown up humans pick the broken toys up and put them in a black bag, This I've seen
But after that I have no idea
They never come back said raggy doll that's what it would appear
Seems some don't have any care for us toys or appreciation
Said the clown with the big red nose and the missing carnation

THE MOTH

Oh tender moth how you fly
In the twig light of the sky
Flying round and round
Above a distance of the ground
Attracted to the lamp or light
Shinning in the darkest night
Is it light or is it heat?
That makes you determined to meet
Your delicate wings pulse to a beat
Your determination makes no defeat
And yet no matter how you try
In the end you get burnt and die
Sad what nature does intend
The way you life seems to end
Oh tender moth how you fly
In the twilight of the sky

THE HAND

A cruel and bitter hand
Casts its shadow across the land
It rules with no compassion
To a fanatical and merciless fashion
Its spreads propaganda and hate
False misgivings it does propagate
With one swift wave it causes mass extermination
Kills without hesitation
Tyranny is its defence
There is no recompense
Behind the face lays a sadistic smile
Evil deeds and thoughts it does compile
Power is its hungry greed
For one so veracious indeed
There's no room in its heart for guilt
Political games and mockery is built
Holding the world to random
And the pleasure of the game seems handsome
Fear makes his tin pot generals quake
For the scape-goat to make a mistake
And in turn the soldiers under his firm hand obey
As the minions are forces to pray
Weapons, hidden of mass destruction
Waiting for this insane leaders instruction
This person you ask? Who is insane?
There's only one, Saddam Hussein

THE CONTRACT

I thought when bosses hired you for a Skill, that they didn't
own you
    Read the small print on this contract through
    I expect you as an employee, to work body and soul each day
    to earn the highest profit, in my pocket that will pay
    I own your life outside the work place
    Early to bed and early to rise, so you can handle the pace
    No social life, no drinking
    Fresh each day for profit making, I want you thinking
    I want you to stop smoking
    No fun at work and no joking
    Sexual cohabitation is only allowed on Saturday
    to rest up on Sundays, be fresh and rearing to go on Monday
    All these things you need to know
    Sign on the dotted line below
    And when you all worn out, I will sack you in style
    To be thrown out on the reject pile
    While I live in style and the comfort you have made
    Knowing that your hard work has paid

THE AD

I am putting in this Ad
Someone wanted to take, this late 1950s model in hand
A late model but not a vintage type
Needs regular servicing and some amount of hype
A good runner under the hood, sturdy and reliable
Quite adaptive and fairly pliable
Loyal and trustworthy
Some times witty and a little wordy
I have done quite a few miles on my clock but still got room
for more
As you'll be surprised how far I can go and what I have in store
My engine is so young at heart can go as far as required
And I'm very easy to start and active once fired
Not a racing model more like a saloon car
Nothing fancy, just slightly tarnished star
Paint work is nice and clean
Bodywork still trim and lean
Tires have good tread
Sturdy engine with a good head
I need someone caring
To polish those places wearing
Someone not too eager to over accelerate
But not keep a foot on the break just to keep me at a steady rate
I have stood under a dust sheet for 13 months with my for-
sale sign
I suppose it must slightly off-putting by the line of my design
I look a little worn and used
And have been slightly abused
But if someone gives me TLC (tender loving care)
There's always room for improvement somewhere
I'm sure I'd offer many years of pleasure
Some Love, Fun, and Happy times of leisure

Treat me gently with respect
And I'll give you more in return I expect
I can't always promise a smooth and comfortable ride but I will do my best
It all depends on who and how much they want to invest
if you're tired of those sporty types who leave you far behind
Those super flashy models that sweep you off your feet you'll find
Then dump you in the middle of nowhere in some dark wood
Then find another driver to make themselves look good
Then I'll be here If you decide that is not the car for you
And you got better things to do
If you want a more reliable model that's easy to keep and run
And you will have a trustworthy model here, for loyalty, life, and fun
No time wasters as the ad will say
You can come for a test run, anytime of day

A TEAR

A single tear drops cascades
From a glassy eye that displays
One single pearl roll's down the cheek
As inner emotions reach a peak
The light makes it glisten and gleam
Crisp, Transparent, sterile, and clean
A prism of rainbow colours reflects
Of warm solution the eye rejects
Softly it ascends on a downward trace
Mapped on contours of the face
Always on a downward flow's
The direction a tear falls always goes

SNATCHED AWAY

*When something comes into your life and makes you happy
as life could
     And there for once inside you feel rather good
     And you think "YES!" This is what I've searched for
     Over the moon, you can't ask for more
     It took a long time in the search to find
     Of what you want to hold on to, and not leave behind
     To find that someone special that really seems to care
     That makes your life worth living and able to bear
     The one you need to trust
     As you think they would give their all or bust
     Gently as you drift in to a loss of reality
     Of that persons kindness and hospitality
     Prepared to sacrifice all
     But unknown to you, you're heading for a fall
     Happiness snatched away
     Dropped like a hot stone, and heading to dismay
     Left behind to pick up the pieces
     Feeling like a piece of human faeces
     As is proved you were never compatible, but you tried
     Once again you feel cheated and broken, and you cried
     Wondering what's really so wrong again, as your rejected
     Once again you heart has been ejected
     And yet, you pick up those pieces and carry on
     As you face another situation that's has been and gone*

RUBY

It seems that through life's events and fate
Life brought our paths together, we did not anticipate
Your heart smarts from your last romance
Seems someone destroyed your chance
Devastated and in tears its hard
Destiny played that card
Well I hope I've lifted you pain
Set you on your feet again
That I have softened that blow
And stopped you feeling so low
And you are strong enough to walk that course
Gave you the will and force
And you carry that personal aftermath
So you can walk that path
One day I hope we will meet
And you will not give in to defeat
As for me all I can do is accept
Me being resilient and adept
Whatever the outcome in the end
I will be here your loving friend

PUPPIES

Little puppies small and sweet
Unsteady, slightly stumbling on their feet
Coats so soft and dowdy and incomplete
Always playing, wagging tails to greet
Big eyes that make your heart melt
Innocence of a child, and still in whelp
Antics they get into, funny things that they do
Daily learning, they go through
Naughty Puppy peeing there
Of natural motions they are un a were
Anything that they can chew
It may be something personal to you
It's just their way of getting closer to
They don't understand wrong or right
Sometimes tries your patience it might
But as they grow a personality does arise
As they grow and develop before your eyes
Mans or woman's best friend
They always get there in the end
Try to respect them, be patient and kind
They will treat you the same as you will find
A member of your family they will become
Loving, affectionate, and lots of fun
Sensing emotions that you emit
Being there and doing their comforting bit
As the saying goes, they are for life
They need you there please don't give them strife
Enjoy them, watch them, love them, be as one with them as
they really care
Regardless of anything they will be there

CONTENTS

POLITICS

Isn't it a dirty business, politics?
Those who make empty promises, they know they cannot fix
Instead they spend time to dig out the sleaze
Bring those who oppose them to their knees
It's a really dirty game to shame
Digging up the dirt is their aim
Stabbing those in the back, as they stand in front of you and smile
Making you think you're all safe for a while
These people take the affairs of our countries in their hands
While those, who are grovelling sheep follow their demands
Who is running who?
Isn't it time you knew?
Wasn't the government for the people's wishes?
Looks like we ended up washing those politicians dirty dishes
We work for the People; on us it's been engraved
But really we have become enslaved
All those mistakes covered up and hidden
And those who stand in their way, got ridden
Or personal details leaked out to the press
As those who are victims torn apart by the media, no less
Who is the scape goat to take the blame?
Because politics is a dirty game
Now I've quoted this, if anything happens or I disappear?
Then all this, to you all will become clear
I wrote this when i was a member of a 3D chatroom

PASS THE BLAME

You can't run, and you hide
Because someone's hurt your pride
Accusing others in your reside
It's never the fault of what you do
It's others who suffer your blame, and what you put them through
Where is the incriminating whispers and gamma that I could use?
Where are the insults and indignant, I could abuse
I wouldn't sink that low
From all the accusations and the games you throw
I don't need to put any one down
I feel as if I have nothing I need to prove, to anyone
After all what's done is done
Keep the games going?
By using all personal things of others, you are showing
In the end it will bring you down, and make you fall
Truth will come to a loud resounding call
So my confused, illusive friend
When will you let it end?

OH THE FEELINGS

Oh the feelings that make you fall apart
That seems to test you tender heart
Confusions running through your brain
Mind numbed with gentle pain
All Jumbled up inside
As mixed emotions ride
And the heart flutters
To orated nervous stutters
And pulses race
To a flushed and reddened face
And the only word that seems to fit, like a glove
Is the word LOVE

THE END OF A YEAR

As the old year draws to a close
Looking back at those days of problems posed
Those trial and tribulations thrown at every individual one
Success of those trying days, that's gone
Times of happiness, magical, or sad
Some of the best or worse times ever had
Those days that brought tears
And the facing days of inner fears
Days of illness or good health
Poor times, with the odd pockets of wealth
Moments of love and joy
The use of stealth and ploy
All those 365 days have passed and gone
And yet another day moving on
Another day and another year
On our doorsteps very near
Let's see what next year brings
I hope you all have happiness and good luck in all things
May you all prosper in all what you do?
And hope that success comes to all of you
Well, we will just have to see
All the best from me

MY FATHER

father those times we reminisced
About the times we spent or missed
Spending those moments together
Father and son forever
Times you were my hero
When you watched me grow
Passing on your knowledge and advice
And helped me through difficult times to suffice
You were there when needed
Listened and heeded
How I looked up to you
In all the things you did do
Who would have thought our time together?
Was short and not would be forever
Life passed swiftly by
I now, left behind to cry
Now that you have passed on
You left behind a grieving son
I will always think of you while my sole survives
To remember all about our lives
Our special times spent together
Father and Son forever

MUSIC

How can we put the rhythm of music into word?
Sounds put into describing, what you've heard
Those sound bouncing in your ears
Tempo, rhythm, word and rhyme that one hears
Heavy rock to purge the soul
Exciting, rhythmic, as the beat loud and whole
Acid house to garage beat
That makes you dance intensely of your feet
Classical takes you away to another place
Slowing you down to gentler pace
Rock and Roll that's the one that makes you swing
Jumping and jiving makes you do your thing
Reggie that West Indian rhythm and blues
Sings of slavery and going back to their roots
Soul that feeling of slight sadness of love
Sung with emotions form heaven above
Country and western with its lively spring
As those Cowboys and Cowgirls with a twang they sing
Jazz that uniform sound
They play it as is called underground
And then there Ballads, melancholy to make you dream
As you drift off to romantic scene
All the different sorts' lyrics we address
Are all related to one thing no less
They all have one meaning to each role it plays
To touch our emotions in different ways
Music written on a page for all time
From the first to the last line
To affect us in the life and the way we live
From personal experiences those artists give
From the first to the last
Both in the future to the past

A poem, a verse, and written song
Ever short or ever long
Now a part of history for ever more
Those words of music written on a score

MENOPAUSE

Disclaimer: I don't intend to offend any parties concerned, just trying to lighten what is normally classed as Taboo.

There isn't a get out clause
In the contract of the one you love, when in menopause
And Guys isn't it frustrating
When the one you love is menstruating
Hormones up and down, and raging
The Danger of the word PMT is paging
And in the bathroom packs of many strange things
Tiny little hammock thingies, and cotton wool bullets with strings
All shapes and sizes, colours and sticky bits, even some with smiley faces
All manner of things, to stick in strange places
A BIG BADGE comes free with every purchase, neatly packed
Just to advertise the fact
"I'm a Lil-Latté girl and very proud"
To show off amongst the busy crowd
And yet GUYS we know what pain inside makes them want to die
No wonder they scream, shout, and cry
And YES, they say with great demand
You're a man you don't understand
No matter what GUYS you still got to love me
Little darlings, little gem
And YES Ladies, understand, we do
Diplomats for piece, is what we go through
Three more weeks at best
It's time to make the moment and rest

LONELY HEARTS

Here I sit by my charismas tree
Longing for someone to be with me
Thinking of past partners and lovers
Those happy times spent with others
This my second noel alone
Lonely hearts for Christmas being on my own
So here I sit and after all maybe it's the best way to be
Saves me being hurt again you see
What really does sadden me is those in the same position
You all out there get my hopes and recognition
Maybe next year will pick up for us all
Maybe that someone special will knock your door and call
That special person to make you Christmas complete
Someone to knock you off your feet
Well, another year for me now
And I have healed and How
Well like others I hope you all see it through
No more lonely hearts for Christmas especially for me and you

KITTEN

Tiny little kitten how small and sweet you are
Wide innocent bright eyes, you melt our eyes by far
Watching you while you romp and play
Stalking and pouncing is your learning way
Tiny claws and needle teeth that grip and chew
Makes us laugh by the things you do
Everything to you is a new adventure
Lively you jump into every exciting venture
Miniature paws you tap and swipe
As you run wildly about in your usual hype
Then when tired you curl up into a tiny ball
Fast asleep and ignoring all
When you hear the sound of food being served
You rub yourself against ankles unreserved
As you tiny meows and purrs make us heed
To make us known your hungry and need to feed
Watching you grow every day
Means you will be exactly like your parents in every way
Oh you tiny delicate ball of fur
Wonderful when stroked to hear your purr
How your looks and antics really do appeal
We love to hold you and this is how we feel
Our bonding to you as we watch you grow
To an adult cat is what we know

TWO TINY BUDS

*This poem is dedicated to the sad loss of Jessica Wells and
Holly Chapman*

In the field of flowers seedlings grow
Young and developing so
Leaves of the older flowers protected them from the sun
Loved and neutered until each day was done
Supplying all to those dependant needs
Helping them grow by doing parental deeds
Them, tiny and perfect and yet to live
As any loving parent would give
Tiny blooms that grow and made
Each new day the sun in the sky was laid
Those tiny buds unopened and small
Not ready to open yet at all
*The cruel hand that plucked away those buds, and made
them died*
The whole community of the field of flowers, wept and cried
Tarnished and ruined, delicate petals lay in the hand
Left to be blown and scattered across the land
Picked for no purpose at all
And those petals were left where they fall
*But flowers are always remembered for their beauty and
always set in mind*
The wonderful smell of perfume left behind to remind
To hold such beauty is no regret
Always to be remembered and not forgotten is a bet
And in the brief moment they did live
For the wonderful moments in their life did give
These things will stay forever in our memory of those times
Not ever to be forgotten in our minds

I WISH

If wishes were given to me
I would wish for us to never part
I would wish for you to hold my heart
As I would hold yours too
I would wish for you to be happy
And we would stand together
Forever no matter what we do
I would wish our love to be ignited
A flame of passion that would always burn
I would wish for your passion in return
I would wish you would always be the same
And never change
All these wishes and more
But I would want nothing in return
I would wish you just you the way you are
And as for wishes, why would I need to wish?
When I have you here with me, all my wishes have come true
Now I'm here with you

HOW DO I FEEL?

I sit alone here at night
Lost in a world full of fear and fright
I used to have a purpose in life to abide
A love, a reason
Waking up was once, by your side
And all my love I had to give and show
Where I went wrong, I do not know
I wanted us to be together for life
You for me, the wanted wife
Now cast me out without a word
The nasty rumours that I have heard

.....
And you ask me how I feel?

.....
Thanks for making me insecure
But I am now working on a cure
Thanks for changing my life
Filling it full of hurt, confusion, and strife
But I am on the mend
At least it's just myself that I can depend

......
And still, you ask me how I feel?

......
I don't think it's any of your concern
In life we tend to live and learn
The web of lies you had built
Just to hide your actions, and justify your guilt

....
So, ask me how I feel
Now to your conscious does it now appeal?

A HAPPY CHRISTMAS

December brings thoughts of Christmas
Roast golden turkey and chestnut stuffing
Christmas pudding topped with creamy white fluffing
Presents given on Christmas morn
The day that Christ was born
White snow of Christmas scene
And a reminder of what the old years been
Children's faces lit with excited smiles
Open presents and Christmas paper piles
Crackers pulled with a loud crack
Love and greetings given back
Tinsel and lights on decorated spruce pines
Trimmings and decorations hung in lines
Cheese and old port wine
Feast and fare that's Oh so fine
The one day of strife and problems put to one side
All feelings of malice and ill feelings kept inside
One day of peace on earth
Happy laughter, fun, glee, and mirth
Christmas day a day for giving
The one day of the year worth living
May you all have a wonderful New Year's Day
This message I say to you all I pray
Peace, love, and good will to all mankind
These are the thoughts that come to mind

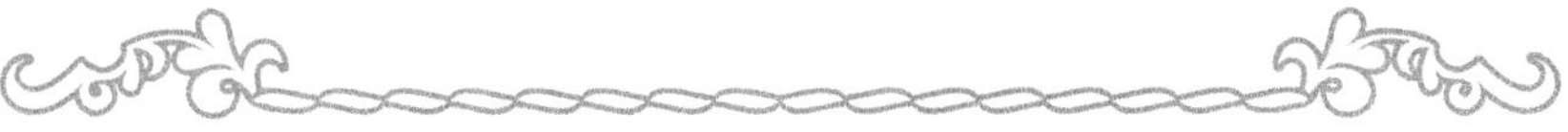

DISABLED

The difference to you and I, we fit and abled
But its hard work for those who are disabled
Disability and infliction of constant pain
Would drive a person insane
After all they have the normal mind of a human being
Despite what's on the outside seen
They like us are a person, clever and out going
With a sense of humour glowing
All they ask for is acceptance
In the normal structure of life's expectance
There's something I have to admire
The way they excel and aspire
Drive to set soles on fire
No sympathy, just acceptance and desire
After all they work harder than most do
For the normal things we take for granted
They just get on, and work harder for the things they wanted
Frustration, trapped in a body that doesn't work
And ridicule of some unsympathetic jerk
That's all to lack of that persons understanding
They could never know to a disabled person, how life is so
demanding
Courtesy and understanding is the only way
To be treated as a normal person would help them get through
their day
Respect for them no matter how different they appear
They have as much right to life as any one here

DENIED LOVE

I met a special lady on a chartroom line
She was fraught with pain of life; I thought I'd give her time
I patiently listened and heard her cries of plea
Thinking she's the one for me
But conflicts of her own culture and hurt by one she once revered and had
Had given her insecurity and had slightly driven her to anger and made her mad
That pain she carries is the price I helped to bear
Showing her that there is kindness and honesty in the world some where
How I share her pain of sadness and woe
I long to give her affection so
To kiss away her broken tears and show her there is one who cares
That there is someone Honest and truthful who fares
My rugged looks tend to deceive the eye
But like most it's what's inside from one who doesn't lie
I know in my heart of hearts that this is one I could never have to hold
As this person has been spurned and her love has left her cold
Still, this is my price
From a guy who's been constantly told by others I am too nice
As I'm told I'm a giver not a taker
A healer not a hater, a creator and a maker
A guy with good humour and laughter I hold
Some one who's got a heart of gold?
A person of certain morals that I have give
Giving honour and courtesy is my way to live
That's my station in life I guess, this makes my heart breech
For the one you really want, is too far out of reach
You can't always have love in your life it seems to me
And maybe to stay single is my destiny

DECEIVED

What is this turmoil all about?
Left behind confused, hurt, and full of doubt
The broken promises you made
The empty plans you laid
You used me for your games of mental play
I really didn't think you would be this way
You absolutely pulled the wool over my eyes
As you betrayed me with deceit and lies
I truly loved you and honestly believed
The clever way you manipulated me and deceived
I fell for you with all my heart
For ever you said "we will never part"
I gave up and sacrificed all I had to be with you
Now you have no idea what you've put me through
You took advantage of my good nature
I thought you were more mature
You will never whiteness the damage you have left behind
That looks in my children's eyes always in my mind
How could you? I trusted you so much
You with your persuasive voice and tender touch
All those letters, cards, and flowers you sent
Those gifts and jewels from your heart, was they Meant?
Were they really to bide you sometime
Or just another ploy to undermine
All those promises to my children and me you broke
Not the actions of an honest Bloke
Only to find you replaced me with another
While you kept me hanging on as the other lover
All a sham you were to me
And how stupid and gullible I must have been

BELIEF

Each religion from each race
Each belief in a different face
Each growing in a separate pace
Each worshipped in a different place
Each falling from grace
Each held in its own embrace
All fanatics in their own belief
All creating misery and grief
All for murder swift and brief
All taking like a thief
All headed by a chief
All expecting no relief
One of its own perfection
One in its own conception
One of its own protection
One of growing conception
One breeding its own reflection
One with its own preconception
The need of will
The deed to kill
The name of religion to fulfil
The turning of that treadmill
The climbing of that hill
The burning of soles on a grill

THE BATTLE

As our guys and the guys of the USA have gone to war I wrote this poem

Now our young brave Soldiers go to the battle, we fly our Union jack

Fighting tyranny, US soldiers with us at our back

UN, American, British, and others too, Fight for our Freedom as well

Taking those who oppose us and sending them to hell

As common cause brings us together

We bear our Arms to face the stormy weather

To seek out and the grasp of a modern HITLER, BINLADEN is our goal

And he the Coward hiding like a frightened sewer rat in his little hole

He now sends others, innocents, to death for his own means

As he the way he uses other Human beings.

We are coming BINLADEN there's nowhere to run and Hide

You Pray to your GOD for mercy you'll Need it I can confide

As you will never go to heaven

Hell holds a place for you

Because we will WIN that we can rest assured too

WE ARE COMMING, BE SCARED, RUN, and HIDE, we will get you in the end

As our boys and one of many others ARE COMMING for you, that you can depend

And you BINLADEN in the end you'll pay

But not on just here on earth, but in Hell I can truly say

So, Boys May GOD and Justice Make you win the battle there

As a just saying goes "He who wins dares"

As today is a sad day on the carnage in America I wrote this to tell the people they are not alone

Today the 11th of September
This day we will always remember
The children of America Injured and maimed
Injustice at all, at those innocents aimed
MOTHERS we shed a tear
FATHERS our arms are around you, we are near
SONS and DAUGHTERS, we hold you tight
To protect you this day this night
GRAND PARENTS it's you that has to be strong
To help rebuild lives and help your families get along
GOD will hold those innocents involved
He will love and take those he holds
WE holding hands all over the world as one together
Our hearts and feelings at these events forever
A tear falls down one individual's face
But we cry as well, the entire human race
Well sons and daughters of America
Stand strong and we will stand by your side along
Hands are joined all over the world and hold you dear
We have your sadness in our hearts it would appear
Your grief is understood
As we feel, ourselves as part of the human brotherhood
We hold our tears for you and cry
To carry the grief in our hearts for you In America as we can only try
That's all I can say to you all

AGONISED

How agonising is the day
For those who lock themselves away
Those who are scared
Who don't want feelings and time-shared
To close that front door, and leave it all behind
As each new morning comes the bind
How the lonely soul little by little dies
All to hide from mistrust and lies
Too scared to trust happiness
To let an invitation or party pass
The Human sole a sensitive part
For those who suffer with a broken heart
One step forward and two steps back
Forwardness is something that is slack
How hard it is to trust
It's better to be safe, than have a heart bust
It all becomes a muddle
In that daily struggle
Each new day a battle
Something new each day to tackle
How we wish someone could take the pain away
Just to fight and live another day

THE LETTER TO AN EX

I sit alone in this room writing you a letter
In the hope now your life is getting better
As a friend told me, that you let yourself go
For what reason I'll never know
The beautiful home that we both worked hard to complete
Is left ruined, declined and in defeat
You think your happy now?
But I wonder how?
And I'm sorry your feelings, ran high in you that way
Please believe me when I say
I know the guilt that you're hiding inside
And I know that your life is in downward slide
You think you're happy but, I know you're not
I may not be there, but I've not forgot
I hear the times of hardship that passes through your life
And you think you're happy, in your struggle through the strife
This new guy treats you like a fool
Some times he's hard and cruel
And he thinks you like this, that you seen to thrive
He thinks he keeps you alive
But I would have treated you better
That's why I write this letter
Don't be fooled that I want to come back to you
Because that's one thing I would never do
And I'm not doing this for any kind of return
I'm doing this out of sheer concern
It's just that you at one time, was so special in my heart
And this situation you're in, is tearing me apart
Good luck my ex-love, I hope you find your way
And in the future have just one small bit of true happiness
one day
And ok you chose your way in life and yet

I'm still the guy who can forgive and forget
I'll always remember those days
I wish you happiness in many ways
Give my good wishes to all the rest
All my Best. Terry.

WHISPERED ON THE WIND

Your name was whispered on the wind
It gently brushed my hair
Caressed my cheek
Softly touched my ear lobes
And echoed gently in my ears
It excited me
My heart picked up the pace
Adrenaline did with in me rise
I saw you're face
It was a moment captured
Trapped for ever in my mind
There is no release
Face and Name held
You reminded me of a lost youth
Those days
Now times have passed
I cannot hold you
I cannot have
But your name was whispered in the wind
You're face I saw
I can't be there any more
Forbidden is love

WHAT IF

What would the future bring?
If I could not sing
What if I could not dance?
Or take a chance in love or romance
See no works of art
Or if poetry has no heart
No TV
No PC
No creativity
No longevity
Not allowed to play and have fun
A sense of humour, that is over and done
And yet they are all part of giving
Makes one's life worth living
And if all these things are lost, what would we see
You might as well lock yourself away, and throw away the key
No stories to tell
Wouldn't that be hell?
So, let's keep our heritage in tact
To teach our children how to act
Teaching the value of these things
That fun, culture, and laughter brings
And our world will be a better place
To make our life's more enriched in the human race
Enjoy what life has to offer every day
To live life to the full in every way

WE DO NOT FORGET

After the 11th of September
Something history will never forget, and will always remember
The loss of all innocent soles was lost
At the hands of a fanatical mad man's cost
For some the pain too much to bear
Months of painstaking clearing from workers who care
The once Twin Towers of Americas pride
Lost now, where ground zero does reside
Finished at 10.29am on Wednesday the 29th of May
One solitary steel beam stands defiantly on display
A sign of resistance to all
Regardless of the fate that did befall
That beam standing to the last
Against all odds of this tragic past
A struggle to succeed to endeavour
That America and its people will stand for ever
An epitaph of sad regret
We will always remember, we do not forget

VISIT TO THE DENTIST

The dentist gave me a filling
When he started drilling
Before that, he gave me a shot
The drill inside my mouth was getting hot
And all manner of utensils hanging from my lower lip
Me now sweating, hoping he doesn't slip
Head now vibrating
As the drill is grating
Screeeeeeeeee goes the sound
As my heart starts to pound
And the pipe sucks all the time
Toothache was the crime
All the time I became a were
Me hanging on, and gripping the arms of the chair
Thinking at the time, it's just not fair
All I could do is sit and stare
Then the drilling ceased
Now the silence of the screaming beast
Porcelain or metal filling?
Anything to get it over, I am willing
Then the heater thingy stuck on the filled tooth
And the pink and rinse stuff
As I walked out, thinking it's not so bad
All over, relieved, and glad

TWO FLAGS

Oh, you banner of red white and blue
Two flags together steadfast and true
Nations together you fight and stand
Fighting hand in hand
Come on you glory boys
United in strengthened armies' ploys
As the battle inches forward
Never ceasing onward
Gathering the weaker crop
Pushed ahead and never stop
Reap the harvest sown
Cut down the tyranny that has grown
And strong in battle gave
Steadfast will never cave
Fight for determination
For the lesser nation
And don't stop for anyone
Till those oppressors are dead and gone
On Lads On, drive the enemy out
So, they would never return, without a doubt
The Eagle and the Lion stalk
There is no time to waste on talk
And sadly, our boys do die
They still persevere and try
My hands applaud you all
May you live and never fall

TROUBLE

Who stuck jam all over the kitchen floor?
Who squeezed toothpaste all over the bathroom wall?
And placed spiders in Mum's draws
Who stuck stickers on all the doors?
And let the tyres down on my bike
Took the wheels off his new trike
Who put a red top in the white washing and turned it all pink?
Who is always causing trouble, and kicking up a stink?
Who fed the dog, all of mum's chocolates and made him sick?
Who had drawn a moustache on granny's pic?
Who ate twenty-four packs of crisps (chips), and hid the wrappers in my bed?
Who served up sandwiches up, with worms in between slices of bread?
Who broke the TV remote, and tried to fix it with tape and string?
Who covered axle grease all over the garden swing?
Who is this person who is always bursting my happy bubble?
Always lays the blame on me, and getting me into trouble
He is seven
And I am only eleven
And he can be the only one, and I'm glad I don't have another
It's my brother

THE ZIPPER

I know a guy
Who got his JOHN THOMAS caught in his zipper fly
"ZIP"!!! And there was a trapped piece of skin
What agony he must have been in
The best of it was he was in the public library Loo
He panicked and didn't know what to do
The zipper stuck fast and wouldn't move
Using soap to free it was difficult to prove
So, with a hand in a tactical place
He walked through the library with embarrassing haste
To find a hospital near by
To explain his predicament, he would have to try
The sniggering nurse tying to keep a straight face
Led him off to the cubical place
Cream applied to freeze the offending part
While the nurse attending him tried not to fall apart
Then "ZIP"!!!! And a quick burst of Pain
The prisoner JOHN THOMAS was free once again
Now Sir? Asked the Nurse
Trying to hold back the laugh as she tried to converse
Would you like a plaster cast or a splint?
Or better still shall I put it in a sling or wrap it in lint
Well, that was the final straw
Nurses and Doctors rolling about on the floor
But my mate took it at heart
I guess he seen the funny part

THE RECLUSE

Sitting here alone thinking back
What in my life the things I lack
My world a while ago crumbled and fell
Turning my feelings to a life of hell
Loneliness is my companion now
Insecurity I know this very well
As I hideaway in my little flat
Safe, secure, now, I know that
I've been told many times to get a life
But who knows the root of my Strife?
I once believed in life, because I'm a giver
Giving all, I could deliver
But rejection weighs heavy on my sole
This fear I carry, scared inside as a whole
Now I sit here as a recluse
That's my safety in this life and my excuse
But I was asked a question the other day
Was I afraid to commit myself in any way?
Oh no, I want to, God Knows I am
To someone genuine and honest and who gives all they can
But you must understand
I don't like those who play under hand
Scars burn deep inside
Although I'm positive and applied
I can't blame anyone that wouldn't be fair
Not all are tarred with the same brush as far as I'm aware
Time to come out of my protective shell
Time for these feelings inside to rebel
Against this situation in that I've been
Time to join into the human race's scene

THE HYENA

The hyena is on the prowl
He laughs and scoffs, with a scowl
Inflictor of misery, and pain
As he pompously struts around his domain
But well-made enemies, lie in wait
The complex game he's played, he now can't anticipate
The eagle takes to the air
The lion waits in ambush, beware
Eyes on the ground and in the sky
Fly eagle fly
Wait patiently, lion wait
Time will make the hyena surface, that reprobate
This formidable team, will bring him down to he knees
As he will scream for mercy and scream his pleas
The eagle with claws embedded in his back
And the lion with teeth at his throat, in the joint attack
He will die alone in baron terrain
Others will eventually forget his name
And happy ignorance will remain
Normal time and life will once again retain

THE BLACK PEARL

The ghostly galleon sails the Caribbean seas
The black pearls shredded sails dancing in the breeze
Those unfortunate to cross her path, could never live to tell the tale
A curse of the Inca gold hangs on her crew, like a dark shrouded veil
Pirate un dead skeletons dance by the light of the moon
All but one, Captain Jack Sparrow, who they cruelly did maroon
William the Black smith and Jack, pursue the kidnapped lady
A secret island and a crew who was shady
No let up, No rest
Until the fulfilled adventure in their quest
For Captain Jack his return of the Black Pearl
And for will his beloved girl
The lifting of the immortal curse
Retuning every last coin of gold, from the pirates' purse
This the story of the Black Pearl's story told
As the swashbuckling venture is bold

SPRING

Here comes spring to warm mother earth
New plants, blossoms, and animals given birth
Crocuses and snow drops of white purple and yellow bed
Cherry blossom of pink and white on trees spread
Pussy willows blow in gentle breeze
New young shoots and buds spring forth on trees
New born calves and lambs skip in the fields
The time of the year that brings new yields
February's frost has now gone
Windy blustery March blows on
Rainy April then through to May
Children Dance round the maypole and play
Winters harshness now has passed
That white and cold shroud melted to the last
To bring warm spring air
The start of summer fruits to bear
Ploughed and rutted soil
The season of sowing and seedlings toil
Ready for new growth
New produce for you and me both
What wonders of mother nature will we see?
Of yet to come from its mystery

SCHOOL HOLIDAYS

Well Parents, Schools and Colleges are back in swing
6 weeks of hell, that prison thing
All those weeks of pressures
Looking after your little treasures
As those kids get bored
Extra cost and expenses you can't afford
More meals supplied
Extra washing or laundry applied
The fighting amongst the kids gets more intense
The slightest thing becomes a major offence
And you coping with the insanity day by day
Wishing the turmoil would go away
Hoping the days would just whiz or fly
But as time draws nearer those days get longer and slower as they pass by
Then comes the final day
All the kids start Schools and colleges, off they go on their way
Pity we don't have Summer Camps here in the UK
Like they do in the USA
It's us parents we need the break
Can't we have 6 weeks off instead? The change we would all love to make
16 to 20 years the ritual of what we have endure
A long time that's for sure
96 weeks of summer holidays in our lives
But they the ones who bear the brunt of this, is Girlfriends, Partners, and wives
Well, it's all over and done
Getting back to normality seems to be the number 1
"Till next year"

SAD GIST

Why do you haunt me?
Why don't you let me be?
This my life of tragedy
To endless suffering and misery

.

All I want is Happiness
A tiny glimmer of hope no less
A way out of this daily stress
Something to fill my emptiness

.

This life of being alone
I think this is my destiny is prone
Although I'm not one to moan
That lonesome, constant companion I have known

.

As taken without opening doors
Another time in life to pause
Unhappiness is the cause
The shadow of my sadness does applause

.

Must it always be like this?
All those joyous occasions I must miss?
Must I with frustration shake my fist?
This Void, of this constant sadness gist

REMEMBRANCE AT GROUND ZERO

A small child looked up at his mother
One of three, himself, Mum, and his brother
Stood in the wide and empty place
The ground zeros lonely space
Mummy where has daddy gone?
He's gone to heaven my little one
Why can't I see him? I wish he were here
He's here my son, looking over us and very near
Mummy said the little boy, why are all these people around?
They have come to this place to remember those lost and never found
Is daddy lost?
Yes my son, at a great deal too many and mine family's cost
What did they do mummy, was god angry with them?
Not our god my little gem
Our god would never do this to innocent soles
He has taken Daddy and many more and in has filled many empty tender heart holes
Mummy asked the little boy, have all these People lost Daddies and Mummy's?
They have lost all that were once dear to them loved ones and honeys
A tear fell down his delicate cheek
The questions from some one innocent and meek
I won't be seeing my daddy ever again
And I know Mummy you have a thing called pain
I can see all the colours of a rainbow in all these flowers all around
That decorates this ground
A lot of people must love daddy as well
There's lot of others who miss him as well
The Mother looked down at the small child

With a tear in her eye she smiled
You are on of the special children amongst the many here
Who have lost some one special and it brings us all closer and
near
All those Daddies and mummy's smile down on you and the
other children in this place
And look on you with tender grace
So lets us always remember
The day of 11th September

RELIGION

All this conflict in the world today
In the name of religion, I have to say
Those of different belief
It all brings misery and grief
Some times fanatic in the some need for hope
As other sects in their struggle to cope
Wars, conflict, misery, death and pain
All caused by gods and religion remain
And yet apart from wielding fear, but preaching love and
peace
Love thine enemy sayeth the priest
What did we worship before these religions sprung and grew?
Each evolving in different ways from new
What existed before man wrote books for?
Each of the individual religious core
Most are not more than four millennia old
And yet man is over two million years of age I'm told
Doesn't it make you think?
This excuse that brings nations to the brink
All in the many names of God
Don't you think it odd?
And if God made a person in his image or of his genetic
Then like us all he must be schizophrenic
Prone to good and evil thought
As we are lectured and taught
All no doubt back in time, from some one's minds
Some where from the dark annuals of histories times
As we all have the need
For some one beyond proof to lead
So please excuse my point of view
Freedom of speech is what we are entitled to

RACIAL TENSION

Before I read this poem I don't submit to any racial overtones
And hope that no one takes offence I am just putting a point
of view over

What politician gave our small Isle a reason to Mix?
An Attempt of a multi racial fix
Small pockets of others race to integrate
Those small communities trying to relate
Are we guilty of those?
What different Ideals that separate cultures pose
Small sets living in a different base
Those of alien ideals in a human race
Intermixing that's has come about, and we have created
Half casts as we call them have lost their identity, not debated
Neither one or the other of any race to others
In an even small minority of sisters and brothers
Lost confused and alienated
Not of one race or the other related
And yet those individual racial sects
Each and everyone have different religious respects
Not really wanting to be part, of the majority's scheme
Wanting to live in there in their own cultures it seems
Breeding mistrust and separate views
Clashing racial tension always in the news
This multiracial society does not want to mix
And our government think it's a thing that they can fix
It could never be so
As I'm sure if the truth be known they seem to know
They could never get it right
A losing battle that they do fight

OUR OWN POOR

*Disclaimer: If there are those who are offended by this poem
then all I can say is that there's a lack of understanding*

*Have you noticed every time our declined economical situa-
tion has an affect?*

On our own countries Poor, they lose their self-respect

And as we pump money to those poor and needy aboard

Depleting our own treasuries valuable hoard

To busy helping 3rd world countries in need

*Really neglecting those pensioners, single mums, and those
fallen on hard times indeed*

And as our cost of living does rise

Worry and pressure sets in that minority's eyes

And those who live in comfortable lives, Have no idea

Of the struggle on those who are on low-income, live-in fear

*It's those who live above incomprendable wage who set the
standard and decide*

Of those poor saying it's ample and will have to abide

They brag about the rises they give

But take away those in other costs that the poor need to live

*As they give in one hand, they take away in the other hand
That so called rise*

*Given grudgingly with a feeling of despise, and they spread
lies*

They look to lay blame and disgust

Treating them with contempt and mistrust

No position, No identity, No self dignity, and No rights

As they struggle with daily financial fights

Some get so desperate to do what they can

Crime, Prostitution, Fraud, or a loan shark man

A scape goat in the government's propaganda machine

Someone to pass the blame on in its regime

Some never wanted to fall into this trap

Down hearted are they and living in this crap
The adopted view of keeping them peasants down
The government took over from the Aristocrats crown
So, if I get arrested for saying my piece
Then you can support me, if arrested by police
Whatever happened to freedom of speech?
From a member of those, who is a so-called leech?

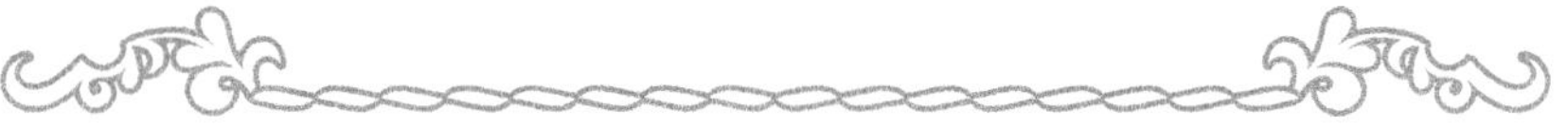

AUTHOR'S BIOGRAPHY

Thank you for taking some interest in me, and my back ground, I started writing poetry almost by accident. I joined a 3D chatroom 2002, 20 years ago and was approached by one of the hosts. She told me that if I wrote a poem and joined the poetry session that evening, I could possibly win a VIP. I entered a poem called Worlds that is published on the 1st page of my 2nd book called A Complete Works of My Poems part2. There is a part 1 as well. And to my surprise I won. After entering several more poems, I seemed to have a hidden talent as I was told by many people, for creating or writing poetry. Eventually I ended up hosting poetry in this 3D chatroom, with a Canadian Colleague called Kath. Over a time of 4 and half years of hosting I managed to create well over 560 poems, 582 pages in my latest book. And now the final book, Anthology of All My Poems in Softback.

Writing a new poem for each of the 2 days a week over a period of 4 and half years. Tuesday for the UK and Europe and Thursday for the US, Canada, Australia, and New Zealand. I have 9-10 books published including one 24-page book created on an epic poem Called Hogarth's Epic Poem. I also working on creating another book based on a poem that was a challenge, by my friend Kath called The Food and Veggie Ball. I once won a cheque for £50 from a competition from poetry.com.

I stopped sending in other works because I came to realise that I was supplying poems to fuel vanity publishing. It has taken a long time and a hard journey through the rigors of publishing. I never thought I was talented enough, and never thought that I would get anywhere. It's nice when I am congratulated and appreciated by people that have either read or heard my poems. However honest criticism is always accepted. If you google me Terry J Powell you will find out who I am. I am still moving forward I am also about to work on a very controversial triple novel. Untitled at the moment.

My most favourite comment is a line written in a poem called Breathless Wonder a poem about one of the most rugged but wonderful part of the UK in a place called Wales. "The sky burns red with the dragon's flight."

My other controversial saying is "How can I be racist if I'm only telling the truth".

I love traveling the world and have travelled most of the earth, it's been brilliant. Exploring places, I could only dream about. I have met quite a few people and made many friends. I have lectured twice about poetry while on cruise ships. Distributed books to many of my book shops throughout the world. It's taken more or less to have my books published over a period of nearly 15 years or more. The reason why it's taken so long is because of affordability. I must point out that getting self-published can be a minefield I have a list of scammers of over 150 or more people prepared to scam authors here is the link, check them out. https://accrispin.blogspot.com/2019/08/from-phil-ippines-not-with-love-plague.html I hope they all get prison.

The problem is that there is that many scammers out there, you don't know who you can trust. They all say that they are there to help you, but in reality, they are there just to take your money. If they are genuine, it should be the case of they are willing to pay you for the use of your material. I have heard horror stories that people are willing to buy up the rights of your book so they can take the rights of you book away from you. This situation has created mistrust for all the honest people who would love to publish you hard earned book or materials.

The proudest moment of my life was to have two titles conveyed one in December 2021 Lord Metley and the second title Lord Wollaston, (pronounced Woolaston)

Many thanks for your time, Terry (Lord Metley Wollaston)

https://www.facebook.com/terry.powell.180/
https://mobile.twitter.com/TerryJPowell
google.co.uk/terry j Powell/poet
https://wordpress.com/view/terrypowellpoetry.wordpress.com

www.ingramcontent.com/pod-product-compliance
Lightning Source LLC
Chambersburg PA
CBHW071956190726
48293CB00001B/48

9 781957 956138